Heisenberg *Probably* Slept Here

Heisenberg *Probably* Slept Here

The Lives, Times, and Ideas of the Great Physicists of the 20th Century

Richard P. Brennan

John Wiley & Sons, Inc.

New York • Chichester • Brisbane • Toronto • Singapore • Weinheim

Copyright © 1997 by Richard P. Brennan

Published by John Wiley & Sons, Inc.

Library of Congress Cataloging-in-Publication Data

Brennan, Richard P.
    Heisenberg probably slept here : the lives, times, and ideas of the great physicists of the 20th century / Richard P. Brennan.
        p.   cm—(Wiley popular science)
    Includes bibliographical references and index.
    ISBN 0-471-15709-0 (cloth : alk. paper)
    1. Physicists—Biography.   2. Physics—History—20th century.
I. Title.   II. Series.
QC15.B74   1997
530'.092'2—dc20
    [B]   96-42935

Printed in the United States of America
10 9 8 7 6 5 4 3 2 1

It is the most persistent and greatest adventure in human history—this search to understand the universe, how it works, and where it came from. It is difficult to imagine that a handful of residents of a small planet circling an insignificant star in a small galaxy have as their aim a complete understanding of the entire universe, a small speck of creation truly believing it is capable of comprehending the whole.

Murray Gell-Mann

One thing I have learned in a long life: that all our science, measured against reality, is primitive and childlike—and yet it is the most precious thing we have.

Albert Einstein

My message is that science is a human activity, and the best way to understand it is to understand the individual human beings who practice it.

Freeman Dyson

Acknowledgments

I am grateful to Carolyn F. Brennan for the illustrations that accompany the text, as well as for her critical review of the manuscript. I am also greatly indebted to my editor, Emily Loose, for her many significant contributions.

Contents

Contents

Preface

Mention the words *physics* and *history* in the same sentence, and the average reader's eyes will glaze over. Yet, the story of the evolution of human thought, especially in physics, is a dramatic tale filled with interesting characters and exciting discoveries. The prime objective of this book is to show that physics and history can be both stimulating and thought provoking.

This book presents portraits of eight physicists who have contributed in a major way to the twentieth-century revolution in physics that led to a whole new understanding of reality—of the laws of the universe. Physics is the science that deals with matter, energy, motion, and force—everything from the immensity of the cosmos to the smallest indivisible particle of nature. As an intellectual activity, physics is the search for the fundamental laws of nature, and no phenomenon in the universe is foreign to the physicist. The scope of our subject, then, depends on how able we are, as writer and reader, to stretch our imaginations.

But in addition to ideas, we are going to be dealing with people —a collection of colorful characters who are the players on this stage. Specifically I have chosen Isaac Newton, Albert Einstein, Max Planck, Ernest Rutherford, Niels Bohr, Werner Heisenberg, Richard Feynman, and Murray Gell-Mann, each of whom represents a major breakthrough or change in world view. These men share a common intellectual passion to know and understand—just as great artists are driven to create. What were the unique human qualities of each of these scientists that made them so outstanding and makes each of their stories so fascinating? They were all strikingly original thinkers who, in each case, deviated sharply from previous thinking to provide the world with entirely new views of reality and new truths to ponder. They are in short those individuals who led the intellectual world, sometimes reluctantly, to the continuity of ideas, observations, speculations, and syntheses that constitute the body of knowledge now called *modern physics*. What does this mean for us? Admittedly I am a science buff and as such I may be accused of having a tunnel vision of history. I submit, however, that it is almost impossible to overstate the contributions of these eight scientists. Their contributions, I suggest, are far greater than all the kings, queens, generals, and politicians that are the usual subjects of history. Almost everything around us in the modern age, from automobiles to household appliances, from jet aircraft to power plants, owes its existence in some part to these scientists.

Isaac Newton is popularly known as the man who saw an apple fall from a tree and somehow thereafter worked out the laws of celestial motions. His contributions—mechanics and the calculus—can be truly appreciated only when they are viewed as ushering in the Machine Age and the Industrial Revolution. Max Planck's revolutionary theories introduced quantum electronics, without which modern industry would not exist. The combined legacy of these men is astounding.

This book is intended for that most wondrous of creatures, the "intelligent layperson"—the nonscientist who might never have had a course on the history of science but who nonetheless possesses the intellectual curiosity to wonder about how we came to our current concept of the natural world, and, equally interesting, who were the scientists who led us to this point. This book, then, is the history of physics told through abbreviated biographies that concentrate on the personalities of the physicists and their scientific accomplishments. It is written in nontechnical language, and my goal is to explain and interpret the work of these remarkable scientists in language understandable to all. No science or mathematical background is required for this laymen's guide. I am in full agreement with science writer Timothy Ferris, who has said, "The difficulty of understanding a work of science, as opposed to a work of art, is frequently exaggerated." Newton, Einstein, and Gell-Mann should be no more forbidding than Shakespeare, Tolstoy, or Mozart. Each represents an intellectual challenge and promises rich reward for the effort. This book is for those of us who are not upset by attempts to probe and understand the incredible world in which we live and who are willing to pay a small admission price in thought and effort.

By the way, the title for this book comes from a bumper sticker spotted on the campus at M.I.T., and it proves that despite some evidence to the contrary, the scientifically literate do have a sense of humor. Werner Heisenberg, of course, originated the uncertainty principle, wherein exactitude of measurement is replaced by imprecise probability.

Why begin with Isaac Newton rather than with a twentieth-century physicist? If we think of physics as the effort to find a unified set of laws governing matter, motion, and energy at the microscopic or subatomic level, at the human scale of everyday life, and out to the largest cosmic extragalactic scale, then we see that Newton's achievements span the entire range, from the micro to the macro, and cover as well the middle ground of day-to-day applied physics. Today, the ambitious goal of physics has almost been realized. Although a completely unified theory of physical phenomena has not yet been reached, a remarkably small set of fundamental physical laws appears able to account for all known phenomena.

The body of physics developed up to about the turn of the twentieth century is known as *classical physics*, and can account for the motions of the objects that move slowly with respect to the speed of light and for such phenomena as heat, sound, electricity, magnetism, and light. The development of modern physics, such as relativity and quantum theory, modifies the understanding of these phenomena insofar as they apply to higher speeds and massive objects, as well as the tiny elementary constituents of matter, such as electrons, protons, and neutrons.

Physicist Steven Weinberg, in his book *Dreams of a Final Theory*, put it this way: "It is with Isaac Newton that the modern dream of a final theory [of physics] really begins." Newton, then, provides us with the logical starting place for our intellectual adventure into space, time, and the unknown. To set the stage for the great man, a few pages of prologue—a brief summary of pre-Newtonian physics—is necessary.

Introduction

Standing on the Shoulders of Giants

In 1676, a modest Isaac Newton wrote in a letter to fellow scientist and long-time rival Robert Hooke, "If I have seen further than other men, it is because I stood on the shoulders of giants." The following precis touches on some of the giants to whom Newton referred.

Of course, there was physics before Isaac Newton. Even before the ancient Greeks—in China, Egypt, and Mesopotamia, to name just three geographical locations—people struggled to comprehend the natural laws of the strange world in which they lived. The Arabs, for instance, gave civilization its current numbering system. The great pyramids, which took an incredible amount of mathematics to build, were already quite ancient when the Greeks first began to discuss philosophy and science. From the Western point of view, however, the Greeks were the most important early scientists, the prototypes of physicists, if you will.

Some historians have identified Thales of Miletus (640–546? B.C.)

as the first philosopher and the first scientist. To earn that honor, he offered new perspectives about how to try to understand the natural world. First, Thales did not resort to animism; that is, he did not say that it rains because the rain god is angry or that the seas are deep because the deities so ordained it. Second, he made the bold assertion that the cosmos was something the human mind could understand. His most spectacular achievement, and one that proved his point, was predicting an eclipse for 585 B.C.—it actually occurred. Thales set the intellectual world on the path of thinking about how things worked, a path that it is still on today.

Thales was succeeded by Pythagoras (ca. 582–ca. 500 B.C.) and his followers, who discovered that the real world can be understood in mathematical terms—in fact, perhaps *best* understood in mathematical terms. The Pythagorean school, which outlasted the master by several hundred years, held that the universe is the manifestation of various combinations of mathematical ratios. It has been said that the Pythagoreans turned from religion to mathematics and ended up making mathematics into a religion. Their original insight, however, is considered one of the greatest advances in the history of human thought. Since the Pythagoreans, mathematics has been the *lingua franca* of science. However, it is translatable into a more understandable language. Pythagoras himself is also noted as the first man known to teach that the Earth was a sphere and also to postulate that the Earth moves—both radical notions.

The Greek explosion of knowledge continued with the works of, among other notables, Euclid, Aristarchus, Archimedes, and Eratosthenes. Euclid (ca. 300 B.C.), whose name is, of course, almost synonymous with geometry wrote a textbook called *Elements* that became the standard for centuries. It went through more than a thousand editions after the invention of printing, and Euclid thus is considered the most successful textbook writer of all time. What made Euclid great was his ability to take all the knowledge accumulated in mathematics since the days of Thales and to codify that two and a half centuries of labor into a single work. Euclid's axioms, such as "The whole is equal to the sum of its parts" or "A straight line is the shortest distance between two points," were once considered mathematical laws. In the nineteenth century, scientists came to understand that axioms are actually only agreed-upon statements, rather than absolute truths. Little is known of

Euclid's life, but one story concerns his reply to King Ptolemy of Egypt when the latter, studying geometry, asked if Euclid could not make his demonstration a little easier to follow. Euclid said, uncompromisingly, "O King, for traveling over the country, there are royal roads and roads for the common citizens; but in geometry there is one road for all." This thought is often expressed in the shorter form, "There is no royal road to geometry."

Aristarchus of Samos (ca. 260 B.C.) is generally considered the most successful of Greek astronomers. Aristarchus worked out the actual size of the Moon by noting the size of the shadow thrown by the Earth during an eclipse of the Moon. Most revolutionary of all his concepts was his suggestion that the motions of the heavenly bodies could be interpreted most easily if all the planets, including the Earth, were assumed to revolve about the Sun. This heliocentric hypothesis was too radical to be accepted by the scholars of the time, and his book on that subject did not survive.

Next among the Greeks we have Archimedes (287?–212 B.C.), considered the most eminent scientist and mathematician of ancient times. He was in many ways the first scientist-cum-engineer in that he turned many of his theoretical ideas to practical use. For example, Archimedes worked out the principle of the lever. He showed in mathematical detail that a small weight at a distance from a fulcrum (or support point) would balance a large weight near the fulcrum and that the weights and distances were in inverse proportion. Archimedes is reported to have said in connection with the leverage principle, "Give me a place to stand on, and I can move the world."

Archimedes is also credited with inventing a water pump in the form of a helical cylinder that, when rotated, could move water from one level to a higher level. This device is still known as the "screw of Archimedes." During his time, he was most famous as an inventor of weapons of war, catapults and the like. He was in effect a one-man military–industrial complex. But he is most popularly known today for the amusing story of his discovery of the principles of buoyancy. The story is that Archimedes' patron, the King, had asked him to determine whether a crown just received from the goldsmith was really all gold, as it was supposed to be, or whether it contained a diluting mixture of silver. He was to do this without damaging the crown in any way. Archimedes had no idea how to accomplish this task until one day, stepping into his full bath, he noticed that the water overflowed. Legend has it that on making this observation he jumped out of his bath and ran naked through the streets of Syracuse to the palace shouting, "Eureka, eureka! (I've got it!)" He had made the brilliant deduction from this casual observation that the amount of water displaced was equal in volume to the portion of his body that was submerged in the bath. From this, he concluded that if he dipped the King's crown into water he could tell by the rise in water level the volume of the crown. He could then compare the crown's volume with the volume of an equal weight of gold. If the volumes were equal, the crown was pure gold. If the crown had an admixture of silver (which is bulkier than gold), it would have a greater volume. As a footnote to this famous story, it should be noted that the crown in question turned out to be partly silver and the goldsmith was executed.

Another famous Greek thinker of interest is Eratosthenes (276?–195? B.C.), the astronomer, geographer, and historian. He was the scholar in charge of the Library at Alexandria and tutor to the son of King Ptolemy III. Most important of all, though, and the reason for his inclusion in most lists of important ancient scientists is his achievement in determining the size of the Earth. He did this by noting the fact that on the day of the summer solstice, the Sun was directly overhead in the city of Syene in southern Egypt at the same time that it was seven degrees from the zenith in Alexandria. He reasoned that the difference was due to the curvature in the surface of the Earth between the two cities. If the distance between the cities was known to some degree of accuracy and if one assumed that the Earth is a sphere with equal curvature on all parts of its surface, it was possible to calculate the diameter of the Earth. Using this method, Eratosthenes calculated the circumference of the Earth at a little over 25,000 miles, which is almost correct. The problem was that no one accepted his figures at the time because to do so meant that the then-known world occupied only a small portion of the Earth's total surface, and much of that was sea. The other three-quarters of the Earth's surface was either entirely water or contained some vast unknown lands—and these two alternatives were both unacceptable at the time.

From the time of the ancients to the major discoveries of Nicholas Copernicus, Johannes Kepler, and Galileo Galilei, some 1,700 years passed—centuries during which the theories of Claudius Ptolemy (A.D.

127–151) dominated the thinking world. In Ptolemy's version of reality, the Earth is at the center of the universe, and all the planets revolve around it in circular orbits of various size, depending upon their distance from Earth. This theory was neat and orderly. It could even be used to predict the orbits of the planets, albeit with crude accuracy, and it was, of course, completely wrong. It was not until 1,700 years later that observations of the planets were made with sufficient accuracy to call into question Ptolemy's version of the universe.

Polish astronomer Nicholas Copernicus (1473–1543) was the one who kicked off the scientific revolution that was to dethrone Greek science and to set thinking man on a more productive path. In 1507, he noted that tables of planetary positions could be calculated more accurately if it were assumed the Sun, rather than the Earth, was the center of the universe. This was not a completely new idea—Aristarchus had suggested this radical notion many years before. But it was Copernicus who worked out a system in full mathematical detail in order to demonstrate and support the new concept. Copernicus's new ordering of the planets outward from the Sun—Mercury, Venus, Earth and Moon, Mars, Jupiter, and Saturn—replaced the traditional Earth-centered order and provided a simple and coherent solution to the previously ill-resolved problem of why Mercury and Venus always appeared close to the Sun.

The Copernican system also explained the puzzling motion of the planets, in particular the apparent backward movement of Mars, Jupiter, and Saturn. If the Earth was traveling around the Sun in a smaller orbit than those of Mars, Jupiter, and Saturn as Copernicus postulated, it would periodically overtake those planets and cause them to appear to be moving backward in the night sky. Furthermore, the phenomenon of the precession (or earlier occurrence) of the equinoxes could now be explained by a wobbling of the Earth as it rotated on its axis. The equinoxes, you will remember, occur when the Sun crosses the plane of the Earth's equator, making night and day of equal lengths all over the Earth. This happens twice a year, on about March 21 for the vernal equinox and September 21 for the autumnal equinox. The problem was that these events were occurring a little earlier each year and this could not be explained by the old Ptolemaic theories. The seasons on Earth could be better explained if the Earth moved around the Sun once a year and was, as is the case, tilted on its axis in relation to the Sun.

For most of his life, Copernicus held back from full publication of his extraordinary views. Not until 1543 was *De Revolutionibus* published, and, ironically, it was largely ignored at the time. The ideas expressed in Copernicus's work were too radical to be taken seriously. For decades, there was little indication in Europe that an unprecedented concept had been put forward and that a drastic change in world view was now necessary. The Roman Catholic Church did take note of the heretical nature of Copernicus's opus and, because it clearly contradicted the Church teaching about an Earth-centered universe, banned it. Not until 1835, almost 300 years after Copernicus's death, was the book removed from the list of banned books. Four years later, when a statue of Copernicus was unveiled in Warsaw, no Catholic priest would officiate on the occasion.

However, two young astronomers in different parts of the world were early converts to Copernicus's views: Kepler in Austria and Galileo in Italy. Johannes Kepler (1571–1630) was the inheritor of a vast body of unprecedentedly accurate astronomical observations collected by his mentor and predecessor as mathematician and astrologer to the Holy Roman Emperor, the Danish astronomer Tycho Brahe (1546–1601). Using this treasure of data and armed with his faith in the Copernican theory, Kepler set out to discover the mathematical laws that would solve the problem of the behavior of the planets. As great as Copernicus's heliocentric concept was, the observable data still did not perfectly fit the theory. Kepler devoted ten years of hard and patient work to the empirical investigation of the movements of the planets and the mathematical laws behind that movement. He did this entirely on his own, supported by no one and understood by only a few. Kepler's stroke of genius was to discover that the true shape of Earth's orbit around the Sun was an ellipse rather than a neat circle as had been postulated. He did this by calculating the positional relationships of Earth, Mars, and the Sun and concluding that only an elliptical orbit would match the observable data. This accomplished, Kepler went on to calculate the orbits and motions of the rest of the known planets. This was a monumental achievement, especially considering the limited state of mathematics at the time. In addition to discovering that the observations precisely matched orbits shaped as ellipses, Kepler also discovered that each planet moved at a speed that is proportionate to its distance from the Sun.

On the basis of these findings, Kepler developed a set of three laws: (1) Planets orbit the Sun in ellipses, with the Sun at one of the two focal points of the ellipse. (2) The line joining the Sun and a planet sweeps through equal areas in equal times. (3) The cube of the mean distance of each planet from the Sun is proportional to the square of the time it takes to complete one orbit.

The second law can be restated as follows: When a planet is moving through the outer end of its ellipse, the line to the Sun will be longer and the planet will be moving more slowly; as the planet swings closer to the Sun, the line will get shorter and the planet will speed up. These changes in speed mean that the area a planet covers in any period of time, no matter whether close or far from the Sun, will stay the same.

Kepler's third law can also be restated: If the average distance between the Sun and any planet were cubed and if the time it took that same planet to complete its orbit were squared, the ratio of the two resulting numbers would always be the same, no matter which planet were involved. In effect, Kepler's laws brought order and harmony to humankind's concept of the universe.

As a young man, Kepler made his living as a mathematics teacher in a small town in Austria. To supplement his meager earnings, he issued astrological calendars that predicted, among other things, the

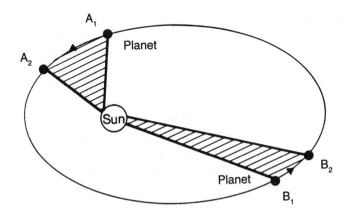

Kepler's Second Law Time between A_1 and A_2 equals the time between B_1 and B_2. Speed between A_1 and A_2 is faster as it is nearer to the Sun.

weather, the fates of princes, the dangers of war, and uprisings of the Turks. His fame spread, and he eventually cast horoscopes for Emperor Rudolf and other prominent members of the court. The pseudoscience of astrology remained Kepler's source of income when all else failed. "Prognosticating," he is reported to have said, "is at least better than begging." His excursions in fortune telling notwithstanding, Johannes Kepler takes his place among the giants as the first man to discern the real architecture of the solar system and to formulate laws that accurately predict the motions of the planets.

At about the same time that Kepler was publishing his laws of planetary motion in Prague, Galileo Galilei (1564–1642), universally known by his first name only, turned his newly constructed telescope on the heavens above Padua, Italy. He had not invented the telescope; it had been invented in Holland in 1608. However, he did make his own better telescope in 1609 and pioneered its use as an astronomical instrument.

Before he turned to astronomical observations, Galileo had been busy establishing his reputation as the world's first experimental physicist. He experimented with everything he could think of: with sound, with light, with temperature, and most importantly, with motion. There is an interesting story, which unfortunately turns out to be a myth, about Galileo dropping objects of different weights from the leaning Tower of Pisa to demonstrate that they would fall to Earth at the same velocity. This story is not mentioned by Galileo in any of his notes; it was, in fact, attributed to him years later. At any rate, the experiment, if he had performed it, would not have had the reputed results, because objects of different weight would fall at the same rate only in a vacuum.

What Galileo did do was study how objects move, not by allowing them to fall free from the Tower or anyplace else, but by using an inclined plane. By rolling balls of different weights down an inclined plane, he slowed the motion down to the point where he could measure it. This was not a perfect experiment because friction was involved and heavier objects would be more affected than lighter ones. Galileo did his best to eliminate this factor by polishing the slanted board to a high gloss. He started with a gentle incline and then repeated the experiment with increasing inclinations until the speed became too great to measure with any precision. From these slanted-incline experiments, Galileo was able to extrapolate to a hypothetical thought experiment to conjecture what would happen to objects in a free fall. Galileo discovered that a falling object does not simply drop—it drops faster and faster over time. In other words, it accelerates, and the acceleration (increase in speed) is constant. He further observed that the rate of increase in speed is the same for all spheres, regardless of weight or size. Being a mathematician, he put all of his conclusions into a formula, which is now known as the *Law of Falling Bodies*. We need not detail the mathematics or the formula, but we should simply note that Galileo's observations and deductions are now credited with initiating the science of mechanics and that they would greatly influence Isaac Newton.

On the nights of January 4 to 15, 1610, considered by many to be among the most important in the history of astronomy, Galileo made startling observations with his newly constructed telescope. These observations made available to astronomy the first qualitatively new evidence it had known since the ancients. Galileo interpreted each of his observations—the craters and mountains on the surface of the Moon, the moving spots on the Sun, the four moons revolving around Jupiter, the phases of Venus, the almost unbelievably numerous individual stars of the Milky Way—as powerful evidence to support Copernicus's concepts and to disprove the old Ptolemaic theory. With Galileo's telescope, the heliocentric *theory* became the heliocentric *fact*. The Copernican universe could no longer be dismissed as merely a computational convenience.

In 1632, Galileo published his findings in a book called *Dialogue on the Two Chief World Systems*, and immediately got into trouble with the Roman Catholic Church. By the way, despite its import, this is a far from somber book. It is full of what would now be called corny jokes and leg pulling. The leg pulling, however, was at the expense of the Church and Pope Urban VIII, and that is where the trouble began. Galileo was brought before the Inquisition on charges of heresy. The issues at the trial had little to do with scientific theories. In fact, Copernicus, the heliocentric concept, and an Earth that moved were never discussed. The issue at the center of the trial was obedience to the Pope. Galileo had tried to separate the domains of Church and state when he said, "Religion tells you how to get to Heaven, not how Heaven got there," but he failed.

As part of their effort to convince Galileo of the error of his ways, the Inquisitors took the upstart astronomer, then nearly seventy, to the dungeons and showed him the rack. Galileo was not actually tortured. He was, however, twice threatened with torture. He might also have been reminded that the Pope (then still Cardinal Bellarmine) had sent the unfortunate Italian astronomer Giordano Bruno to be burned at the stake in 1600 for heresy in connection with his thoughts and teaching of the heliocentric theory. With little choice, Galileo renounced his views and was condemned to house arrest for the rest of his days. The story that Galileo rose from his knees after his recantation and muttered under his breath *"E pur si mouve"* ("Nevertheless it does move") is another myth that did not surface until 1761, some 130 years after the trial.

While under house arrest, nothing Galileo wrote was allowed to be published. The forbidden doctrine of a heliocentric universe was not to be discussed, and Galileo was not even allowed to talk to Protestants. The result of all this was the end of Catholic scientific research. Galileo's great contemporary, René Descartes, took the warning to heart, stopped publishing in France, and moved to Sweden. It took until 1985 for the Vatican to acknowledge that Galileo was a great scientist and that he had been wronged by the Church. In 1986, His Holiness Pope John Paul II called for a "fruitful concord between science and faith." Today, the Catholic Church maintains astronomers and other scientists to advise it about the physical world.

If further advancements in human understanding of the natural universe were to occur in the seventeenth century, however, the Scientific Revolution had to move to Northern Europe, and it did. Galileo died, still a prisoner in his villa in Arcetri near Florence, in 1642. On Christmas Day of that same year, in the hamlet of Woolsthorpe, England, Isaac Newton was born.

Chapter One

Isaac Newton

Nature and Nature's Laws lay hid in Night,
God said, Let Newton be; and all was Light

Alexander Pope

Isaac Newton has been called the preeminent scientific genius, the supreme intellect of the Age of Enlightenment. What sort of a man was he to arouse such awe? When his great book *Philosophiae Naturalis Principia Mathematica* (Mathematical Principles of Natural Philosophy)—*Principia*, for short—first appeared in 1686, it astounded the world of scholarship. In this book, Newton solved the greatest problem in the history of science up to that time—the problem of the mechanics of the universe.

He had actually solved the basic problem twenty years before during a plague-enforced seventeen-month vacation in the Lincolnshire, England, countryside. Subsequently, the young Newton returned to Cambridge to teach mathematics at Trinity College. He carried out his duties quietly and, one can assume, well, but he published nothing of his work. He was, it seems, on a monumental sulk at the time. Newton did not feel like telling the rest of the world what he had discovered during that brief stay in the country. What is more, because of the complexity of his calculations, he had to invent an entirely new system of mathematics—now called the *calculus*. He did not tell anyone about that either. Here was a strange scientist indeed.

In the present days of rushing into print, often prematurely, the idea of discovering the basic laws that govern the universe and then keeping them a secret seems preposterous. Why was the quarrelsome and crusty Newton so reluctant to share his discoveries? Stephen Hawking, in his best seller *A Brief History of Time*, observed that "Newton was not a pleasant man" and that he was given to "deviousness and vitriol." Newton's manner could not have stemmed from a failure to be recognized and honored in his own time, because he was. In fact, he was the first English scientist to be knighted by a British sovereign. So why was Newton reputedly so eccentric? Knowing something of the background of this extraordinary man will help to answer that.

Omen of Success

On Christmas Day 1642, Hannah Newton (née Ayscough) of Woolsthorpe, near Grantham, Lincolnshire (about sixty miles north of Cambridge), England, gave birth to her first child. She named the boy Isaac in honor of his father, a farmer who had died two months earlier at the age of thirty-six. The baby was premature, so small and frail that his mother worried that he might not live out his first day. He was so tiny that, as he told his biographer many years later, "they could put him in a quart pot." According to family legend, two servant women who were sent to fetch something for the new baby from nearby North Witham sat on a stile by the way and said there was no reason to make haste as the child would be dead before they could get back. Live he did, however, and although he had bouts with ill health from time to time and was a lifelong hypochondriac, Newton defied their prediction and lived to be eighty-four years old. By that time, there must have been many who thought it was his temper that kept him alive so long.

Isaac did not have a happy childhood. When he was three years old, his mother married Barnabas Smith, a well-to-do minister twice her age, and Isaac was sent to live with his maternal grandmother.

He was separated from his mother for nine years, until the death of his stepfather in 1653. It is apparent that the separation severely affected his personality development and almost surely shaped his attitudes toward women. He had little to do with them throughout his life. If his diaries and notes are indicative, he spent little time even thinking about women (as contrasted with his contemporary and fellow diarist Samuel Pepys, who apparently spent little time thinking of anything else). Newton never married, although he might have been engaged at least once (possibly twice), and he seemed to have focused his attentions exclusively on his work.

Some historians have examined Newton's ancestry in efforts to explain his brilliance as genetically inherited, but such investigations have been fruitless. The branch of the Ayscough family from which Newton's mother came, though on the whole better educated and more prominent socially than the Newtons, produced no one else of any exceptional merit. As for the Newtons, although they were quite successful farmers, they had little, if any, formal education and were in fact illiterate—all signed their wills, composed by village scribes, with their mark. Hannah herself could write a little, judging by a few scraps of notes she sent to Isaac when he was away at Cambridge. She did sign her own will, but it is not likely that she had much formal education, nor that she put much stock in it.

The important point for our story is that Newton was raised almost entirely by the Ayscoughs, and, because of this, he was probably held to a different set of expectations than if his father had lived. There were educated relatives among the Ayscough family, most importantly the Reverend William Ayscough, who lived only a few miles away. The Ayscoughs might have taken it for granted that the boy would receive at least a basic education, whereas there is some doubt that the Newtons would have considered this necessary.

Although the Newtons did not pass on to Isaac a tradition of education, they did leave him an estate. When Hannah remarried, she was careful to reserve the income from this paternal estate for Isaac. Also, as part of the marriage agreement, she insisted that her second husband settle another piece of land on young Newton. Whereas it can be said that as a young widow Hannah deserted her baby emotionally, she certainly did the best she could for him financially.

Almost all of the anecdotes of Newton's childhood years come from two sources: Dr. William Stukeley, a friend of Newton in the physicist's later years, and his first biographer, and John Conduitt, husband of Newton's half-niece, who took notes for an intended biography. Although they interviewed many people who knew Newton as a child, Stukeley and Conduitt both relied on Newton himself for most of the stories that have since become legend. Stukeley and Conduitt reported the then current folk wisdom that a Christmas birth was an omen of future success and that posthumous children were endowed with extraordinary powers that destined them for success and good fortune.

If Newton was aware of these two folk beliefs and if his mother had told him of his almost miraculous survival as a baby, Newton, indeed, might have thought he had been selected by fate for greatness. He knew soon enough that he was different: He seemed to prefer his own company to that of other children and seldom played games or sports with them. When he did play with other children, it was usually with the girls, rather than with the rough and tumble farm boys of the neighborhood. According to those interviewed by Stukeley, Isaac was introspective, shy, temperamental, and high strung. However, he did display manual dexterity and mechanical ingenuity in the construction of mechanical toys, such as waterclocks, model windmills, kites, and sundials.

The nine years that Newton spent in Woolsthorpe, separated from his mother, was a painful time. There are stories that young Isaac climbed a church steeple in order to see the nearby village of North Witham, the new home of his longed-for mother. There was, of course, his grandmother, Margery Ayscough, to take her place, but in assessing the effects of his early life, it is significant to note that Newton never recorded any affectionate recollection of her whatever. Even her death some years later went unremarked.

How important was all this to shaping the character of the genius to come? There is some documentary evidence to support the theory that it was important indeed. In 1662, at the age of nineteen, Newton underwent a period of religious fervor, during which he compiled a list of fifty-eight sins that he hoped to expiate through acts of self-confession. The thirteenth of those sins is revealing: "Threatening my father and mother Smith to burne them and the house over them."

In his book *A Portrait of Isaac Newton*, Professor Frank Manuel concluded that the remarriage of his mother was the most critical episode in Newton's entire life. According to Manuel's analysis, based on a Freudian perspective, the sense of deprivation dominated Newton's life. He had been robbed of his most precious possession, and he spent the rest of his life finding surrogates on whom to vent the rage that he had not been able to express against the real object of his hate, Barnabas Smith. Manuel thinks Newton's unreasonable attitude toward rivals Robert Hooke, John Flamsteed, and Gottfried Wilhelm Leibniz, as well as his total lack of pity toward the unfortunate counterfeiters he encountered later in life, can be explained by Newton's frustrations as a young child. This is an interesting interpretation of the facts, but the problem is that there are so few facts. Whatever the cause, Newton grew up to be a tortured man with a neurotic personality.

When the Reverend Barnabas Smith died in 1653, Hannah returned to Woolsthorpe to live. Newton was ten when his mother came back. However, a half-brother and two half-sisters now shared her attention. Newton was supposed to play the role of older brother, caring for and helping his younger half-siblings. This was apparently not a role he enjoyed, but it lasted for only a short time. In less than two years, Isaac was sent off to grammar school in Grantham.

Newton's previous introduction to formal education had come by way of two small schools in Skillington and Stoke Rochford, villages close enough to Woolsthorpe for the young student to walk back and forth each day. There is no record of who his teachers were or what he learned from them. Newton does not mention them in any of his later interviews with Stukeley or Conduitt. It might be that Newton's powers of observation and his curiosity about the world around him had yet to manifest themselves. It might also be that the introverted young Isaac lived in a world of his own daydreams, little disturbed by whatever the teachers were trying to teach him. Whatever the case, his master at

King's School, Grantham, was so unimpressed with his new charge (and his educational background) that he not only placed him in the lower form, but also put him next to last there. Newton was to start his real formal education at the bottom, or close to it.

Grantham, being about seven miles to the north of Woolsthorpe, was too far for the young student to walk every day. Arrangements were made to board Isaac at the house of Mr. Clark, the village apothecary. Clark's wife was a good friend of Isaac's mother, and his brother Joseph, a physician, was an assistant teacher at King's school. Isaac had a garret room of his own, and the freedom from farm chores left him the time to undertake various projects that he found of interest.

Newton's formal education was now in the hands of one Henry Stokes, master of King's School. Not much is known of Mr. Stokes because he died at age fifty-three, a decade before his star pupil became famous. He did have an excellent education himself, and his reputation as an educator was a good one. What sort of education did the pupils at King's School receive? The curriculum probably consisted of the Bible, Latin and Greek, classical literature, and a limited amount of instruction in arithmetic. Scholars seem to think that Newton had not studied geometry before entering Cambridge. This was a remarkably small amount of mathematics education for someone who was to invent the calculus only four years after he left grammar school. How could Newton have conceived of the calculus without a thorough grounding in the mathematical culture of the times? This is one of the great unsolved mysteries of Newton. But whatever he was taught at King's School, Newton's intellectual interests clearly were awakened and nurtured under the keen eye of Henry Stokes.

An important feature of grammar school education in the seventeenth century was the teaching of the Bible. It is known that Isaac studied the Bible, in the classical tongues, and developed a lifelong interest in theological questions. Latin was the other essential element of Newton's formal education. It was the language of science and mathematics throughout the Western world, and Newton's proficiency in it not only permitted him to study on his own, but also provided him with the means to communicate with the scholarly community of the day.

As was mentioned, Newton began his education by being placed close to the bottom of the class. But an important incident took place at about that time that helped shape Newton's subsequent academic career. As Newton recalled the event some seventy years later, he and another boy got into a fight on the way to school in the morning when the other boy "kicked him in the belly, hard." As soon as school was over for the day, Isaac challenged his attacker to a fight and won—he forced his opponent's face against the church wall, rubbed his nose on it, and made him cry "enough." But this stinging physical victory was not enough. The opponent in question (it was very likely Arthur Storer) was the top student in the school, and Newton resolved to beat him academically just as he had done physically. Thus motivated at last, Isaac rose rapidly to be first in school. This story has a ring of truth to it, especially as one of the sins Newton listed in 1662 was "Beating Arthur Storer."

At Grantham, Newton became an omnivorous reader of everything he could get his hands on—probably mostly religious books, which would explain his lifelong interest in theology. At about this same time, he developed an interest in medicine and chemistry, traceable to the encouragement of his landlord Clark, as well as to Clark's brother Joseph, a local physician. Grantham was an environment that encouraged Isaac's natural curiosity, and he did well.

His academic accomplishments did not impress his mother, however, and when Newton was about sixteen Hannah decided to call him home to take charge of the more practical business of operating the Woolsthorpe estate. (In a biographical sketch, Isaac Asimov refers to Newton as the "world's worst farmer.") His former headmaster Henry Stokes attempted to persuade Hannah that the boy belonged back in school. Thinking that money was the issue, Stokes even offered to remit the annual forty-shilling fee required for all boys not born in Grantham. This would have been no small sacrifice for a teacher of modest means. But money was not the issue, and Hannah was stubborn. Her long-cherished plans for her son were falling to pieces. She turned to her brother, the Reverend William Ayscough, for advice. When even he supported the idea of Newton returning to school and preparing for higher education, Hannah at last acquiesced.

Most biographies of Newton state that he was unrecognized as a genius in his early days. They might be correct, but it seems that Newton's mentors recognized something special in him. Their efforts on his behalf went well beyond the call of duty. The story is told of Newton's final departure from Grantham, Henry Stokes placed his star pupil at the front of the class and with tears in his eyes made an impassioned speech in his praise to motivate the other boys to follow his example. So it was that in the summer of 1661 the eighteen-year-old Newton journeyed sixty miles south to the university town of Cambridge, to a new world and a new life.

Cambridge

All the educated individuals with whom young Isaac had close contact were graduates of Cambridge University: His uncle William Ayscough had studied at Trinity College, his teacher Henry Stokes had attended Pembroke, and Joseph Clark had been a student at Christ's College. So there was probably little doubt about which institution he would attend.

In 1661, Cambridge was more than 400 years old. Originally it had been what would now be called a spin-off from the older Oxford University. But Cambridge had multiplied several times in size and had reached an enrollment of more than 3,000 by the time Newton arrived. Cambridge had outstripped Oxford and had become the heart of English Puritanism as well as the center of English intellectual life.

Two colleges dominated the Cambridge scene in those days: St. John's and its neighbor, the College of Undivided Trinity (founded by Henry VIII in 1546). Newton attended Trinity, as had his uncle, the Reverend William Ayscough. Another Newton sponsor is believed to be Humphrey Babington. A fellow at Trinity, Babington was the brother of Newton's landlady in Grantham. Apparently he had been impressed by Newton when he had met him at his sister's home, and Babington became a powerful ally to the otherwise friendless student.

Newton needed all the support he could get. He entered Trinity as a *subsizar*, a poor student who earned his keep by performing menial tasks for the Fellows and the more affluent students. Subsizars were at the bottom of the rigid Cambridge social structure. Why Newton had to endure these conditions is not clear. His family was quite well off by the rural standards of the day, and Newton's position as a servant/student was not an economic necessity. Possibly Hannah was not completely reconciled to her son's academic ambitions and was determined that he prove himself.

Subsizars were not allowed to eat with their fellow students nor to sit with them in chapel. Some colleges even had special gowns for the poor students so that the "gentlemen" students could avoid being seen talking or walking with them.

His lowly status had only one noticeable influence on Newton—it made him even more of a loner than he already was. At home he would have had his own servants and, as heir to the manor, a social status far above that to which he was subjected at Trinity. If he was being put to a test, he rose above it. Trinity was where he would stay, come what may.

Newton's strict Puritanical lifestyle would have set him apart from his peers in any case. Cambridge had its share of off-campus temptations for students. Taverns, coffee houses, and bawdy houses abounded. Attendance at these distractions was forbidden the undergraduates, but the laws were impossible to enforce. Newton's own diary and notes do not indicate a wild life. If he treated himself to a custard dessert or even a little wine, he noted the expenditure.

The town aside, what was going on at the colleges? Officially, little that was new or innovative. Like thousands of other undergraduates, Newton began his higher education by immersing himself in Aristotle and Plato. By this time, the movement now known as the "scientific revolution" was well advanced, and many of the works basic to modern science had appeared. The heliocentric system of the universe had been explained by Copernicus and Kepler. Galileo had confirmed this theory and had established the foundations of a new mechanics built on the principle of inertia. Philosophers such as René Descartes had articulated a new conception of nature as a complex, impersonal machine. But as far as the teachings at the universities of Europe were concerned, all of these new ideas might well not have been expressed. The curricula at Cambridge and elsewhere were solidly based on Aristotelianism, the old geocentric theory of the universe, and a qualitative rather than quantitative view of nature. As usual, however, Newton did not pay much attention to the established routine. From his earliest days at college, he acted more like a graduate student than a freshman. He read what he wanted to read and studied what interested him. Trinity has always employed the tutor system, and Newton's tutor was a gentleman named Benjamin Pulleyn, who was busy overseeing a record number of undergraduates. There is no evidence that the tutor had much influence on the pupil or that the pupil made any impression on the tutor. Pulleyn set Isaac on the required path of classical reading and thereafter paid him little heed. Newton found his own way after that, a way that led to René Descartes, Sir Francis Bacon, Galileo Galilei, and Johannes Kepler. There is clear evidence that they, rather than the official courses of study, profoundly influenced the scientist to be.

Writing in his notebook sometime in 1663 or 1664, Newton entered the slogan "*Amicus Plato amicus Aristoteles magis amica veritas*" (Plato is my friend, Aristotle is my friend, but my best friend is truth). He had reached an important point in his intellectual development. Under that slogan and in a new section of his student notebook, Newton listed a series of questions (*Quaestions quaedam Philosphicae*) that covered all the areas of natural science and theology that interested him. This is a most revealing set of queries and concerns, clearly indicative of Newton's drive to understand and of his obsession to know.

Although he did not make record of the fact in his *Quaestions*, Newton had also begun his mathematical studies at that time. Starting with Descartes and geometry, he quickly moved to algebraic techniques. In a little more than a year, he had mastered the literature of mathematics and had begun to move on to new territories of his own. In his last two years at Trinity, Newton came under the influence of Isaac Barrow, a fellow at the college and the first mathematician at Cambridge to recognize Newton's brilliance.

Though Descartes's writings on math were crucial in Newton's mathematical awakening, Descartes's influence went well beyond mathematics. The French intellectual and other mechanical philosophers of the time viewed physical reality as composed entirely of particles of matter in motion, and they held that all the phenomena of nature result from the particles' mechanical interactions. Newton's diary entries and notes show that he thoroughly mastered all the works of Descartes and that he considered this new approach a better way to explain nature than the Aristotelian philosophy prevalent at that time.

What exactly was Descartes's new approach? One of the ironies in the history of ideas is that Descartes's search for certainty in the world was based upon the principle that everything should be doubted. Descartes had received the finest education that could be obtained in the Europe of his time. It was an education that included an exhaustive study of Aristotelian logic and physical science. But when he graduated at the age of twenty, he felt that he knew nothing with certainty except a few mathematical truths. Why could he not know everything, he asked himself, with this same mathematical certainty? Like the Pythagoreans so many centuries before, the young French intellectual thought that mathematics must be the road to truth. Accordingly, he immersed himself in the study of mathematics and was rewarded by the discovery of an essential mathematical tool—analytical geometry—which proved easier to use than the ancient geometry of Euclid. Without this tool, Newton could not have formulated the law of universal gravitation or written the *Principia*.

In 1639, after much thought and reading, Descartes published his short philosophical masterpiece *Discourse on the Method of Rightly Conducting the Reason and Seeking for Truth in the Sciences* (*Discourse*, for short). In this influential work, he documented the history of his intellectual development—how he began to doubt whether what he had been taught was true, until he arrived at the simple conclusion that all might be doubted except one thing, namely, that he the doubter existed because he doubted. *Dubito ergo sum* (I doubt; therefore, I am) was his way of stating this assertion. He went on from there to discover a method of achieving similar certainty in other realms, based upon the reduction of all problems to a mathematical form and solution. If one could first reduce a problem to mathematical form and then employ the minimum number of axioms, or self-evident propositions, to configure it, one might arrive at a set of algebraic equations. Then, applying the rules of algebra, one solves the equations, and certain knowledge is the result. Descartes saw the universe as a huge, complex, clocklike machine set in motion by the hand of God, but a universe that once in motion would run forever without God's assistance. Descartes, some historians assert, made Newton possible.

Sir Francis Bacon, Trinity College's most famous dropout, also had great influence on Newton. Like Descartes, Bacon was a rebel against established dogma. He urged that the basic scientific approach be changed from deductive to inductive reasoning. The pursuer of knowledge, Bacon argued, should no longer start from abstract definitions and verbal distinctions and, from these deduce concrete solutions. By doing so, he asserted, the facts are forced to support preconceived notions. Instead, one should begin with concrete data, preferably arrived at by experiment, and reason inductively from these data to real, general, empirically supported conclusions. Newton's later experiments with light and sound illustrated Bacon's influence on his methods.

When Newton received his bachelor's degree in April 1665, what might have been the most remarkable undergraduate career in the history of the university came to an end, unrecognized. Because Newton charted his own course in both natural philosophy and mathematics and because he confined the progress of his studies to his notebooks, his academic career was officially undistinguished.

The Year of the Miracles

In that same year, 1665, a resurgence of the dreaded black plague forced the closing of the universities in England. Isaac Newton left Cambridge for an enforced sojourn at home in the quiet village of Woolsthorpe. He had already been judged unsuited for farm work, so the young scholar was left to his solitary reading and thinking. He set up a book-lined bedroom and study for himself, overlooking the apple orchard, and set to work. It is likely that by this time he had already come up with all or most of the pieces of the puzzle that would become the *Principia*.

Galileo had defined the law of falling bodies and had accurately measured the force of gravity at sea level. Kepler had described the elliptical paths of the planets and had postulated that a strange force emanating from the Sun drives the planets in their courses. Moreover, Kepler had derived precise laws for the kinematics of the Sun and its planets. Bacon had shown that the true basis of knowledge was the natural world and the information the world provided through the human senses. Descartes had taught Newton how to apply mathematical methods to physical problems. What Newton needed then was the time, the desire, and the mental ability to think anew about all the knowledge he had inherited. Fate, and seventeenth-century medical precautions, provided the time.

Descartes's analytic geometry was an effective tool in dealing with a *static* universe. Newton had determined that what was needed was a way to quantify the operation of a *dynamic* world, a world constantly in motion. Therefore, Newton was up to the challenge: He invented the differential and the integral calculus, a major milestone in the history of mathematics. The calculus is the most effective mathematical tool available for resolving problems concerning infinitesimal variations in rates of motion and for determining the path of a body in space. The calculus is based upon the concept of considering quantities and motions not as definite and unchanging but as dynamic and fluctuating. In fact, Newton first called this new mathematical method *fluxions*.

In developing the calculus, Newton made use of a principle he had learned from Descartes: When a problem seems too large and complicated, break it down into small problems, and solve each of them. This is what the calculus does. It breaks down a dynamics problem into a very large number of steps and then in effect climbs the steps, each a solvable problem, one step at a time. The more steps into which a problem is broken, the more accurate the final results will be.

The story that the idea of universal gravitation was suggested to Newton by the fall of an apple from a tree seems to be true. William Stukeley, Newton's first biographer, reports that he heard the story from Newton himself. In making this observation, Newton made an intuitive mental leap and asked himself a basic "what if" question: What if the same force responsible for the fall of the apple extended to the orbit of the Moon? First he postulated that the Moon was falling toward the Earth in response to the downward (vertical) pull of Earth's gravity but that the Moon never struck the Earth because of the stronger horizontal pull of the Sun. He calculated that as the Moon falls toward the Earth, it is also pulled horizontally just

Principle of the calculus   The calculus breaks down a change or movement into a large number of steps. The more steps the curve is broken down into, the more accurate the answer.

far enough to compensate for the fall and carry it around the Earth's curvature in its elliptical orbit. Second, he envisioned the gravitational force as emanating from the center of a body (Earth, in this case) rather than from its surface. He then attempted to quantify the difference in force exerted on the apple versus that exerted on the faraway Moon. He accomplished this latter task by building on Kepler's third law of planetary motion to arrive at what has become known as the *inverse square law*. Gravitational force diminishes by the square of the distance over which it propagates. If the apple was 60 times closer to the Earth's center of gravity than the Moon was (which it is), then the gravitational force exerted upon the apple was 60 squared, or 3,600, times stronger than that experienced by the Moon. Converse-

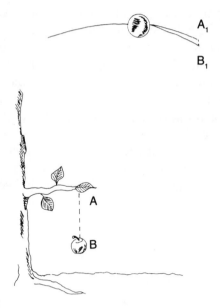

Newton's reasoning The same force that pulls the apple down pulls the Moon, too. But because the Moon is sixty times further away from the source of gravity than the apple and because gravitation diminishes by the square of the distance, the Moon should decline (or "fall") along its orbit 1/3,600th as far as the apple does in the same amount of time. He was right, of course, and, from this beginning, he went on to quantify the laws of motion on all physical bodies—one common scheme for terrestrial and celestial dynamics.

ly then, the Moon should curve downward along its orbit (fall) 1/3600th as far as the apple fell in the same amount of time. From these suppositions, Newton could calculate the exact orbit of the Moon.

Working all of this out mathematically confirmed Newton's grand insight that the same force that pulls the apple down pulls at the Moon. He then took a giant step further for mankind by presupposing that these same mathematical principles applied to every body—planet, moon, or asteroid—in the universe. In effect, Newton had taken Descartes's general picture of the universe and made it rigorously mathematical and precise. He had done nothing less than construct the first modern synthesis about the physical world, a mechanically based view in which the smallest particles as well as the largest celestial bodies all moved in accordance with the same mathematical principles.

Besides developing the calculus and starting on the path to the discovery of the law of gravity, in this same seventeen-month period, Newton arrived at major insights about the properties of light and color—insights that would later form the basis of *Opticks*, his major paper on the subject. How had he accomplished all this so young and working essentially alone? Newton was to recall later: "In those days I was in the prime of my age for invention and minded Mathematics and Philosophy more than at any other time."

Newton then put away all his papers and did not tell anybody about his monumental achievements. Various explanations have been put forward for this strange behavior: He did not like to call attention to himself. He valued his privacy above all else, and he might have been afraid that publication of his ideas would bring notoriety. Also, Newton might not have been confident about his numbers. They fit well enough to convince him of his hypothesis, but because of some imprecise estimates about the distance to the Moon or the radius of Earth, he might have been cautious about submitting his calculations to the critical eyes of his peers. He need not have been concerned. In reality, he had no peers.

It must be noted here that not all historians believe that Newton did all this in his short seventeen-month stay in the country. They put this belief in the category of myth, along with the falling apple story. Indeed, there is little documentation to support either the "Year of the Miracles" story or the opinions of its critics, except that Newton himself (albeit fifty years later) remembered the events that way. Because there is no evidence to the contrary, it is this author's view that Newton's word should be accepted for what occurred and when.

When Cambridge reopened in 1667 and Newton returned there, he was elected to a fellowship at Trinity College. Two years later, his mentor, Isaac Barrow, resigned his chair as Lucasian Professor of Mathematics (the position held today by Stephen Hawking) and recommended Isaac Newton to succeed him. This was a major step up the academic ladder and is illustrative of the close relationship between Barrow and Newton.

Newton entered into few close relationships with individuals his own age. However, he was drawn to older, educated men such as Clark, Stokes, and Babington. At Trinity, Isaac Barrow played the role of mentor. He was more than a dozen years older than Newton and the holder of a prominent position in the rigid academic hierarchy. The two men shared a strict Puritanical background as well as a mutual love of scholarship, and over time Barrow became keenly aware of Newton's mathematical prowess. In letters, Barrow referred to the younger teacher as "my friend" and as an "extraordinary genius."

It is possible that Barrow vacated the Lucasian chair because he recognized that Newton was potentially a greater mathematician than he was. It is more likely, however, that Barrow was a man of considerable ambition and had his eye on higher positions. At any rate, when the opportunity arose, he left Cambridge to become chaplain to Charles II (who, according to history, needed one). Four years later, Barrow was back at Cambridge, having been named Master of Trinity College by the King. Newton then had an even higher placed patron than before. Unfortunately, the situation was not to last long. Barrow became ill on a trip to London and sought relief by taking opium. He died at the age of forty-seven of an apparent drug overdose.

Meanwhile the protégé was gaining a reputation of his own in the field of mathematics. Newton the teacher was no less eccentric than Newton the student had been. He became known as "the odd fellow who lives by the gate." (Newton's rooms were located by the Great Gate at the entrance of Trinity College). He was seen about campus in his disheveled clothes, his wig askew, wearing run-down shoes and a soiled neckpiece. He seemed to care about nothing but his work. He was so absorbed in his studies that he often forgot to eat. On at least one occasion, he recorded in his notes that he forgot to sleep as well: Finding himself unable to solve a relatively simple arithmetic problem, he realized that he had not been to bed for days, and reluctantly took himself off to his chamber.

Eccentric or not, Newton worked hard. Over the years, he advanced the field of analytical geometry, completed his preliminary efforts on the calculus, accomplished pioneering work in optics, and (as historians were to find out many years later) conducted innumerable experiments in alchemy. He did all this without calling much attention to himself, publishing no papers. He might report on his work in one of his infrequent lectures, but few fellow professors or students attended these anyway. His academic colleges apparently found his train of thought difficult if not impossible to follow. His domestic servant told later biographers that Newton, finding himself with an empty lecture hall, would "talk to the walls" or trudge on back to his rooms, evidently unperturbed and eager to resume work. His isolation, however, would soon come to an end.

In 1660, Charles II, a self-styled amateur physicist, chartered the Royal Society of London, an independent organization that became the major center of English scientific activity during the seventeenth and eighteenth centuries. The society members had not yet heard much of Isaac Newton, but they had heard about a new telescope he had made. Always handy at building scientific devices, Newton found himself in need of a new telescope with which to observe the comets and planets. The only type of telescope available at the time was the standard refractor, with a large curved lens at the front end and an eyepiece at the rear. Newton did not like these because of their tendency to introduce spurious colors. So he thereupon proceeded to construct a new kind of telescope, one that used a curved mirror rather than a lens to collect light. He had not originated the idea for this new telescope, but he was the first to actually build one. The new telescope was more efficient and easy to build. The "Newton reflector," as it was called, became the most popular telescope in the world. Newton built three of them, and when the Royal Society asked to see one, he sent them one as a gift. Impressed, the Royal Society promptly elected Newton to membership. It was the beginning of a long and sometimes stormy relationship.

Pleased by the Society's enthusiastic reception of his telescope, Newton felt encouraged enough to volunteer a short paper on light and colors.

The study of light and optics had been a central feature of the scientific revolution and a subject of special interest to Newton since the plague-years hiatus in 1665 and 1666. Newton's contribution had to do with colors and their relationship to white light. The conventional wisdom of the time held that colors arise from a modification of light, which appears white in its pristine form. While staying at his mother's farm, Newton performed a series of experiments in which the spectrum of a narrow beam of light was projected through a prism onto the wall of a darkened room. He observed that a ray of light passing through a prism is refracted (deflected or bent) and that different parts of it are refracted to a different extent. The result is not merely a broadened spot of light, but a band of consecutive colors: red, orange, yellow, green, blue, and violet. When the refracted light passed through a second prism, the different colors recombined to form white light. This discovery led him to the conclusion that light is not homogeneous but complex and that the phenomena of colors arise from the decomposition of a heterogeneous mixture into its simple components. He further concluded that light consists of tiny particles.

The reaction of English and continental scientists ranged from skepticism to bitter opposition to Newton's conclusions, which seemed to invalidate the prevalent wave theory of light. Particular opposition came from Robert Hooke, the brilliant and abrasive secretary (and de facto chief scientist) of the Royal Society and from the Dutch scientist Christian Huygens. Newton never forgot an enemy, and these two antagonists were special objects of Newton's hate for decades.

When the color controversy first started, Newton patiently answered objections with further explanations, but his patience was limited. When his additional arguments produced still more negative responses, he became irritated and vowed he would never publish again. In fact, he even threatened to give up scientific investigation altogether. Not for Newton was the no-holds-barred give and take of scientific debate. Faced with any sort of criticism, he would withdraw into solitude and silence. With the so-called great minds of the Royal Society taking turns assaulting his disconcerting theory of light, the wounded lion retreated to his lair to lick his wounds.

Newton remained in intellectual isolation until 1675 when on a visit to London he was given to understand that Hooke had finally accepted his theory of colors. Emboldened by this news, he ventured to issue a new paper on color, as well as a second piece entitled "An Hypothesis Explaining the Properties of Light." Hooke's response to this article was to claim that Newton had stolen its contents from him. Newton exploded again. Intermediaries controlled the dispute, and an exchange of formal, icily polite letters between Newton and Hooke ensued, letters that do not conceal the complete lack of warmth between the two men.

Newton was also engaged in another controversy at this same time with a circle of English Jesuits in Liège. Their objections to Newton's work were without merit, but what drove Newton to a fury was their contention that his experiments were mistaken. This controversy continued until 1678 when a final blast of rage from Newton ended further correspondence.

Apparently, Newton had the first of his two nervous breakdowns in 1678, and the following year his mother died. For six years, he withdrew from any intellectual commerce, except when others initiated a correspondence, which he always broke off as soon as possible. When he eventually returned to science, it was with his ultimate contribution to humankind's knowledge of the universe.

The *Principia*

Newton might never have rejoined the intellectual world had it not been for the young astronomer Edmund Halley. Halley graduated from Queens' College, Oxford, where he had established a reputation as an outstanding scholar. After Oxford, he spent two years on the island of St. Helena in the South Atlantic. There he made astronomical observations and succeeded in cataloging the stars of the southern hemisphere with an accuracy and completeness never before achieved. King Charles II applauded his work, and the Royal Society elected him a fellow in 1678. A distinguished career lay ahead of him, highlighted by his identification of the periodic comet that has since borne his name. Important to this present narrative were his tact and affability. He was both well known and liked by his colleagues.

In August of 1684, Edmund Halley, who was troubled by a problem in orbital dynamics, visited Newton at Cambridge. This in itself was highly unusual. European scientists had been attempting to initiate correspondence with the noted mathematician for some time without much

success. Newton was apparently flattered that the well-known astronomer Halley had journeyed to Cambridge to seek his advice.

Leading up to this important meeting was a conversation that Halley
had had the previous January with the famous architect and astronomer
Christopher Wren and Robert Hooke. They had lunched together in
London at one of their favorite taverns and discussed the force of gravity and the elliptical orbits of the planets. The problem was that they
could not demonstrate the connection between the force and the orbits
in a precise mathematical manner. Halley and Wren admitted that they
could not do it. Hooke claimed he had a way to do it, but he would not
tell anybody what it was. They all were of the opinion that the inverse-
square law could explain Kepler's elliptical orbits, but they could not
prove it. They ended their luncheon by placing a bet as to who could
first prove the conjecture.

After waiting for seven months for Hooke to reveal his secret system, Halley decided to visit the best known mathematician of the time
and seek his assistance. He had met Newton on one previous occasion
and, of course, knew of Newton's forbidding reputation; but Halley must
also have had confidence in his own diplomatic skills.

At the time of this meeting, Halley was 28 and Newton was 42.
Despite the difference in their ages, Halley fearlessly engaged Newton
in a challenging intellectual discussion. He asked Newton if it was
possible to prove mathematically that planets orbited the Sun in elliptical orbits. Newton's astonishing answer was that it was not only possible but that he had already done it years before. When Halley asked
to see the calculations, Newton rummaged through several of the many
stacks of papers that littered his rooms but failed to find them. He told
Halley that he would write them out anew and send them to him. It is
quite possible that Newton knew exactly where the papers could be
found but he wanted to check his numbers one last time before submitting them to Halley.

Whatever the reason, Newton did not forward his calculations to
Halley for another three months. Much of this time was spent working
on a nine-page treatise that he titled *On the Motion of Revolving Bodies*
(*De motu*, as it was called in Latin). When Halley received this new
paper, he was again astonished. The paper not only contained the solution to the original problem he had posed but much more. In fact, the
short paper contained the mathematical seeds of a general science of

dynamics. The little treatise did not state the law of universal gravitation, nor did it contain any of the three Newtonian laws of motion. It was, however, a brilliant beginning, the precursor of the magnum opus to come. If this was a representative sample, what else could be found in those apparently disorganized stacks of papers in Newton's quarters? To his great credit, Halley recognized the tremendous importance of Newton's work and lost little time in journeying to Cambridge a second time. There, Halley persuaded Newton to organize those stacks of paper, those apparently miscellaneous sketches and diagrams, those endless columns of figures, and to set to work on the definitive book on gravitation and the dynamics of the solar system.

Once Newton started revising and expanding his original short paper, he soon became obsessed. Halley had initiated the effort, but now Newton was fully involved. "Now that I am upon the subject," he wrote to the astronomer John Flamsteed, "I would gladly know the bottom of it before I publish my paper." To get to the bottom of it, Newton nearly cut himself off from human society. From August 1684 until the spring of 1686, his life was completely devoted to the work that would later be known as the *Principia*.

His secretary at that time, Humphrey Newton (no relation), wrote that Newton "ate very sparingly, nay ofttimes he has forget to eat at all, so that going into his Chamber, I have found his Mess untouched." He was a man possessed. Again his secretary reports that he would "fall to write on his Desk standing, without giving himself the Leisure to draw a Chair to sit down in." Humphrey Newton is also the source of Isaac Newton's reputation for not having a sense of humor. In all of the five years he served him, he reported that he saw the great man laugh only once. He had loaned an acquaintance a copy of Euclid. The acquaintance asked what use its study would be to him, "upon which Sir Isaac was very merry." On a later occasion, Isaac Newton was heard to reprimand Edmund Halley for taking the time to express a witticism while they worked on an experiment together.

To write the *Principia*, Newton had to synthesize all the work he had done over the preceding twenty years. He had to recalculate, review, and rethink all of the problems, and he had to gather new data—all the new astronomical data he could get his hands on. He must have known this work was to be his magnum opus, the sum total of all he knew or could figure out about the natural world.

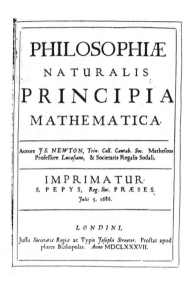

Title page of the *Philosophiae Naturalis Principia Mathematica*—1686.

The book was not to be a best-seller in the current sense of that term. Newton wanted to communicate with a select few, an intellectual elite, whose numbers he sought to reduce to an absolute minimum by every means possible. He wrote in classical Latin, and he made no effort to make his abstruse mathematics easy to follow. Only through the tireless efforts of Edmund Halley was the book ever published. When problems arose in Cambridge, Halley journeyed there to encourage Newton and spur him on. When obstacles to publication arose at the Society in London, he overcame them with diplomacy and unstinting effort. In the end, he put up his own money to meet the cost of printing and distribution that the Society had decided it could not afford.

The surviving drafts of the *Principia* illustrate the dictum that genius is one percent inspiration and ninety-nine percent perspiration. The drafts are characterized less by sudden brilliant insight than by constant, indefatigable working away at specific problems. When, years later, Newton was asked how he had discovered the laws of celestial dynamics, he replied, "By thinking of them without ceasing."

Finally published in 1687, the *Philosophiae Naturalis Principia Mathematica* consisted of three books: Book I sets forth a general dynamics of bodies operating in the theoretical condition of no friction and no resistance. Book II is concerned primarily with the more practical problems concerning the motions of solid bodies suspended in a fluid medium, that is, the motion of bodies when there is friction and resistance. It is in Book III that Newton most remarkably displays his genius. There Newton presents his exact quantitative description of the motions of celestial bodies. This description is based upon Newton's three laws of motion: (1) that a body remains in its state of rest or of uniform motion in a straight line unless it is compelled by a force impressed on it to change that state; (2) that the change in motion (the change of velocity times the mass of the body) is proportional to the force impressed; (3) that to every action, there is an equal and opposite reaction.

An example of the first law would be a moving projectile, which will continue to move in a straight line unless it is retarded by the resistance of the air or its path is curved downward by a force (identified by Newton as gravity). Another example is a spinning top that continues to spin unless it is retarded by friction with the surface on which its point spins or by the resistance of air. The large bodies of the planets or comets, meeting with little or no resistance in space, continue their motions, whether straight or curved, forever. Newton further refined his first law with the concept of *mass*, which he invented. In the Newtonian universe, every object is described by its mass, and mass possesses *inertia*, the tendency of an object to resist any change in its state of motion.

Newton's second law of motion asserts that a greater force induces a greater change of motion and that multiple forces produce a change that is a combination of the different strengths and directions of the various forces. A change in motion is expressed as *acceleration*, defined as the change in velocity with time. Newton's second law—force equals mass times acceleration—is expressed in the first equation every student of physics learns:

$$F = ma$$

This has been called the most useful physical law ever written. The equation, simple in appearance, is awesome in its power and sometimes frighteningly difficult to solve.

Also in his second law, Newton introduced the concept of centripetal force. *Centripetal* is a word he coined himself and defined as "seeking the center," to distinguish it from Christian Huygen's word *centrifugal*, meaning to flee the center.

From Newton's third law, it can be seen that gravitational force is mutual. The attractions of two bodies upon one another are always equal, although directed in opposite directions. The apple is attracted to the surface of the Earth, but the Earth is also attracted to the apple. The Earth exerts a gravitational force on the Moon while at the same time it is subjected to a gravitational force from the Moon. The amount of gravitational force exerted by each body—the apple, the Moon, or the Earth—is directly proportional to the mass of that body.

Consideration of circular motion in terms of these laws yielded a formula for the quantitative measurement of the centripetal force necessary to divert a moving body from its straight path into a given circle. When Newton substituted this formula into Kepler's third law, he found that the centripetal force holding the planets in their orbits about the Sun must decrease with the square of the planets' distance from the Sun. The force in question Newton labeled *gravitas* (literally, "heaviness" or "weight"). The law of universal gravitation, which Newton also confirmed from such further phenomena as the tides and the orbits of comets, states that every particle of matter in the universe attracts every other particle with a force that is proportional to the product of their masses and inversely proportional to the square of the distance between their centers.

Newtonian mechanics became the fundamental base of the structure upon which all the layers of physical sciences and technology are built. Newtonian physics was, above all else, a triumph of *reductionism*—the act of taking a complex phenomenon, in this case the cosmos, and explaining it by analyzing the simplest, most basic physical mechanisms that are in operation during the phenomenon. Moreover, it represented a change in the perspective of human thinking, a transition from a static society waiting for something to happen to a dynamic society seeking understanding because understanding implies control.

The *Principia* had a resounding impact on the thinking world. Voltaire wrote a popular account of it, John Locke admired it tremendously, and even such celebrated critics as Christian Huygens and Gottfried Leibniz joined in praise of the awesome breadth and scope of the work. In his "Ode to Newton" prefixed to the document, Halley said in part: "Nearer the gods no mortal may approach."

Others, however, had a bit more trouble appreciating the work. On receiving his copy, Dr. Humphrey Babington, Newton's sponsor at Cambridge, complained that it was going to take him seven years to understand anything of it. Newton himself told of passing a student on the street in Cambridge who was heard to say: "There goes the man that writt a book that neither he nor any body else understands."

Why did the established Church not attack Newton as it had his predecessors Copernicus and Galileo? It was not because his logic and mathematics were unassailable, because so were Copernicus's and Galileo's. The times had changed, of course, and the Church was more receptive to new ideas. More importantly, it did not see the deeply religious Newton as any threat to orthodoxy. Newton constructed his cosmological system on the assumption of God's existence. Matter could not be explained on its own terms but necessitated a prime mover, a creator, a supreme architect. If the universe was a huge beautiful clock, then there had to be a clockmaker. God had established the physical world and its laws, and determining what these laws were was both a religious and a scientific enterprise. Indeed, Newton saw science as a form of worship. The public Newton had no trouble with the established Church. Secretly, as is now known from his unpublished papers, he did question orthodox teachings, but he was careful not to let a hint of his doubts appear in his published writings.

The *Principia* was Newton's monumental achievement. It sold only a few hundred copies, but most historians call it one of the most important books ever written. The publication of the great work did not change Newton's personality, but the magnitude of its accomplishment thrust the former recluse into the public eye for the rest of his life. As a public figure of international prominence, it was time for him to move on to a larger stage.

Parliament, London, Fame, and Controversy

Almost simultaneously with the publication of the *Principia*, Newton helped lead the resistance to the new King James II's attempt to Catholicize Cambridge. This controversy brought Newton on frequent trips to London, where he made the acquaintance of a broader and more urbane group of people. It included the philosopher John Locke and a young admirer named Nicolas Fatio de Duillier, a brilliant Swiss-born mathematician residing in London, who was to establish a close relationship with the newly famous physicist.

Fatio de Dullier was only twenty-five years old when he first met Newton. The two became almost instant friends—an instant close friendship was not something to be expected from the former recluse. In fact, when Newton was returning to London for a session of Parliament, he wrote Fatio and asked him if there might be a chamber for him where Fatio lodged. It is known that Fatio and Isaac spent a good deal of time together on Newton's trips to London, which became lengthier and more frequent. The intensity of their relationship is noteworthy from their letters to each other and, in letters to third parties, about each other. About 1693, there was a crisis: Fatio became seriously ill, and later family financial problems threatened to call him home to Switzerland. Newton was distraught. He suggested that Fatio move to Cambridge where Newton would support him. Nothing came of that suggestion, and then later in the year the close relationship and the correspondence broke off. The break was sudden, and there is no surviving explanation.

There is little doubt that the breakup had a serious effect on Isaac Newton. It was at this time that he suffered his second nervous breakdown. His two friends John Locke and Samuel Pepys both feared for his sanity. Both had received wild accusatory letters from Newton. Pepys was informed that Newton would neither see him nor write to him again. Locke received an even stranger letter:

Sr

Being of opinion that you endeavored to embroil me with women & by other means I was so much affected with it as that when one told me you were sickly & would not live I answered twere better if you were dead.

Pepys and Locke handled the situation with tact and compassion. Locke journeyed to Cambridge to speak to Newton in person and to assure him of his friendship. By the time he got there, the worst of Newton's attack of paranoia was over. Newton explained that his wild letters were due to distemper and lack of sleep. The actual cause of Newton's breakdown can never be known with certainty. There were other strains and stresses on Newton at this period of his life, but the ill-fated attachment to Fatio certainly seems a likely factor.

Newton's career in politics came at a time of significant change in the relationship between the Crown and Parliament, but Newton himself played only a minor supporting role. He had first been elected to Parliament in 1689 as a result of his previous defiance of recognized authority in the James II versus Cambridge issue. Prior to this period in English history, kings ruled by "divine right." But with the coming of William of Orange and his wife Mary, kings were declared by Parliament. Saying that Newton played a minor role in changing the English form of government to a constitutional monarchy might be an overstatement. The records of the House of Commons for that period contain not a single reference to Newton. He is reported to have spoken only once in his entire time in Parliament. The late science writer Isaac Asimov imagined the scene as the acknowledged greatest mind in all Europe rose to his feet for the first time: A hush must have fallen over the assembly as the great man was about to speak. They were to be disappointed. All he did was ask an usher to close a window in the back of the room because of a chilling draft.

However minor his role in great political changes, this was a time of rising expectations for Newton. He was forty-six years old, and it was at this time that he commissioned the leading painter of the day, Sir Godfrey Kneller, to do his portrait. It was the first, and possibly the best, of the many portraits to be painted of Newton and it is an indication of his self-esteem at that time.

Also at this time, the Archbishop of Canterbury offered him the position of Master of Trinity. Newton was forced to refuse this honor because he would have had to take holy orders and, as is known from his secret papers, he harbored doubts about orthodox Protestantism. In particular, he did not accept the concept of the Trinity. For these reasons, he could see that his academic career at Cambridge was at an impasse. He was forced to turn to other fields.

It was suggested that Newton find a position in London, and he was quick to concur. Eventually, through the help of his friend, Charles Montague (later Lord Halifax), Newton was appointed Warden of the Mint. This was in 1696, and, although Newton did not resign his position at Cambridge until 1701, he wasted little time in moving to London and, henceforth, centering his life there. Newton came to Cambridge when he was eighteen and he had spent nearly thirty-five years there. He left without a backward glance, returned only infrequently, and corresponded with almost no one.

As Warden and later Master of the Mint, Newton drew a large income that, added to the personal estate inherited from his mother, left him a rich man at his death. Although regarded as a sinecure and a reward for past services to the Crown, Newton took his new position seriously. There was a new coinage system to install, and Newton took active charge of that project. He became interested in counterfeiting and with time became the terror of London counterfeiters. He sent a number to the gallows and attended the hangings in person.

Although his creative days in science were largely over, Newton reigned in London as the patriarch of English science. In 1703, he was elected President of the Royal Society, where he ruled magisterially if not tyrannically. One of those to feel the lash of Sir Isaac Newton at his absolute worst was John Flamsteed, the Astronomer Royal.

The Newton/Flamsteed quarrel centered on control over the data that Flamsteed had collected in his years at the Royal Observatory at Greenwich. Newton had needed information from Flamsteed during the preparation of the *Principia* and he acknowledged this debt in the first edition of that document. In the 1690s, however, he was having difficulty obtaining data he needed for a paper on lunar theory. Newton became annoyed when he could not get all the information he wanted as quickly as he wanted it. He used his influence with Queen Anne's government to be named chairman of a new governing body (called "visitors") responsible for the Royal Observatory. From this position, the domineering Newton attempted to force the immediate publication of Flamsteed's catalog of stars. This battle continued for ten years, during which time Newton used every dirty trick possible to best his rival. In the end, he had Flamsteed expelled from the Royal Society. Flamsteed's observations, his life's work, were seized and turned over to his long-time rival Edmund Halley for publication. Flamsteed fought back and finally won his point in court. He had the printed catalog returned to him and burned before it was generally distributed—better that it be destroyed than fall into the hands of Newton and Halley. It was not until after Flamsteed's death that his assistant brought out an authorized version of the document. The mere matter of Flamsteed's death did not stop Newton. He systematically eliminated all references to Flamsteed's help in later editions of the *Principia*. Altogether, this was a disgraceful episode in the life of the great scientist.

Even worse was Newton's infamous battle with Gottfried Leibniz over which of them had invented the calculus. Leibniz was an opponent more nearly Newton's match. It is now agreed universally that Newton developed the calculus before Leibniz became involved in mathematics. However, he kept his 1665 accomplishment a secret and did not publish his method. Leibniz later arrived at the calculus independently and published his work in 1684. The ensuing bitter fracas over who had developed the calculus first took on international proportions, with the English scientific community backing their leader and the Continental scientists siding with Leibniz. The controversy soon escalated to charges of plagiarism by both sides. Neither Leibniz nor Newton conducted this battle with any dignity. Accusation of dishonesty had always aroused Newton to fury, and this was no exception. Newton wrote a number of articles for scientific journals in his own defense, publishing them under the names of some of his young followers. As President of the Royal Society, he appointed what he called an "impartial" committee to look into the matter. Newton then secretly wrote the final report himself and later reviewed this document for the scientific journal published by the Society. Needless to say, with a deck stacked like that, Newton won the hand.

Newton's hatred for Leibniz continued even after the German philosopher was dead. Almost every paper Newton wrote on whatever subject for the next twenty years contained at least one furious paragraph attacking Leibniz. "Second inventors," Newton said scornfully of Leibniz, "count for nothing."

Meanwhile, Newton's life-long quarrels with Robert Hooke continued. So sensitive to Hooke's criticism was Newton that he did not publish his definitive work on light and colors, *Opticks*, until after Hooke's death in 1703, although it represented work he had done twenty years previously. Newton was simply unable to confront criticism throughout his life.

Historians have found another aspect of Newton's personality a bit disconcerting. There is little doubt today that he fudged the numbers in some of his important papers, numbers such as those for the acceleration of gravity and the precession of the equinoxes. Also, in the second edition of the *Principia*, for instance, he chose a figure for the speed of sound that was the average of a number of measurements that had been conducted. He then worked the numbers backward to make it appear that his answer had been arrived at by precise mathematical methods. It should be noted that he did not fake experimental data; rather he used dishonest mathematics to make his conclusions sound more precise than they actually were.

There was, in addition to the public Newton, a secret Newton. This was discovered by, among others, the noted economist, John Maynard Keynes. As a sideline to his academic work, Keynes was interested in investigating how great minds worked. In pursuit of this hobby, he purchased, for only thirty-five pounds, over fifty lots of Newton's papers at an auction held at the London galleries of Sotheby and Company in 1936. Keynes then spent many hours poring over the documents. He found to his amazement that Newton had spent at least as much time on the metaphysical, the occult, alchemy, and Biblical minutia as he did on physics. He found that the bulk of these papers were "wholly magical and wholly devoid of scientific value." Keynes concluded that Newton was not really the first of the modern scientists, but rather "the last of the magicians." The bulk of this material now resides in the Hebrew Museum in Jerusalem, unpublished and unread.

A word in Newton's defense might be in order here. Alchemy was a legitimate science in the 1600s. Any serious investigator of that time, trying to fathom the fiendishly complicated laws of chemical elements, would necessarily have to understand the dominant theory of the day, which was alchemy. Many recent science historians have taken a fresh look at the alchemists and at Newton's later years and have realized that, like many a serious alchemist, he was using an arcane notation that, upon closer examination, represented totally valid scientific observations.

Newton supporters say that if many of the alchemists' notebooks were transcribed into correct, modern scientific language, many valid chemical reactions would be revealed. It might be that Newton was not a magician in his later years, as Keynes suggested, but rather an alchemist, like any serious scientist of that time necessarily was.

As to his work in theology and Biblical scholarship, virtually none of it is read today. Voltaire, who was Newton's defender and champion in France, summed up Newton's later work with a witty observation: "Sir Isaac Newton wrote his commentary on the Revelation to console mankind for the great superiority he had over them in other respects."

In any case, it is the public rather than the secret Newton with whom we are concerned here, and the public man had become a success. In 1705 Queen Anne, the popular successor to the British throne, visited Cambridge along with her entire court including her Prince Consort, George of Denmark (about whom Charles II had once commented unkindly: "I have tried him drunk and tried him sober, and there is nothing in him"). The Royal party were on their way to more important activities at the Newmarket race course, but a ceremonial stop off at Cambridge was in order. There the Queen conferred honorary doctorates and formally knighted three distinguished citizens, including Isaac Newton, Master of the Mint, President of the Royal Society, and natural philosopher extraordinaire. An elegant dinner followed the investiture. It was held in Trinity Hall where the newly knighted Sir Isaac, now seated at the High Table, had once served as a waiter in his impoverished student days. He was now the first man of science ever to be knighted by the Crown. The "odd man who lived by the Gate" had returned to Cambridge in triumph.

What was Newton's life like in his long years in London? He was a workaholic. Whether it was secret research into occult matters, experimentation with various approaches to alchemy, or detailed examination of the books of the Bible and esoteric theology, he worked. Newton had no taste for the esthetic temptations of London. He apparently had a deaf ear for music, referred to sculpture as mere "stone dolls," and viewed poetry as a "kind of ingenious nonsense." He was known to have attended the opera but once. He said later that he heard the first act with pleasure, endured the second, and fled from the third. Although he was a prodigious reader in the fields of theology and science, litera-ture meant nothing to him. Newton's library contained no works by Chaucer, Shakespeare, or Milton.

Newton had helped make science and scientists respectable and welcome in the high society of London, and he adopted the life-style of this upper class. He kept a carriage and employed six servants. Newton's fame had become such that all important visitors to London sought a meeting with the great intellect. Royalty were always wel-comed by him, but others sought an audience in vain. Among those who were turned away were Benjamin Franklin and the French philoso-pher Voltaire.

Sir Isaac's keen intellect, however, did not protect him from the mass financial folly of the 1720 Great South Sea bubble. This invest-ment insanity cost the great scientist a whopping 20,000 pounds, pos-sibly a third of his net worth at the time. Of course it was science, not money management, that was Newton's forte. Not too long before his death, Newton looked back over his long scientific life and summarized it as follows:

> I know not what I may seem to the world, but, as to myself, I seem to have been only like a boy playing on the sea shore, and diverting myself in now and then finding a smoother pebble or prettier shell than ordinary, whilst the great ocean of truth lay all undiscovered before me.

There are episodes in the history of scientific endeavor that are of monumental significance. Newton's demonstration of the manner in which gravitational forces could be calculated and that the same laws apply to motion in the heavens and on Earth must be recognized as one of these. Newton taught the world that everything attracts everything else with a force inversely proportional to the square of the distance from it, and that objects respond to forces with accelerations propor-tional to the forces—these are Newton's laws of universal gravitation and of motion. They account for the motions of cannon balls, rockets, planets, satellites, galaxies, and objects. In effect, he brought order to the universe.

The final word on Newton is left to Aldous Huxley. Speaking of Newton, he said: "As a man, he was a failure; as a monster he was superb."

Newton died at the age of eighty-four in London on March 20, 1727, and was buried with high honors at Westminster Abbey. This was the first time that such an honor had been given to a man of science, learning, or art in England. Physics was not to see his intellectual equal for close to two hundred years, until 1905, when a then unknown twenty-six-year-old patent office clerk in Bern, Switzerland, published his thoughts on time, space, mass, and energy.

Chapter Two

Albert Einstein

There was a young girl named Miss Bright,
Who could travel much faster than light.
She departed one day,
In an Einsteinian way,
And came back on the previous night.

Anonymous

Over the past four centuries, a series of astronomical observations and experiments has radically altered humankind's view of the universe. Just as Aristotle's geocentric universe was replaced by the heliocentric universe of Copernicus, Kepler, and Galileo, so too was this view modified and quantified by Newton's mechanical universe. And in the early twentieth century, Newton's universe was replaced by Einstein's. We currently live in Einstein's universe whether we quite understand it or not. It goes without saying that Albert Einstein ranks as one of the supreme geniuses of our time. His contribution to our understanding of time, and his efforts to reconcile the physics of particles with the physics of space, ensure his place in the history of civilization. But what sort of man was he, and, specifically, what did he teach us?

Einstein's theories of relativity (there are two, the special theory and the general theory) became the first scientific subjects that the newly emerging mass media of the 1930s tried to popularize. But because the press found even the simplest explanations of the theories counterintuitive and hard to follow, attention turned to the man himself. The media spotlight created something of a caricature, which became the popular image of a modern scientist. Einstein possessed a playful wit that made him enormously likeable. A reporter from *Reader's Digest* once asked Einstein, then over seventy, for his formula for success. "Let X stand for work, Y for play, and A for success," replied Einstein, who by that time had created the most famous mathematical equation of all time. "Then A equals X plus Y plus Z." "But what is Z?" asked the reporter. "Z is for keeping one's mouth shut," Einstein joked.

He became a peerless myth—Einstein of the rumpled clothes and massive head and wild hair; Einstein naive and absentminded, yet obviously possessed of a superior mind. One obstacle to understanding Einstein better is that we think we already know him, when all we really know is the image created by the press. A puzzled Einstein once remarked that he did not understand why he was so well liked and so little understood. To truly understand Einstein, we must take a crack at understanding his science.

Science, more than anything else, was Einstein's life; and to understand the man, it is necessary to follow his scientific ways of thinking. Can the theories of relativity be understood by the intelligent layperson, using only a minimum of mathematics? I think that they can, and I also think that they are of such importance that they ought to be part of everyone's education. But be assured that relativity, at the level we will be discussing it, can also be great fun. Time warps, curved space, the controversial Twin Paradox—these are all entertaining exercises for the mind.

Young Einstein

Albert Einstein was born in Ulm, Germany, on March 14, 1879, the first of the two children of Hermann Einstein and the former Pauline Koch. The following year, the family moved to Munich, where Hermann and an uncle, Jakob Einstein, established a small electrical plant and engineering works. A daughter, Maria, was born one year later. Always called Maja, she was to become the person closest to Albert throughout their lives. The Einstein family was of modest means; the father's business activities were never very successful. They were, however, a cultured family—they loved books and music, and were proud of their liberal, nondogmatic attitudes. Hermann's dislike of authority, which was manifest as a distaste for religion, might have helped shape his son's later disregard for social conventions, his independent views of religion, and even his lack of reverence for established physics.

The main source of family recollections about Albert's earliest years is a biographical essay written by his sister in 1924 after her brother had achieved fame. She related her grandmother's reaction upon first seeing Albert as a baby: "Much too heavy," she exclaimed. In the same essay are recounted Einstein's mother's fears over the unusually large and angular back of her baby's head (the uncommon shape to Einstein's skull became permanent). The family also feared that Albert might be somewhat mentally impaired because of his slowness in learning to speak. He did not speak until the age of three, and Maja wrote that he did not become fully fluent in German until he was ten years old.

Prior to his school days, a transformative event occurred that Einstein was to remember all his life. "As a child of four or five," he said, "I experienced a miracle when my father showed me a compass. There had to be something behind objects that lay deeply hidden—the development of our world of thought is, in a certain sense, a flight away from the miraculous."

At age six, Einstein entered public school. Although he did not always get along with his teachers at primary school, he did well scholastically. A popular myth about Einstein is that he was a poor student in his early years. In reality, his grades were excellent, and he was consistently placed at the top of the class, despite the fact that rigid discipline and the rote-learning techniques bothered him. Outside of class, he was a quiet child who did not care to play with his schoolmates, preferring instead solitary games that required patience and persistence. One of his favorite games was building a house of cards.

At age ten, Einstein transferred to a typical German secondary school, the Luitpold Gymnasium, where he was subjected to the harsh and pedantic regimentation normal for the times. He reacted to this coercive teaching style by distrusting authority, in particular educational authority. There is little doubt that Einstein's later independent and questioning attitude toward conventional science was nurtured there. Many years later, in an interview with his biographer, Banesh Hoffmann, Einstein joked that, "to punish me for my contempt for authority, Fate made me an authority."

Einstein stayed at the Luitpold Gymnasium until he was fifteen and continued to earn high marks in mathematics and Latin. He had a natural antipathy for sports or gymnasium athletics, claiming that strenuous physical activity made him dizzy and tired. That attitude was partly responsible for the fact that he made few friends at school and felt isolated and alone. He was not always popular with his instructors either. Albert's Greek teacher once told Hermann Einstein that it did not make any difference what field Albert picked as a life occupation—he would fail in any of them.

Two especially noteworthy events occurred during Einstein's secondary school years. At the age of twelve, Einstein decided to devote himself to solving the riddle of the "huge world." Although he did not know it yet, he had become a fledgling physicist. He had been stimulated in these interests not by his teachers but by his uncles Jacob Einstein and Casar Koch, who encouraged his interest in mathematics and science. The same year that he embarked on his life-long study of the "huge world," Einstein picked up a book on Euclidean geometry, to which he later referred as the "holy geometry book." Einstein was impressed by the precision and definiteness of geometry, and he taught it to himself before it was presented in class. He went on to study differential and integral calculus by himself.

Another influence on Einstein at this time was a close family friend, Max Talmud. A medical student with little money, Talmud took one evening meal each week with the Einsteins. He gave Albert books on science, and later philosophy, which the two discussed for many hours. Talmud, who years later wrote of his recollections of this time, said that he had never seen Albert reading any light literature, nor did he recall ever seeing him in the company of schoolmates his own age.

Einstein's major recreational interest both in those early school days and later was music. His mother was a talented pianist who encouraged music in the home. Maja learned the piano while Albert took up the violin. He also taught himself the piano and played both these instruments throughout his life.

In 1894, the electrical business failed, and the Einstein family moved to Milan, Italy. Albert remained behind to finish school in the care of relatives in Munich. Now even more unhappy in school and missing his family, Einstein became indifferent to his school work and his grades began to suffer. One of his teachers eventually asked him to leave the school. Albert accepted that suggestion with alacrity and, without even informing his parents of his decision, he dropped out of the Gymnasium without acquiring a diploma.

Thereafter, he happily rejoined his family in Milan, where he was encouraged by his surprised parents to give some thought to his future. The family was in financial trouble, so he knew he would be expected to make his own way. If science was to be his chosen career, further education was clearly necessary. His biggest problem was the lack of a diploma, without which he could not enter any of the Italian universities.

College Days

After a time, Einstein learned of the Swiss Polytechnic Institute in Zurich, which did not require a diploma for admission. Passing an entrance examination was required, however. In 1895, Einstein traveled to Zurich for the exam. Although he did well on the mathematics and science parts, he failed the examination. This was a serious setback, but he overcame it by enrolling in a Swiss prep school at Aarau for a year. There he seemed to enjoy school for the first time, reveling in the free spirit of the place and the thoughtfulness of the instructors. He retook the university entrance exam in 1896 and was duly admitted to a four-year program of study that would qualify him as a teacher. Einstein said in an essay he wrote at that time, "I imagine myself becoming a teacher in those branches of natural science, choosing the theoretical part of them." He knew his own strengths even then.

The same year that he enrolled in the renowned Polytechnic Institute, Einstein renounced his German citizenship. After a payment of only a few marks, he received a document from Ulm stating that he was no longer a citizen of Germany. He probably would have been willing to pay much more. Now he was a stateless student in Zurich. However, from the beginning of his student days, he had saved a significant portion of his modest allowance in preparation for paying for his Swiss naturalization papers, which he was able to do shortly thereafter.

In his first year in college, Einstein met fellow students Marcel Grossman and Mileva Maric, a good looking young woman who was called Marity. With these friends, he would spend an occasional evening at a concert or theatrical presentation. He was also attracted to a Zurich kaffeehaus where students could spend hours solving the world's problems. For the most part, however, he was a serious student, and he worked. In a letter to a friend, he wrote: "Strenuous labor and the contemplation of God's nature are the angels which, reconciling, fortifying, and yet mercilessly severe, will guide me through the tumult of life."

Although his attitude regarding work in general was mature, Einstein tended to work only on projects he found of interest. Isaac Newton had behaved similarly at Cambridge more than two centuries earlier. But then Newton's tutor had shown little interest in his activities. Einstein's situation was different: He was attending an institution using the formal lecture techniques, and his attendance (or more often absence) at class was noted. His professor in physics, Heinrich Weber, is supposed to have told Einstein: "You are a smart boy, Einstein, a very smart boy. But you have one great fault, you do not let yourself be told anything."

Einstein's independence of mind and attitude made him generally less than popular with his professors. Herman Minkowski, his mathematical professor at the Polytechnic, remembered Einstein as "a lazy dog" who seldom came to class. Einstein was helped by lecture notes supplied to him by his good friend Marcel Grossman, who kept a meticulously organized journal. He studied these just prior to the few examinations and did well enough. On at least one occasion, he received a formal warning on the neglect of his laboratory work. On another occasion, one of his experiments caused an explosion that almost destroyed the lab and badly injured his hand.

Einstein, like Newton before him, did not depend on his professors but relied on self-study. Again, as in Newton's case, the classical physics being taught in the classroom was out of date. To keep abreast of a fast-moving science, one had to read independently, which Einstein did with an unbounded enthusiasm for new ideas.

Einstein graduated from the Swiss Polytechnic in the spring of 1900 and began to look for a job. He had received his degree in physics at the same time as three other students, each of whom had immediately obtained positions as teaching assistants at the university. Einstein had expected to be taken on as a teaching assistant also, but he was not. This was a major disappointment for him, and he never forgave his faculty advisor Professor Weber for seeming to promise an assistantship and then taking it away. Einstein remained jobless for some time, the price to be paid for his lack of reverence for his instructors. On their part, they might have reasoned that if he could not show enthusiasm for class work, he might not show it for professional work.

Einstein did not like being a financial burden to his family, especially because they were still experiencing financial difficulties. He at last found employment as a part-time teacher, but this was only temporary work.

During this arduous period in Einstein's life, there were long separations from his companion and fellow student from the Swiss Polytechnic, Mileva Maric, with whom he had established a romantic relationship early in their student days. An illegitimate child was born to them in 1902, whom they seemed to have put up for adoption.

Finally, in June of 1902, with the assistance of his friend Marcel Grossman, Einstein obtained an appointment as a "technical expert third class" at the Swiss Patent Office in Bern. He could now plan marriage to Mileva. Einstein's parents were opposed to this marriage, possibly because of Mileva's Catholic background or simply because Einstein's mother never liked her. It was only on his deathbed that Hermann Einstein finally consented to the marriage. The couple were married in January of 1903, and Einstein settled into his new job at the patent office.

Einstein had to do a lot of outside reading and analysis to keep up with modern physics. As a student, Einstein read Kirchoff and Hertz on the behavior of electrical currents and electromagnetic waves. He also studied James Clerk Maxwell's theories of electricity, Ernst Mach's views on the basic concepts of physics, and Hendrik Lorentz's ideas about the electron theory of matter.

These and other influential pioneers of the day, in particular Michael Faraday, became Einstein's "giants." Like Newton before him, Einstein had to have shoulders on which to stand. And Einstein was to acknowledge this debt. In a lecture he gave on relativity in London in 1921, he said that relativity was "the direct outcome and, in a sense, the natural completion of the work of Faraday, Maxwell, and Lorentz."

Einstein's Giants

Although they play supporting roles in this narrative, Einstein's giants could each be a star in his own galaxy. Michael Faraday (1791–1867) was the first hero. Faraday was the son of a blacksmith, and, although he had little formal education, he was the Thomas Edison of his day. He taught himself enough science to become the outstanding experimental physicist of his time. As a young man, he had obtained a position as a laboratory assistant at the Royal Institute of Great Britain. He stayed for forty-six years, eventually becoming the institute's director. He is most famous for his discovery of the phenomenon of electromagnetic induction. This discovery was prompted by an earlier experiment (by Hans Christian Oersted) that showed that an electric current deflects a magnetic needle. Faraday had the ingenuity to design an experiment that explored the possibility of the opposite effect, that is, the effect that the magnetic force might have on an electric current. Because of his limited mathematical background, Faraday did not understand or trust mathematical models as proper descriptions of physical phenomena. He, therefore, developed physical models to explain experimental results.

Faraday found that electricity and magnetism were both conveyed by means of invisible lines of force that are called *fields*. With this discovery began field theory, at the time a significant breakthrough. (When high school students today randomly sprinkle iron filings on a piece of paper resting on a magnet, they are illustrating how the filings are attracted to the magnetic field, and they are replicating a Faraday experiment.)

Faraday's major contribution to physics was to focus the attention of the scientific community upon the invisible fields of force, now the prime object of research everywhere, from the subatomic to the intergalactic. Faraday's electrochemical studies also convinced him that matter consists of different kinds of atoms, each of which is an electrically balanced structure with equal numbers of positive and negative units of electric charge. He was in some ways the world's first atomic physicist.

James Clerk Maxwell (1831–1879) had first studied electricity and magnetism by reading Faraday's papers on the subjects. Applying his prodigious mathematical skills, Maxwell derived what are now known as Maxwell's equations. By means of these equations, he demonstrated that electricity and magnetism are aspects of a single force, electromagnetism, and that light itself is a variety of this force. The hitherto separate fields of electricity, magnetism, and optics were now united.

Maxwell's discovery that the speed of electromagnetic propagation was exactly the same as the speed of light led to his conclusion that light is but one example of an electromagnetic radiation. He further concluded that electricity need not be confined to wires but could be disseminated as waves through space, as light is. With these conclusions, Maxwell opened the possibility for radio (first called *wireless*) communication.

The scientific world was skeptical of Maxwell's radical ideas until Heinrich Hertz (1857–1894) conducted a series of now famous experiments that confirmed all of the theoretical predictions of Maxwell's theory. Electromagnetism comes in waves, and all waves have a wavelength, the distance between the waves' crests. If electromagnetic waves are thought of as ocean waves, then the crests can be visualized as being about twenty or thirty feet apart. The difference among various electromagnetic waves—infrared, microwave, X rays, radio waves—is a matter of their wavelengths and frequencies. Visible light, which is in the middle of the electromagnetic spectrum, is spread over wavelengths called colors—blue, green, orange, and red.

Heinrich Hertz developed a method to generate electromagnetic waves and at the same time measure their speed. He showed that these waves had the same reflection, refraction, and polarization properties as light waves and that they could be modified or focused. Hertz took Maxwell's ideas, subjected them to a series of rigorous experiments over a period of ten years, and proved them.

Einstein became aware of these breakthroughs through his independent reading. Herr Professor Weber at the Polytechnic neither recognized nor lectured on Faraday or Maxwell. Many years later, Einstein expressed the degree of his appreciation of the importance of Maxwell's equations when he said: "Maxwell made the single most important contribution of the nineteenth century."

The work of two more supporting players must be described, and then the stage will be set for Einstein's entrance. The first involves the Dutch theoretical physicist Hendrik Lorentz (1853–1928), who first suggested the concept of the electron. He had studied Maxwell's equations regarding the electromagnetic field and had looked for ways to extend these mathematical insights to other areas of physics. In the 1880s, the twin towers of physics were believed to be Newtonian mechanics and Maxwell's equations of electrodynamics because the only two basic forces in nature known at that time were gravity and electromagnetism.

Electrons, as Lorentz showed, are essential to the structure of neutral (uncharged) atoms. They contribute little to the total mass of an atom, but they are necessary to contribute the negative electric charges, thus compensating for the positive charges of the protons and making the atom electrically neutral. Lorentz was the first to suggest that the mass of a charged particle would increase with speed, a revolutionary concept. Einstein found Lorentz's work in incorporating the electron into the Newtonian–Maxwellian physics of the time central in his own work. The only physicists mentioned by name in Einstein's first relativity paper are Maxwell, Hertz, and Lorentz.

The Michelson–Morley Experiment

The last key supporting role is played by the famous Michelson–Morley experiment. Though the experiment did not contribute directly to Einstein's ideas, it did prepare the scientific community to accept Einstein's theories.

Albert Michelson was a professor of physics at what is now the Case Institute in Cleveland, Ohio, and Edward Morley was teaching chemistry at the nearby Western Reserve University. The two teamed up to design and conduct an experiment intended to measure the force of ether wind. Conventional science at that time held that space was filled with an invisible substance called *ether*. This hypothetical ether (sometimes spelled *aether*) was postulated to account for the propagation of electromagnetic radiation through space. Physicists reasoned that an object moving through this ether must encounter an "ether wind" blowing in the opposite direction. Michelson and Morley knew that the Earth, in its orbit around the Sun, was moving at a speed of about 18 miles (30 kilometers) per second; therefore, an ether wind of about the same speed should be created.

In 1887, in Morley's basement laboratory, Michelson and Morley set up an experiment intended to detect and precisely measure the force of ether wind: A beam of light was optically split. The two resulting light beams were reflected at right angles from each other, then recombined and brought to focus at an eyepiece. One beam of light is oriented parallel to the Earth's supposed motion through the ether. The theory being tested was that the beam of light that had to travel into the force of the ether wind would be slowed down with respect to the other beam. The analogy used by Michelson to explain this principle compared the two beams of light to two swimmers in a race against each other—one swimmer has to go upstream and back, while the other swimmer covers the same distance but across the current and back. If there is no current, the race will end in a dead heat. If there is any current in the river, the second swimmer will always win. (This reasoning can be verified algebraically if the reader is so inclined.)

To the astonishment of the two experimenters, there was no difference in the time it took the two light beams to travel the specified distances. Either the ether was moving with the Earth, which made no sense at all, or there was no such thing as ether. (A third possible conclusion from the results was that the Earth did not move, but Galileo and others had convinced them that it did.) Michelson and Morley repeated the experiment again and again, always getting the same results. If there was no such thing as ether, some of Newton's concepts had to be rethought, and that prospect was daunting. Isaac Asimov calls the Michelson–Morley observation "the most important experiment-that-did-not-work in the entire history of science." It did, however, open up the possibility that Newtonian physics might be incomplete. Einstein did not know about the Michelson–Morley experiment at the time he formulated the ideas behind his theories of relativity. On his own, through thought experiments, he concluded that there was no such thing as ether; and when the time came the Michelson–Morley results helped the scientific community accept Einstein's theory.

In his *Essays In Science*, published in 1934, Einstein said: "The theory

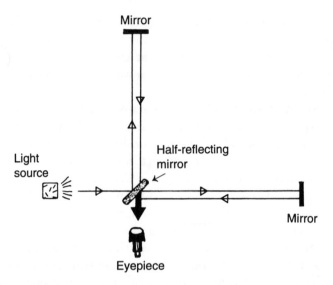

Michelson–Morley experiment Light from the source is split by the half-reflecting mirror and travels along two perpendicular arms. Mirrors at each end reflect light beams back. Negative results of this experiment indicate that there is no ether wind.

of relativity resembles a building consisting of two separate stories, the special theory and the general theory. The special theory, on which the general theory rests, applies to all physical phenomena with the exception of gravity; the general theory provides the law of gravitation and its relation to the other forces of nature." We will start on the first floor and work our way up.

The Special Theory of Relativity

By all accounts, Einstein enjoyed his work at the Swiss Patent Office. It provided security, was often interesting, and allowed time and energy for some serious thinking and writing on physics. In particular, he was thinking about many puzzling problems that had to do with light and motion. By 1905, he was twenty-six years old and highly respected in his work at the patent office. Although his salary was small and his marriage less than perfect, he would look back on his Bern days as among the happiest of his life. Above all during these days, he was productive.

In May of 1905, Einstein completed a pap   .1at would earn him the Nobel Prize seventeen years later. In June of 1905, he finished an article that would gain him his Ph.D. from the University of Zurich. Then, in the prestigious German physics journal *Annalen der Physik*, he had four more papers published, the third of which, now known as the *special theory of relativity*, would forever change humankind's view of the universe. He accomplished all this working alone in the back room of his small apartment in Bern. The only period in the history of physics comparable to this one is Newton's 1665 to 1666 sojourn in Woolsthorpe.

Unlike Newton's *Principia*, which was recognized almost at once as a revolutionary document, the publication of Einstein's special theory of relativity did not immediately startle the scientific community. To Einstein's chagrin, the paper was largely ignored. Where he had expected controversy there was silence. Instead of hundreds of letters questioning or applauding his ideas, he got one—a note from Professor Max Planck in Berlin asking for more information on some of his points. Those few scholars who understood Einstein were skeptical, and even they resisted his stunning conclusions until definitive proof of his theories could be obtained by experiment. As for the greater body of the scientific establishment, they were committed to Newtonian mechanics and Maxwellian electromagnetism, and they did not give up their fortified positions easily. After all, if Einstein's mathematics held up, a lot of rethinking would have to be done.

Much of the special theory of relativity evolved from a thought experiment that had occurred to Einstein at age sixteen. He had asked himself then what he would see if he were to chase a beam of light at the speed of light. Classical Newtonian physics said that he would see light at rest. In thinking about this in 1905, Einstein concluded that that answer could not be correct. Einstein knew from Maxwell's equations that light was movement, that velocity was inherent in light. Einstein saw that Newton's concept of absolute space and time and Maxwell's equations could not both be correct. He solved this paradox by concluding that one cannot accelerate to the velocity of light and that the velocity of light was constant for all observers, regardless of their relative motion. Once he reached this conclusion, the rest of the

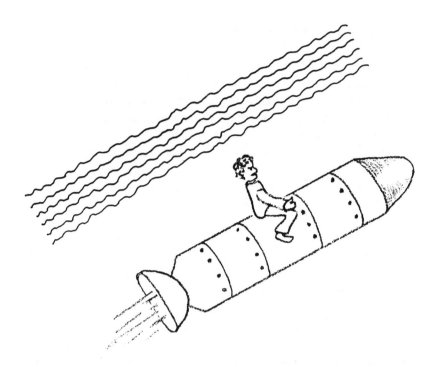

Einstein's famous *Gedanken* experiment At the age of sixteen, Einstein had wondered what he would see if he could chase a beam of light at the speed of light. Would he see light "standing still"? Going back to this idea in 1905, he reasoned that, because Maxwell's equations showed that velocity was inherent in light, one could not accelerate to the speed of light. He further concluded that the speed of light was constant—the same for all observers regardless of their relative motion. Einstein called this idea his "invariance theory." Murray Gell-Mann has said that once Einstein reached this conclusion, the rest of the special theory of relativity fell into place logically.

special theory of relativity began to take shape. For example, Newtonian mechanics assumes that an object can travel at unlimited speed as long as enough force is used to accelerate it. Einstein said that nothing can travel faster than the speed of light. He pointed out that an infinite amount of energy would be required to accelerate an object to the speed of light and that this was impossible because the amount of energy available in the universe is finite.

Einstein realized that fundamental changes in how one thought about space and time would be necessary if the Newtonian principles of absolute space and time were to be ~ ~tioned. Special relativity can best be understood by the use of thou, ~ experiments, some of which were developed by Einstein himself. This technique will be utilized here to illustrate what are considered to be the five most important special relativistic effects: (1) the relativity of simultaneity, (2) time dilation, (3) length contraction at speeds close to the speed of light, (4) increase of mass of a fast-moving body, and (5) the relationship of mass and energy.

If I had to summarize the special theory of relativity for a physics student's notebook, it would read:

The speed of light is always constant.
At the speed of light, time stands still.
At the speed of light, mass is infinite.
$E = mc^2$

The special theory of relativity does not state, by the way, that everything is relative. It states only that some things the world had thought of as absolute, such as time and space, are relative, and some things the world had thought of as relative, such as the speed of light, are absolute. The theory does hold that if, for all frames of reference, the speed of light is constant and if all natural laws are the same, then both time and motion are found to be relative to the observer. This is simply stated, but the implications are profound, and the terms *relative*, *absolute*, and *frame of reference* need a few examples to illustrate the concepts.

Relativity

It is easy to understand size as a *relative* term. Something is large or small only in reference to some other object. A basketball is large compared to a pea, but small compared to the moon. There is no way to measure an object and say it is *absolutely* large or *absolutely* small.

Speed is another example of a relative term. Nothing can be said to be fast or slow without comparison to another object. My car is fast compared to my bicycle, but slow when compared to a rocket ship.

Up and *down* are both obviously relative terms. Here on Earth, *up* is the direction toward the sky, whereas *down* is the direction toward the center of the Earth. But, as has been seen from television pictures of astronauts on board a space shuttle, there is no absolute *up* and *down* in space because there is no *frame of reference*.

How about motion? Is that a relative term? We can see at once that it is. Imagine a train moving east at 100 miles per hour. On board the train, a man walks west at 4 miles per hour. How fast is the man traveling? We cannot answer that question unless we choose a frame of reference. Relative to the ground, the man is moving east at 96 miles per hour, but, relative to the train, he is moving west at 4 miles per hour.

The Relativity of Simultaneity

The *relativity of time* is a more difficult concept to grasp. Newton's universe assumed that absolute time was being ticked off by an unseen universal clock. If it was 1:02 on Earth, it was 1:02 on Venus or Mars or anywhere else in the universe. Einstein showed us that this is not true. One of the examples Einstein used to demonstrate his new ideas deals with simultaneous events. In Newton's universe, two events could be said to occur simultaneously because absolute time was being measured by the universal clock. Einstein showed us that this idea of absolute time and simultaneous events produces a paradox. If the speed of light is absolute (constant) under all conditions, then something is wrong with the Newtonian concept.

Einstein pointed out that light takes time to travel from point to point, and he cited the case of two bolts of lightning striking near a railroad track. To a person standing beside the track and midway between the two strikes, the two flashes would appear to strike at exactly the same time. But an observer on a fast train would see the lightning bolt up ahead—the one he was rushing toward—strike before the one from which he was rushing away. To that observer, the two bolts struck at different times. Then consider another train going in the opposite direction. The order in which an observer on the second train would see the two bolts strike would be opposite to the order seen by the observer on the first train. Einstein went on to state that there is no privileged observer of these three—in other words, they are all correct. Thus, two events are simultaneous in one frame of reference but not in two others. There is no such thing as absolute time, and there is no universal clock ticking away out in space somewhere.

Because this concept is a little tricky, let's consider another example. Imagine a railroad passenger car with an observation dome. Sitting in the middle of the car on a side-facing seat is our trusty observer. Two large light bulbs are in place, one at the front of the car and one at the rear. From his position, our passenger can see both the front and the rear of the car. If a switch is thrown connecting the lights to an energy source, the train passenger will see the lights come on simultaneously. It does not make any difference if the train is standing still or moving down the track at 200 miles per hour, because relative to the passenger the train is not moving.

Now, let's assume a stationary observer watching the train go by. If we assume that the passenger and the stationary observer are eye to eye when the switch for the lights is thrown, then our stationary observer will not see a simultaneous lighting of the bulbs. Rather, he will see first the rear light come on and then the front light. Remember, the rear light is traveling toward him at 200 mph, whereas the front light is receding from him at the same speed. Because it is moving toward him, the rear light will have a shorter distance to travel than the receding front light. If the distance is shorter and the speed of light is constant

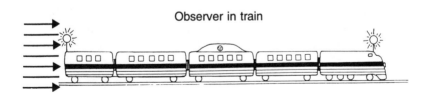

Observer in train

Observer on ground

Einstein's relativity of simultaneity To an observer in a moving train, both lights appear to come on at the same time. To an observer on the ground, the rear light appears to come on slightly before the front light.

under any circumstances, then he will see the rear light flick on before the front light does. Thus, two events seen to be simultaneous from the point of view of the passenger on the train are not simultaneous when viewed by a stationary observer. And, what is most important, both observers will be correct. Simultaneity is a relative phenomenon.

For another example of this principle, consider the space shuttles in the illustration. From the point of view of the observer in the command shuttle, the light signals arrive at the other shuttles simultaneously. However, from the point of view of an observer on a space station, the light signals arrive at shuttle A well before they arrive at shuttle C.

Of course, these conclusions are based upon the speed of light being constant. Is light, then, the one invariant measuring rod for everything in the universe? Here, the term light refers to the visible portion of a spectrum of electromagnetic radiation. This radiation includes radio waves, radar, infrared and ultraviolet light, and gamma rays. They all propagate through space at the same speed and that speed, a little more than 186,000 miles (300,000 kilometers) per second, is constant, regardless of the motion of the source of the radiation. Imagine a bullet fired straight ahead from the front of a jet airplane. The ground speed of the bullet is obtained by adding the speed of the plane to the speed of the bullet. In the case of light, however, the velocity of the light beam (or any other electromagnetic radiation) is not affected by the speed of the object that sends out the beam. If instead of firing a bullet, the airplane in our example turns on a headlight aimed straight forward, the speed of the light is not added to the speed of the aircraft. This concept has been tested many times in many different ways and the results are always the same—the speed of light is constant.

How Fast Is Fast?

Speed of light in a vacuum = 3×10^8 meters per second, or
186,000 miles per second, or
668 million miles per hour

1% of speed of light = 6.7 million miles per hour
Speed of sound in air = 330 meters per second (Mach 1)
Muzzle velocity of rifle bullet = 660 meters per second (Mach 2)
Escape velocity of Earth = 25,000 miles per hour, or 7 miles per second

---

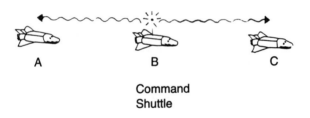

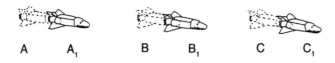

A   B   C

Command
Shuttle

A   A₁   B   B₁   C   C₁

Space Station

Einstein's relativity of simultaneity   Imagine three space shuttles (A, B, and C) passing a space station in deep space. This flotilla is moving in a straight line at a constant speed. The middle space shuttle (B) is the command vehicle. The distances from the front and rear space shuttles to the command vehicle are equal. At a given time, a light signal is emitted from B simultaneously backward in the direction of A and forward in the direction of C. From the point of view of an observer in shuttle B, the signals arrive at A and C at the same time. However, from the point of view of an observer on the space station, the light signal arrives at A well before it arrives at C.

Uniform Motion

Uniform motion is motion that is not changing, neither accelerating nor decelerating. Classical or Newtonian physics made it clear that if you are on a uniformly moving conveyance, say a train car that is closed on all sides and so does not allow you to see the scenery go by, there is no mechanical experiment by which you could prove that you are moving. (Of course we're assuming a smooth ride with no sound or other clues to motion.) If you were to toss a ball straight up in the air on the train, it would come straight down again—no matter if the train were in motion or standing still. Einstein carried this idea forward a step. He showed that not only are we unable to detect the train's motion by mechanical means, it is also impossible for us to detect its motion by any other experiment. The special theory of relativity tells us that it is not possible to measure uniform motion in any absolute way.

Take, for example, the case of two spaceships moving toward each other at uniform speed. There is no way that the astronauts on either ship can determine: (1) if their spaceship is at rest with the other spaceship coming at them, (2) if their spaceship is hurtling forward while the other spaceship is at rest, or (3) if both spaceships are moving. There is no experiment with light or any electrical or magnetic phenomenon that will prove that any one of those three choices is better than the other two.

Now let us consider what the relativity of motion can tell us about the relativity of time. We have seen how observers differ in their estimates of the time of the occurrence of an event (such as the lightning bolts or lights in our earlier examples), and that each observance is just as "true" as the others. Time, in other words, is relative to the frame of reference of the observer.

Time Dilation

Having demonstrated the relativity of time, Einstein went still further and challenged our imaginations with the concept of time dilation. He predicted that the keeping of time by clocks would be affected by motion and by gravity. According to the time-dilation effect, a moving clock will tick more slowly than a stationary clock.

Today, the world keepers of the official time use high-precision atomic clocks based upon the microwave emissions from caesium-133. These devices measure time to an accuracy of a millionth of a second per day. With precise instruments available, the world should have an absolute standard by which to measure time, right? Wrong. Even with such sophisticated measures, no absolute can be determined. Einstein did not know about atomic clocks when he postulated his special theory of relativity, but he had realized that there are inherent variations in timekeeping in concert with motion.

Einstein's concepts about the keeping of time were confirmed by an experiment carried out in 1971 when caesium clocks were placed aboard two jet aircraft flying around the world, one eastward and one westward. At the beginning and end of the trips, the clocks were compared to a reference clock at the U.S. Naval Observatory in Washington, D.C. At the conclusion of the experiment, the clocks no longer agreed about the time of day. The eastbound clock lost an average of 59 nanoseconds (billionths of a second) when compared to the reference clock, and the westbound clock gained 273 nanoseconds. These results were close to the numbers predicted by the scientists conducting the experiment. Subsequent experiments have confirmed this phenomenon with even greater precision.

According to Einstein, relativity allows events to occur more slowly for one observer than for another, including the events of life, such as aging. The effect of high-speed motion on time has led to the famous Twin Paradox. In this theoretical example, an astronaut leaves his twin brother on Earth and takes off at high speed for a long journey to distant stars. On his return home, the astronaut finds his twin is an old man, whereas he himself is still in his prime. The astronaut's clocks, atomic and biological, have registered fewer hours and years than have the clocks on Earth.

Another example of the same phenomenon is the Clock Paradox: A manned space vehicle is imagined to be on an interstellar trip to Arcturus, a first-magnitude star located thirty-three light years from Earth. If the space ship travels at a velocity close to the speed of light (possible only in science fiction), it will arrive in the vicinity of Arcturus a little over thirty-three years after lift-off, Earth time. If it returns immediately, it will have been gone about sixty-six years, Earth time. Because the space ship has been traveling at high velocity relative to

Earth, all time processes on board have been slowed down. It would not seem to the crew that the trip to Arcturus and back took sixty-six years. It would seem to them that only a day had passed on this journey. When the crew emerged from the spacecraft back on Earth, they would find that their spouses, who were young when they left, were now sixty-six years older, or had died. Some of the crew would see their sons and daughters some sixty-six years older than themselves. No wonder that the Twin Paradox and Clock Paradox have generated more perplexity and controversy than any other ideas in the theory of relativity.

Preposterous as these ideas might seem, Einstein's relativistic time has been verified by experiment. In order to check the Twin Paradox, scientists needed an object with a short life span that could be measured precisely. The experiment would then attempt to prolong that life span by means of high-speed travel. The subatomic world of particle physics provided the object. Many subatomic particles are unstable, have built-in obsolescence, and decay after a lifetime fixed by nature. A convenient example turned out to be muons, heavier cousins of the electron. They decay into electrons after a life span of two millionths of a second. An experiment involving the longevity of muons was conducted at CERN, the huge high-energy accelerator near Geneva, Switzerland. In this experiment, muon particles were accelerated to 99.4 percent of the speed of light, while traveling in an orbit 46 feet in diameter. If the muon particles were unaffected by high speed, a typical muon would make fourteen or fifteen trips around the ring before its two-microsecond life expired. In the CERN experiment, a typical particle traveling at speeds close to the speed of light survived long enough to make more than 400 orbits. Its life had been extended nearly thirty-fold, confirming Einstein's theory.

Length Contraction at High Speeds

This part of Einstein's theory states that if an object were to travel at a speed close to the speed of light, it would appear to a fixed observer to shorten in the direction of motion. In other words, a yardstick moving at nearly the speed of light would seem to be less than 36 inches in length. *Length contraction* is another relativistic phenomenon that can be demonstrated by thought experiment and verified in the laboratory.

Increase of Mass With Speed

Einstein proposed still another difficult-to-comprehend theory. Not only does time slow down with speeds close to the speed of light, but mass increases—a body in motion increases in mass as it increases in speed until, at the speed of light, mass becomes infinite. The concept of *increasing mass with speed* has also been well demonstrated in particle accelerators. As particles move faster, they increase in mass. In fact, the theory is verified every time an accelerator propels particles to superfast speeds. At the Stanford Linear Accelerator in Palo Alto, California, particles are accelerated to speeds close to the speed of light in the first few inches of the two-mile-long track. During this process, they pick up detectable energy and mass but, of course, no more speed.

If all this is true, you may ask yourself, why doesn't your automobile's mass get bigger when you step on the gas pedal? The answer is that the effect of increased mass is only significant for objects moving near the speed of light. At 60 miles per hour, your car is traveling at a relative snail's pace (1/60 mile per second), and change in mass is undetectable.

At low speeds, the laws of motion remain almost exactly as specified by Isaac Newton. But where high-speed travel is concerned, the universe belongs to Einstein. In the words of the Polish mathematician Herman Minkowski, "Henceforth, space by itself, and time by itself, are doomed to fade away into mere shadows, and only a kind of union of the two will preserve an independent reality."

$E = mc^2$

In his 1905 paper on relativity, Einstein included a sort of mathematical footnote to the special theory. In this paper, Einstein established the relationship of mass and energy and provided a formula for quantifying this relationship—the energy (E) of a quantity of matter with a given mass (m) is equal to the product of the mass and the square of the velocity of light (c). This formula is commonly expressed as $E = mc^2$. When this concept was finally understood, it became clear that an enormous amount of energy was contained in a small amount of mass. Mass is, in effect, frozen energy. Einstein's contemporaries questioned this theory. "You mean," they asked him, "that there is more energy in a small block of lead, for instance, than is contained in a major coal mine." "Yes," he replied, "but it is only theory, as there is no way to utilize that energy unless one could split the atom and that's, as we all know, impossible."

Einstein knew that if this energy could be released slowly in a controlled manner, the world would have a new source of power. He also knew that if the energy could be released suddenly, the world had a new weapon of awesome potential. But this was 1905, and both the benign and the deadly potentials represented by Einstein's equation, although theoretically possible, were a long way from becoming technically realizable. Today, $E = mc^2$ is mainly thought of in reference to the atomic bomb. Actually, this misses the main impact of this famous equation. It is a mathematical explanation for why the Sun and the other stars shine. It is the formula for the energy source of most of the universe. $E = mc^2$ was an impressive afterthought to be tacked on to the special theory of relativity.

Today, of course, Einstein's 1905 paper is accepted as a statement of the fact of relativity, not just as a theory. Special relativity is as fundamental to contemporary science as is the existence of atoms.

Postpublication of the Special Theory of Relativity

News of Einstein's work spread fairly slowly throughout the universities of the world. Einstein continued to work at the patent office until 1909. He had been granted several salary increases, and his position was now secure. However, his interest lay with the academic world of theoretical physics, and when he was offered the position of associate professor of physics at the University of Zurich, he lost little time in accepting.

From Zurich, Einstein moved on to the University of Prague when he was offered a full professorship, and then, in the winter of 1912, he moved back to Zurich to a position at the Polytechnic. Colleagues remember him as a happy man in those days, delighted with his two young sons, Hans Albert and Edward. In 1914, Einstein was offered a post at the Prussian Academy in Berlin, a position that permitted him to continue his research with only occasional lectures required at the University of Berlin. He accepted and, despite the fact that war threatened, the family moved to Berlin. Mileva, however, could not stand living in Berlin. Because their marriage had been in trouble for some time, she left Einstein, took the children, and moved back to Switzerland. A few years later, this enforced separation led to divorce.

With the outbreak of World War I, Einstein became an outspoken critic of German militarism. He was at that time a pacifist and did not think that any war could be justified. (He modified these views in 1930 when he reluctantly concluded that war was necessary to stop Adolf Hitler.) In Berlin in 1916, he joined antiwar movements and passed out antiwar pamphlets on street corners. His Swiss nationality protected him from official backlash for these actions. During this time, he was primarily occupied in perfecting his general theory of relativity, which he eventually published in *Annalen de Physik* under the title "The Foundation of the General Theory of Relativity" in 1916. It was called *general* because it is a generalization (or extension) of the special theory. The general theory is considered by historians of science to be a much greater intellectual achievement than the special theory, monumental as that was. In the short sixty-page document, Einstein postulated that gravity is not a force, as Newton had said, but a curved field in the space–time continuum, created by the presence of mass. What exactly he meant by this can be challenging, but it also can be understood.

General Theory of Relativity

For many years, the general theory of relativity was regarded as too opaque and difficult even for most scientists to understand, let alone the rest of us. However, at the nonmathematical level at which we will discuss it here, I suggest that this attitude is unjustified. I further suggest that some episodes in the history of scientific endeavor are of surpassing significance to our cultural heritage. Instead of objects of art, paintings, sculpture, or music, Einstein left us scientific ideas and concepts. These were his legacy to us and to ignore them because we think they seem to be abstruse would be the same as ignoring a Michelangelo painting or a Mozart concerto.

Einstein proved his theories mathematically but we can, if we choose, concentrate on the ideas that form the basis of the theory, taking Einstein's word for the mathematical proofs (and, of course, the words of many of the physicists who, over the years, have verified his numbers).

What Einstein was trying to do was generate a theory of gravitation that would fit with the special relativity theory that he had developed in 1905. In this effort, he conceived the idea that when a thing is falling freely, everything inside it seems weightless. For example, when the space shuttle in orbit is falling freely in Earth's gravity, the astronauts inside it feel weightless. The astronauts, in fact, weigh just as much as they ever did, but because the laws governing the fall of the astronauts and the shuttle are the same, the astronauts appear to be floating about the inside of the cabin. They are not falling *with respect to the space shuttle*.

What happens in a spaceship that is accelerating? The engines are on and generating a thrust so that the spaceship is no longer coasting in free fall. If the spacecraft is accelerating at the rate of 1 g (one times gravity, or the force equivalent to what is felt on the surface of the Earth), then an astronaut will be able to stand on the floor of the spacecraft and will feel his or her normal weight. Also, if the astronaut drops an object, it will fall toward the floor. This is because the ship is accelerating upward, and, in effect, the object, with no force on it, is being left behind.

All of this is logical and easy to follow. But then Einstein made a creative intellectual leap. He compared the situation of the accelerating spacecraft with a like spaceship sitting at rest on the surface of the Earth. Einstein pointed out that everything is the same. The astronaut's feet would be pressed to the floor, an object dropped would fall toward the floor with an acceleration of 1 g. In fact, if there was no way the astronaut could see out, there would be no way to tell the difference between a spaceship sitting on the Earth and one accelerating in free space. According to Einstein, there is no experiment that can be performed and no measurement that can be made that would tell the difference (as long as these experiments or measurements are confined to inside the spacecraft). Stated with mathematical precision, as it is in the general theory of relativity, this idea is Einstein's *Principle of Equivalence.*

Einstein concluded that the reason gravity and inertia (*state of rest,* in this usage) seem to be the same thing is that they *are* the same thing. Let's get back into Einstein's elevator, accelerating upward in space at a constant rate. What would a beam of light do in this elevator? To an outside observer, it would cross the elevator cab in a straight line. But inside this same elevator cab, the light beam would appear to bend downward, because the elevator is accelerating upward away from it. Einstein concluded that if our accelerating elevator is the same as an elevator at rest in a gravitational field, then light must also bend in a

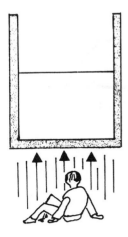
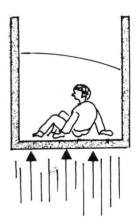

Behavior of a beam of light in an elevator accelerating in space   To an outside observer, the beam of light appears as a straight line. To an observer inside the accelerating elevator, the beam of light appears to bend downward.

gravitational field. From this equivalence, Einstein went on to conclude that space–time must be curved.

Curved Space

Curved space is not actually as difficult a concept as it at first seems. After all, the Earth is a spherical globe on which the shortest distance between two points is not always a straight line as it is in the old Euclidian, flat-world geometry. On a globe, two parallel lines (longitudinal lines, for instance) can come together and meet (at the poles). Of course, we know that the Earth does appear to be approximately flat on the small scale, but it is actually curved on the large scale. On the surface of a globe, the shortest distance between two points is the arc of a great circle, called a *geodesic*. If, using a globe, we stretch a string as tautly as possible from San Francisco to London, it will describe the geodesic.

To assist us in thinking about curved space, we can imagine a rubber sheet stretched and held taut at the edges. If a heavy weight such as a bowling ball is placed on the sheet, it forms a depression in the area of the weight. If we now imagine shooting a marble across the sheet, we will see that it tends to curve in toward the depression. We can think

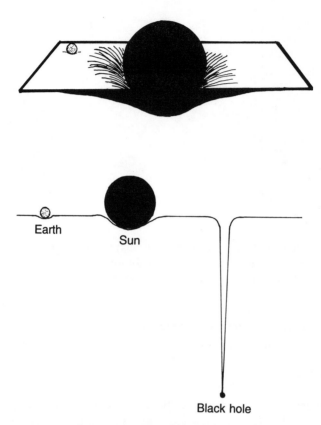

Einstein's curved space   Imagine a rubber sheet held taut at the edges. If objects such as a baseball or a bowling ball are placed on the sheet, they form a depression relative to their weight.

of the large rubber sheet as a trampoline and the weights we use to deform the sheet downward as representing stars, planets, or black holes. This is not a bad mental picture of curved space, but it does not show the slowing of time.

The curvature of space is so small that its effects are imperceptible except over relatively long distances. In traveling the distance from New York to Los Angeles, a beam of light bends only about 1 millimeter due to the curvature of space induced by Earth's mass. Over a much longer distance, however, the curvature is more measurable. When the 1987 supernova was detected, scientists calculated that the small curvature through which the light from the supernova passed as it traveled from one side of the Milky Way to the other to reach Earth was sufficient to delay its arrival by about nine months. Had it not been for the curvature of space, the 1987 supernova would have been visible from Earth in 1986.

Summary of the General Theory of Relativity

The essence of what Einstein showed in the general theory is this: First, *gravity* and *inertia* are two different words for the same thing (the Principle of Equivalence). Second, in thinking about space, four dimensions must be considered: length, width, height, and time. Time is the fourth dimension, and every event that takes place in the universe is an event occurring in a four-dimensional world of space–time. Third, space-time is curved or warped by the presence of large masses like the Sun. This warping is the gravitational field. A planet, such as Earth, moving around the Sun is not traveling in an elliptical orbit because the Sun "pulls" on it, but because the field (the depression created in space by the mass of the Sun) is such that an ellipse is the shortest possible path the planet can take in space–time.

Einstein versus Newton

Generally speaking, Einstein's equations defining gravity gave results in agreement with Newton's mechanics. However, there were differences. Three discrepancies first pointed out by Einstein have been experimentally confirmed: (1) The orbit of Mercury is not a fixed ellipse. (2) Starlight passing near the Sun is deflected twice as much as Newtonian mechanics predicted. (3) The rates of clocks depend on their location in a gravitational field. As Richard Feynman was fond of pointing out in his lectures on physics at Caltech: "Whenever the predictions of Einstein have been found to differ from the ideas of Newtonian mechanics, Nature has chosen Einstein."

Expanding Universe, Big Bang, and Black Holes

Almost as soon as he completed the field equations confirming his concepts, Einstein realized that his calculations showed that the universe must be expanding. Because he did not quite believe his own numbers—it must be remembered that this was some twelve years before the American astronomer Edwin P. Hubble and others established the fact of the expansion of the universe—Einstein added a monumental fudge factor, his cosmological constant, to force his figures to conform to a static universe. He later regretted this mathematical sleight of hand, saying it was "the greatest blunder of my life."

By 1922, the Russian mathematician Alexander Friedmann, solving Einstein's cosmological equations, realized that the expansion indicated by Einstein's formula necessarily implied an explosion at the beginning of time. Friedmann's solution was rediscovered in 1929 by Abbé Georges Lemaître and George Gamow. They postulated the theory that the universe began as a superdense clump of matter that for unknown reasons exploded, hurtling across space the material that became the stars and galaxies. Gamow later labeled the theory the "Big Bang."

Still another theory that evolved directly from the consequences of Einstein's cosmological equations is the concept of *black holes*. Barely a year after publication of the general theory, the German astronomer Karl Schwarzschild proposed an explanation of Einstein's equations that led to what is now known as the black-hole solution. Further refinements were made over the years (by J. Robert Oppenheimer, Hartland Snyder, and John Wheeler), but the black-hole idea dates back to Einstein and Schwarzschild.

Nervous Breakdown

In addition to the general theory, Einstein published two other significant papers in 1917. One paper dealt with the stimulated emission of light, a concept that would eventually provide the basis for lasers. The second paper dealt with the structure of the universe and is generally considered to be the basis of modern cosmology. All this intellectual effort over a short period of time took its toll. Like Newton and Maxwell before him, Einstein suffered a nervous breakdown as the result of difficult intellectual work. His physical health was also poor, and this period lasted for several years. His poor health included a stomach ulcer that was a problem for the rest of his life. The mental part of the collapse was short-lived, and for the duration of his physical weakness, Einstein was remarkably productive.

Second Marriage

With the help of his second cousin Elsa Einstein Lowenthal, Einstein slowly recovered his health. He had moved to an apartment next door to Elsa's in Berlin, and she took over his household, cooking all his meals and generally looking after him. The two cousins had always been fond of each other, and now they drew extremely close. In 1919, the forty-year-old Albert and the forty-three-year old Elsa were married. Although this marriage was to last until 1936 when Elsa died, it was neither a particularly close nor an especially happy marriage. It was said that the main reason Einstein married his cousin was the convenience of having his shirts done at home. For her part, Elsa enjoyed being the wife of a great man. Taking care of her Albert and basking in his fame were her pleasures. For his part, Albert liked being taken care of and delighted in the many social gatherings at their apartment. Einstein was apparently not an easy man to live with, however, and all was not harmonious. Many years later, writing to the family of his life-long friend Michele Besso who had just died, Einstein said: "What I most admired about him as a human being was the fact that he managed to live for many years not only in peace but also in lasting harmony with a woman—an undertaking in which I twice failed rather disgracefully."

Probably the main reason Einstein was difficult to live with was his mania for work. He was remarkable for his powers of concentration and could work steadily for many hours and even days on the same problem. Some of the topics that interested him remained on his mind for decades. For relaxation he often turned to music and sailing, but even in those moments his mind was at work. He always carried a notebook in his pocket to jot down any idea that came to him. Elsa told how Einstein would come downstairs, strike a few notes on the piano, stop to jot something down, and then return to his study. His reputation for absentmindedness is not all myth. His wife told about how she used to bundle him up in his overcoat and leave him in the foyer, only to find him standing there half an hour later, lost in thought.

When discussing his thought processes in evolving the principles of relativity, Einstein said, "How did it come to pass that I was the one to develop the theory of relativity? The reason, I think, is that a normal adult never stops to think about problems of space and time. These are things which he has thought about as a child. But my intellectual development was retarded, as a result of which I began to wonder about space and time only when I had already grown up. Naturally I go deeper into the problem than a child with normal abilities."

Experimental Proof and Fame

Although the General Theory of Relativity was published in 1916 and drew attention and approval from the world of physics, Einstein did not achieve international acclaim until 1919 when the Royal Society of London announced that its scientific expedition to the South Pacific would test one of Einstein's theories under eclipse conditions. Einstein had predicted that starlight grazing the Sun would be bent by the Sun's gravity more than Newtonian physics had forecast. A total solar eclipse would occur on May 29, 1919, during which time the Sun would stand against the bright stars of the Hyades cluster. English astronomer Arthur Stanley Eddington led an expedition to the Principe Island off West Africa to observe the eclipse. A second set of observations was made from Sobral, Brazil. The Eddington expedition results would prove or disprove a major point in Einstein's theory, and scientists worldwide awaited the results with considerable suspense.

There had been one previous confirmation of the general theory when Einstein noted a phenomenon where general relativity worked better than Newton's theory did. Physicists and astronomers had been puzzled by Mercury's movement around the Sun. Newtonian physics predicted that the point of Mercury's closest approach to the Sun (its *perihelion*) would change every Mercurial year. Observations found that the gravity pull from other planets was moving Mercury's perihelion, but by a puzzling amount more than Newtonian physics predicted. In the course of his work on the general theory, Einstein had calculated how much Mercury's perihelion would change if space–time were curved. The answer exactly matched the observations, and Einstein knew he was on the right track. But this had been a case of observations first, mathematical confirmation second. The real test of Einstein's theory would be the observations made by the Eddington astronomers.

It is interesting to contrast the difference in behavior between Max Planck, the father of quantum physics, and Albert Einstein on the eve of the eclipse experiment. Planck stayed up all night to see if the results of the expedition would confirm Einstein's prediction on the amount the light would bend as it passed the Sun. Einstein, on the other hand, went to bed. He *knew* he was right. Of his good friend Max Planck, Einstein said, "If he had really understood the way the general theory of relativity explains the equivalence of inertial and gravitational mass, he would have gone to bed the way I did."

In the event, the British team found that the degree of bending of light was exactly what Einstein had predicted. When Einstein received a telegram announcing the positive outcome of the Eddington expedition, he showed it to a student who asked, "What would you have said if there had been no confirmation?" "I would have had to pity our dear Lord," Einstein replied. "The theory is correct."

The announcement of this discovery made headlines worldwide. It was the beginning of the perception by the general public of Einstein as a world figure and a new phase of his life was about to begin.

World Fame and Controversy

By 1920, signs of trouble were evident for Einstein in Germany. A disturbance occurred during one of his lectures at the University of Berlin when a group of Nazi students interrupted his talk. Einstein attempted to play this down, saying that expressions of anti-Semitism had not occurred. This was only the first of an intensifying anti-Einstein campaign in the growing Nazi party in Germany. His work would eventually be condemned as "Jewish physics" by the party, and any German scientist who showed an understanding of or agreement with the theories of relativity would risk his academic career at the least. At this time in Germany, a book was published with the title *100 Scientists Against Einstein*. The ever-confident Einstein reacted by laughing and saying, "If I were wrong, only one would be enough."

Now world famous, Einstein was much sought after for personal appearances, lectures, and papers on any subject that he cared to write about. He traveled widely in Europe during this period to lecture on relativity, usually arriving by third-class rail carriage, with a violin under his arm. Many of these invitations he turned down because he was still interested in doing further work in physics. However, he did become involved in the Zionist movement to establish a Jewish nation in Palestine, and he lent his name to fund-raising activities for the proposed Jewish state. As part of this effort, he visited the United States in 1921 along with Chaim Weizmann, a fellow scientist who was later to be Israel's first president. On that trip, every politician or celebrity in the United States wanted to have his picture taken with Einstein. On disembarking back in Europe after an Atlantic crossing together, Chaim Weizmann told reporters, "During the voyage, Einstein kept explaining his relativity theory to me again and again, and now I believe that he has fully understood it."

Nobel Prize

On the heels of the confirmation of the general theory came the 1921 Nobel Prize in Physics. The prize was not actually awarded to Einstein until 1922 and then not for the theories of relativity, but rather for Einstein's contributions to mathematical physics and especially for his discovery of the law of photoelectric effect. It was thought at the time that the Nobel committee could not see how the theory of relativity had improved the condition of humankind as specified by Alfred Nobel as a condition of the award. Einstein's reaction to the award is of interest. He did not even mention it in his diary or in any letters to friends. Some years later, he even forgot to include it on a form listing honors he had received. It is not that he did not expect the prize. He knew that he would eventually win it. In fact, when he divorced his first wife, Mileva, he had promised her the Nobel Prize money as alimony.

The Great Debate

Early in the 1920s, Einstein met Niels Bohr, the prominent Danish physicist. At that time, they started their great debate over the implications of quantum theory—a controversy that was to last over the next three decades. It was to be one of the most important scientific dialogues of the twentieth century, although the issue was more philosophical than scientific. Bohr believed in a "probabilistic" universe in which chance plays a role in the occurrence of events. This offended Einstein's sense of order and contradicted his belief in a "deterministic" universe, as evidenced by his much quoted remark that "God does not play dice with the universe." Most physicists today agree with Bohr, but Einstein remained unconvinced.

In 1927, while on a visit to the United States, Einstein attended a meeting at the Mount Wilson Observatory in California. At the meeting, the Belgian physicist Abbé George Lemaître first presented to a prestigious scientific audience his theory of an expanding universe that had begun in the explosion of a primeval atom (now known as the Big Bang Theory). Einstein jumped to his feet, applauding. He stated that this presentation was the most beautiful and satisfactory explanation of creation he had ever heard, and he rushed forward to shake Lemaître's hand. As pointed out earlier, Lemaître's theory was a direct result of Einstein's cosmological field equations of 1917.

The year of Einstein's fiftieth birthday, 1929, marked the beginning of a number of setbacks for the great scientist. His first published paper on a unified-field theory had not been well received. This did not bother him inordinately because he considered it a preliminary work and was prepared to "go back to the drawing board." What did bother Einstein was an ominous trend in world affairs. Arab attacks on Jewish colonists in Palestine, the growing strength of the Nazis in Germany, the weakness of the League of Nations (which caused Einstein to resign from its Committee for Intellectual Cooperation as a protest against its timidity), and the stock market crash in the United States all presaged worldwide crisis. More important on a personal basis was the mental breakdown of his younger son, Edward. Einstein's son was suffering from lifelong paranoid schizophrenia. The last decades of Mileva's life were largely shaped by this tragic fact, caring for him and making special arrangements for him. Edward Einstein had worshipped his father from a distance, but now blamed his father for deserting him as a boy. Einstein's sorrow in this sad event was eased, if only slightly, by his good relationship with his older son, Hans Albert.

The Coming of the Nazis

Remaining in Germany until 1933, when Hitler came to power, Einstein received numerous death threats and was often vilified at staged meetings of "Aryan" scientists who competed in exposing the "fundamental flaws in the theory of relativity." Einstein found these anti-Semitic ravings to be scientifically pathetic, but he did recognize that he had become a focal point of Nazi hatred and the time had come to leave Germany forever. Shortly after he left, Nazi brown shirts raided Einstein's summer home, announcing that they were looking for weapons. When told of this later, Einstein, who never owned a weapon in his life, was amused. As he well knew, and they did not, his ideas were not hidden under the bed. The Nazis later branded Einstein a public enemy with a price of 20,000 marks placed on his head, and his home and belongings were confiscated.

Einstein saw Hitler for the threat that he was, and the rise of Nazism in Germany caused him to change his political views from absolute pacifism to qualified support for defensive wars. This philosophical change distressed his pacifist supporters, who charged that he had violated his ideals.

Move to the United States

Toward the close of 1933, Einstein accepted a position with the Institute for Advanced Study at Princeton, New Jersey. He, Elsa, and an assistant named Helen Dukas, who had started to work for Einstein in 1928, moved to the United States. By the time he arrived in Princeton, he was a noticeably aged man. It was as if something had deadened in him. He was not laughing anymore. Both personal and world affairs had taken their toll.

Except for a few trips around the United States, Einstein remained at Princeton until his death in 1955. His work at Princeton over the twenty-two years involved a search for a mathematical framework that would unite both electromagnetism and gravitation—the so-called "unified field theory." There has been some criticism of Einstein for spending twenty-two years working on a problem to which he never did find a solution. In my view, this criticism shows a lack of understanding of scientific endeavor. The essence of science is not just in finding answers, but in asking questions. Today, there is a large school of thought that is reanalyzing Einstein's great quest. Possibly he was onto something important, perhaps the greatest philosophical quest of all time. The current consensus among scientists is that Einstein was on the correct path, but that he made key mistakes based on what was then known about the nuclear force.

Einstein's life in Princeton was placid and largely routine. He lived with his wife (and after she died with his sister Maja) in a simple, two-story frame house. Most mornings, he would walk to the Institute. He never owned a car. (He never owned a TV set either, which may have given him an unfair advantage over the rest of us when it came to sustained thinking about tough theoretical problems.) At the Institute, he worked on his unified-field theory, talked with colleagues, and carried on worldwide correspondence on both scientific and political affairs. Once his immediate needs were met, he did not seem to care much about money. His salary at the Institute was modest, and he never wrote a best-seller explaining his theories. In short, he never capitalized on his celebrity. For recreation, he played his violin and sailed his small boat on a local lake.

Although not actively involved in religion, Einstein did possess a sincere sense of the spiritual. "Science without religion is lame," he once said, "while religion without science is blind." He often referred to God in his writings, sometimes alluding to the Deity as "the Old Man." In discussing the relationship of science to religion, he once said, "Subtle is the Lord, but malicious He is not." I think he meant that nature might seem to hide secrets from the inquisitive scientists, but these secrets are neither unfathomable nor incomprehensible. That is, it is difficult but not impossible for humankind to discover the laws of nature.

Eventually Einstein acquired American citizenship, but he always thought of himself as a citizen of the world. Quietly he pursued his own line of theoretical research outside the mainstream of physics, which had flowed on by him. He took on an air of fixed serenity, and claimed that among his European friends he was known as the "Great Stone Face." Even his wife's death in 1936 did not seem to disturb his outward calm.

Splitting of the Atom

In 1939, Niels Bohr brought Einstein the news that the German physicist Otto Hahn had split the uranium atom. Lise Meitner had worked closely with Hahn before she had been forced to flee the Nazis, and it was she, then living in Sweden, who made public the information that it was possible to split the atom. Bohr suggested that if a controlled chain-reaction splitting of uranium atoms could be accomplished, a mammoth explosion could result. Einstein was unconvinced, but other physicists were already thinking and worrying about the feasibility of atomic fission.

In the summer of 1939, the eccentric Hungarian physicist Leo Szilard—once Einstein's assistant at the Kaiser Wilhelm Institute in Germany— and his colleague Eugene Wigner sought out Einstein at his summer cottage on Long Island, New York, and conveyed to him their fears that Nazi scientists might be at work developing an atomic bomb. Convinced of the danger, Einstein signed the letter to President Franklin D. Roosevelt that they had brought with them. It was Leo Szilard who had written the letter, but he and Wigner knew that it would take Einstein's prestige to bring about some high-level reaction. Szilard carried the letter around in his pocket for months before entrusting it to the financier Alexander Sachs to deliver to the President personally. Historians still refer to this document as the Einstein/Roosevelt letter, but Einstein himself said that "I really only acted as a mailbox."

Wrote Einstein, "Some recent work by E. Fermi and L. Szilard leads me to expect that the element uranium may be turned into a new and important source of energy in the immediate future. . . . This new phenomenon would also lead to the construction of bombs. . . ." This is the recommendation that would lead to the initiation of the Manhattan Project. Einstein took no part in the Los Alamos bomb-building project, nor did he know that a nuclear-fission bomb had been constructed until after Hiroshima.

Final Years

After World War II, Einstein joined those scientists seeking ways to prevent any future use of the bomb. He urged the formation of a world government under a constitution drafted by the United States, Great Britain, and Russia. Once more, the former recluse was on the world stage; but his views were treated by many as naive, and he was regarded as a well-meaning old man devoting his last years trying to bring harmony to a world not ready for peace.

In 1952, he was offered the presidency of Israel, a largely ceremonial position. Einstein declined, saying that he was too old and frail to move to Israel. There were those in the Knesset who were concerned about this offer. Perhaps he had become disillusioned with politics by this time. "Equations are more important to me," he once said, "because politics is for the present, but an equation is something for eternity."

His health had now deteriorated to the point where he could no longer play the violin or sail his beloved boat. On April 19, 1955, at the age of seventy-six, Einstein died in his sleep at the Princeton Hospital. The last document he signed before his death was a proclamation against the use of nuclear weapons.

Einstein was more than a scientist, more than a philosopher, and more than a world statesman. He had recognized his own position in the history of physics, and acknowledged his great predecessor in 1949 when he wrote,

"Newton, forgive me; you found the only way which in your age was just about possible for a man with the highest powers of thought and creativity. The concepts which you created are guiding our thinking in physics even today, however we now know that they will have to be replaced by others farther removed from the sphere of immediate experience, if we aim at a profounder understanding of relationships."

Someday, a brash young physicist might write, "Einstein, forgive me; you found the only way which in your age was just about possible for a man of the highest powers of thought and creativity." It has not happened yet. Since our space age began, dozens of experiments have tested relativity, primarily by checking predictions based on it, and it has never failed. Nor has a more powerful theory of the architecture of the universe replaced it.

Radio transmissions from spacecraft sent to Mars, Venus, and Mercury have refined measurements of the bending of light by the Sun to within 0.1 percent from about 20 percent in 1919. The discovery of pulsars in 1974 provided scientists with a new measuring reference. (*Pulsars* are two extremely dense stars rotating rapidly around each other and emitting a radio signal every 59 thousandths of a second.) Using pulsars as a celestial clock, scientists confirmed the warping of time, predicted by the special theory, and the gravitational stretching of light waves toward the color red, predicted by the general theory.

One experiment yet to be conducted is Stanford University's plan to put four extremely precise gyroscopes on a satellite in a polar orbit in 1999. If general relativity is correct, as most scientists believe it is, the gyroscopes will change their angle relative to distant stars by a tiny fraction of a degree each year.

All this does not mean that physics as a science is over. As we have seen, general relativity is concerned with one force of nature—gravity—but it does not incorporate the other natural forces such as electromagnetism and the forces that hold atoms together. The search for a more complete theory, one that will link general relativity to the quantum of relativity, is continuing.

Even if only those mathematicians and physicists who have mastered the theories of relativity are in a position to completely understand it, the rest of us can still appreciate Albert Einstein's monumental success—he forever changed the way we contemplate the universe.

Biographical Overview

1879   Born in Ulm, Germany.

1902   Unable to obtain academic position, he went to work as a technician in the Swiss Patent Office in Bern.

1905   Published five scientific papers, including the special theory of relativity and an addendum that said that the energy content of a body is equal to its mass times the velocity of light squared ($E = mc^2$).

1911   Described the principle of equivalence, which equates gravity and acceleration, a keystone in the general theory of relativity.

1914   Moved to Berlin to accept an appointment to the Prussian Academy of Sciences.

1916   Published his most famous paper, "The Foundation of the Theory of General Relativity."

1919   Solar eclipse provided British astronomers with the first confirmation that space is curved by gravity and that light bends in presence of large mass as Einstein had predicted.

1922   Received, one year late, the 1921 Nobel Prize in Physics, not for relativity theories but for his work on photoelectric effect.

1933   After repeated attacks by Nazis, he left Germany for the United States and took up residence at the Institute for Advanced Study in Princeton, New Jersey.

1939   Signed a letter to President Roosevelt pointing out the potential for an atomic bomb, his only involvement in the Manhattan Project.

1955   Died in his sleep at the Princeton Hospital.

Chapter 3

Max Karl Ernst Ludwig Planck

It's as if one could drink a pint of beer or no beer at all, but were barred by a law of nature from drinking any quantity of beer between zero and one pint.

George Gamow on *quantum physics*.

Quantum physics is a term that many nonscientists find a bit daunting. It need not be so. Although the implications of the theory are profound, the concept itself is almost as easy to grasp as George Gamow's analogy. The impact of this theory on physics, however, might be said to match that of relativity. Although many scientists have achieved fame by applying quantum theory to different phenomena, one man alone was responsible for the source of this radical doctrine, and a most reluctant revolutionist he was.

Quantum physics began with Herr Professor Max Karl Ernst Ludwig Planck on December 14, 1900, when the then forty-two-year-old physicist presented a strange new concept to the imposing body of the German Physical Society. This date would later be regarded as the birth date of the quantum, and Planck has come to be universally regarded as the father of quantum theory.

In his lecture that day, the diffident, soft-spoken Planck presented a mathematical exercise that explained a phenomenon that had been plaguing thermodynamicists for years. Planck explained why heat energy does not always get converted to invisible ultraviolet light waves. This accomplishment by itself does not sound revolutionary, but in the process of investigating this phenomenon, Planck had discovered that matter absorbed heat energy and emitted light energy discontinuously, in other words, in discrete bits. He later called these bits *quanta*, from the Latin for "how much." With this discovery, the quantum revolution in physics was underway.

The Scientist's Scientist

In many ways, the life of Max Planck presents a striking contrast to those of Newton and Einstein. Where Newton and Einstein were widely regarded as geniuses, Planck was a dutiful and diligent scientist. He was no shooting star in the night sky of physics. Also, where Newton and Einstein were loners, Planck was a well-liked and respected academic manager. And, despite the conventional wisdom that physics is so intellectually demanding that practitioners must make their contributions in their early twenties, Planck did not make his most significant mark on the history of physics until he was forty-two.

Planck was born in Kiel, Germany, in 1858, the sixth child of Wilhelm Planck, a professor of jurisprudence at the university there. His mother, Wilhelm's second wife, came from a long line of pastors. Max Planck might have inherited some of his father's legal talents, including the ability to screen large amounts of evidence and distinguish the relevant from the irrelevant facts. Whether that influence was significant or not, the influence of a solid, upper-middle-class, professional family life can certainly be seen in his career. The Plancks had a high respect for education and culture and for conservative family values. All this they passed on to their young son. Planck's letters offer a glimpse of the family's life-style. They speak of summers spent at the Baltic resort of Eldena, playing croquet on the lawn, evenings reading novelists such as Sir Walter Scott, and plays and musicales put on by the family members.

Student Days

During his high school years, Planck attended the Maximilan Gymnasium in Munich, where his interest in science was awakened. Planck credits his mathematics teacher, Hermann Muller, for first giving him an understanding of the meaning of the laws of physics. In introducing the law of the conservation of energy, for example, Muller used the image of a bricklayer using a great amount of energy to lift a heavy block of stone. Muller showed that the energy used to lift the stone is not lost but rather is stored up in the stone until it is dislodged and falls back to Earth. This principle impressed Planck because it represented an absolute—a fundamental law of nature. From that time on, as Planck recounts in his memoirs, he considered the search for fundamental laws of nature to be the noblest quest that any scientist could pursue.

As I pointed out earlier, Planck was not a prodigy. His teachers at the Maximilian Gymnasium ranked him near, but never at, the top of his class. His teachers noted no special brilliance or aptitude, except in his personal attitude and extreme diligence. His social skills must have been first rate, however, as he was a favorite of both his classmates and teachers.

After graduation from the Gymnasium in 1874, Planck had not yet decided in what subject he wanted to continue his studies. He had by then displayed considerable talents in music and was an excellent performer on the piano and organ. He was seriously considering a musical career until he sought advice from a professional musician about the choice. "If you have to *ask*," the musician told him, "you had better study something else!"

Eventually, he decided to attend the University of Munich as an undergraduate and later the University of Berlin. He studied experimental physics and mathematics, and after he moved to Berlin he was able to attend the classes of two world-renowned physicists, Herman von Helmholtz and Gustav Kirchhoff. Planck credited these two scientists with kindling his interest in thermodynamics. He did not say that they taught him all that much, but he was awed by their reputations and wanted to be like them, respected figures of the academic community. Helmholtz and Kirchhoff were not particularly inspired lecturers, and Planck found his interest in science faltering in their dull lecture halls. Like Newton and Einstein before him, Planck turned to independent study of the subjects that interested him. In this way, he came across the thermodynamic treatises of Rudolf Clausis. Planck was impressed both with the content and with the lucid style and clarity of reasoning in Clausis's work, and he turned to thermodynamics as his major field. The study of the second law of thermodynamics became the subject of Planck's doctoral dissertation at Munich in 1879. Planck settled on thermodynamics despite the fact that his professor at the University of Munich, Philipp von Jolly, had counseled him against a career in physics on the ground that the discovery of thermodynamics had completed the structure of theoretical physics. Planck told Jolly that he had no wish to make discoveries, but only to understand and perhaps deepen the existing foundations of physics.

The Problem of Entropy

Planck's dissertation reviewed the two principles of classical thermodynamics. The first states the conservation of energy; the second establishes a direction in time by defining a quantity called *entropy* that increases in all real physical processes. *Entropy* can be defined as a measure of the degree of disorder or as the tendency in any physical system toward breakdown. The effect of increased entropy is that things evolve from a state of relative order to one of disorder, and with this disorder there is increased complexity.

Planck's ideas on entropy and his proposals for experiments to be made in this field did not impress his distinguished faculty advisors. Planck claimed that Professor Helmholtz did not even read his dissertation, and he also indicated that although Kirchhoff did read it, he did not like it. Even Rudolf Clausis, Planck's inspiration, was not the least interested and did not respond to a copy of the dissertation sent to him for comment. This was altogether an inauspicious debut for a man who was to change physics fundamentally.

Planck took the reaction to his dissertation with characteristic equanimity and returned to work with even more zeal. He did suffer a two-year delay in his college career because of illness, but in 1879 he was awarded his doctorate *summa cum laude*.

In 1880, he joined the faculty at Munich as an associate professor, and five years later he received a professorial appointment at Kiel University. About this time he met a young student of physics named Wilhelm Wein, who was a friend and collaborator for over forty years. It was Wein's experimental and theoretical work that would later provide the starting point for Planck's most important contribution to science.

In 1889 Planck's old advisor Gustav Kirchhoff died, leaving his chair at the University of Berlin vacant. By this time Planck's other faculty advisor, Herman von Helmholtz, had come to admire both Planck's tenacity and the work he was producing. Helmholtz was instrumental in securing Kirchhoff's chair for Planck. Planck would remain there, gradually accruing notice, honors, and finally world fame, until his retirement in 1926.

It was at the University of Berlin where one day Planck, having forgotten in which room he was supposed to lecture, stopped by the department office and asked, "Please tell me in which room does Professor Planck lecture today?" "Don't go there, young fellow," an office worker told him firmly. "You are much too young to understand the lectures of our learned Professor Planck."

Black Bodies, Ultraviolet Catastrophe, and Quanta

Settled into his chair appointment, Planck turned to the classic physics problem, first raised by Kirchhoff, of black-body radiation. A *black body* is a theoretical object that absorbs all frequencies of light; therefore, when it is heated it should radiate all frequencies of light. However, there was a problem with black-body theory. The number of different frequencies in the high-frequency range is greater than the number in the low-frequency range. If a black body radiated all frequencies of electromagnetic radiation equally, then virtually all the energy would be radiated in the high-frequency range. This theoretical situation was referred to as the *ultraviolet catastrophe* because the highest frequency radiation in the visible light spectrum is violet, and theoretically a heated black body would then radiate only invisible ultraviolet light waves. I said "theoretical situation" because in actuality it didn't work that way (the "catastrophe" part of the term) and physics theory at the time could not explain why.

Let's take a quick look at the background to the problem. Although physicists knew that hot things glow and that they glow in different colors as they are heated, they did not know the exact relationship between heat and radiated light. Sunlight produces a balanced spectrum of colors, and the equal amounts of all colors cause sunlight to appear white, or colorless. When sunlight passes through tiny prisms made of water droplets (raindrops), the spread of colors that result is called the light spectrum (a rainbow). Studies had shown that the characteristic color of any object changes in a predictable manner as it is slowly heated to higher temperatures. A hot branding iron, for instance, glows red at first. At higher temperatures it starts to glow orange-yellow, and at still higher temperatures, it glows blue. The hotter an object becomes, the whiter its color and the more balanced its spectrum.

Physicists determined that the connection between the temperature of a material and the color it emitted had to be a mechanical one. They knew that higher temperatures produce greater kinetic energy or more rapid motions of heated materials. At a more fundamental level, this means that the atoms are moving or oscillating to and fro more rapidly. From these facts, it followed that the differences in color in materials at different temperatures were somehow determined by the movements of the atoms composing the heated material. Physicists also concluded that the frequency of the light at different temperatures must be the same as the frequency of the vibrations of atoms in the material. After all, Maxwell had shown that a light wave is really electromagnetic oscillation. Therefore, it seemed reasonable that the different colors of light emitted by a heated object were caused by different vibrational frequencies. For instance, red light was thought of as having a lower vibrational rate or frequency than blue light.

As this explanation makes clear, the prevailing theory at that time for understanding hot glowing objects and the colors they emitted was based upon the wave definition of *light*. According to this theory, the light energy emitted by a glowing body should tend to be given off at a higher frequency rather than a lower one. The reason for this is the direct relationship between the frequency of a wave and its length. The higher the frequency of a wave, the shorter its length. It was thought that light waves with very short wavelengths (very high frequencies) would prevail. That is because there would be more ways for short waves to fit within any volume of space than for long waves. What this meant was that a red-hot branding iron should not be red at all, but blue. Moreover, an iron glowing blue should not be blue but should instead be glowing in the really high frequency ultraviolet range, ultraviolet being, of course, a color that vibrates at a higher frequency than violet and is invisible to the human eye. In other words, any hot object should give off its electromagnetic energy at beyond ultraviolet frequencies. The fact that in reality heated objects did not give off their energies exclusively in the higher frequencies was known as the "ultraviolet catastrophe." It was a "catastrophe" because Lord Rayleigh, the then prevailing expert in fields of the behavior of sound and light, had predicted that any heated object would soon emit all of its energy at frequencies beyond the visible, and the experimental evidence did not match the prevailing theories—this is always a problem in science. Today scientists would call this phenomenon the "ultraviolet anomaly." Finding the solution to this puzzle was the challenge Max Planck took up, having no idea at the time that the solution he found would revolutionize the concepts of classical physics.

Many modern developments in physics have been concerned with investigations of the properties of the radiation that travel through empty space, and, in particular, with their relationship to matter. Radiation is described in terms of its wavelength and frequency, that is, the distance between successive wave crests and the number of crests that arrive per second. When the wavelength is short, the frequency is high, and vice versa. Various forms of radiation compose the electromagnetic spectrum, from radio waves with very long wavelengths (very low frequencies) to gamma rays with very short wavelengths (very high frequencies).

All objects radiate energy. The hotter they are the more energy they radiate. You and I, for instance, emit about 200 watts of radiation in the invisible infrared region of the spectrum. All objects absorb energy from their surroundings. If the temperature of the object is higher than

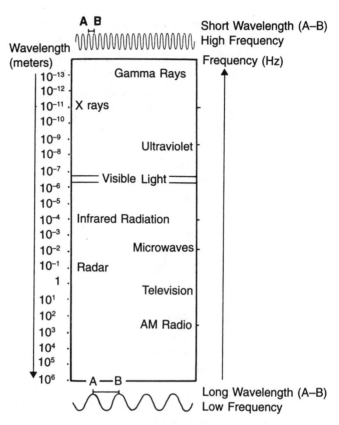

Electromagnetic spectrum Radiated energy in terms of wavelength and frequency. When wavelength is short, the frequency is high, and vice versa. Forms of radiation range in wavelength from less than a billionth of a micron for gamma rays to many miles long for radio waves.

its surroundings, it cools because it radiates more energy than it absorbs. The technical term *black body* means an ideal absorber, one that absorbs 100 percent of the radiation falling on it. Also, this ideal black body must, if heated, radiate as much of every kind of radiation as possible, more than any other kind of body at the same temperature would radiate.

A black body, when cold, appears black because it reflects no light. Therefore, physicists like to use this ideal black body as a standard for measuring emitted radiation. What is of particular interest about radiation from a black body is the color spectrum of light, that is, how much light it gives off at the various wavelengths. As an object is gradually heated, it first gives off a dull red glow, then, as the object gets hotter, a bright red, then yellow, then blue-white, then bright white. This shift along the color spectrum means that, as the temperature is raised, the peak intensity of light is moving from infrared to red to yellow to blue.

In 1893, Planck's physicist friend Wilhelm Wein had worked out a theory that yielded a mathematical expression for the energy distribution of black-body radiation, that is, the amount of energy radiated at each particular wavelength. This theory provided a formula that accurately described the distribution of energy radiation at the violet end of the spectrum but, oddly enough, not at the red end. At about this same time, the English physicist Lord Rayleigh developed an equation that described the distribution at the red end of the spectrum but failed completely at the violet end. This was the situation when Planck started looking into the question of the ultraviolet catastrophe. The best theories available could explain one half of the radiation or the other half, but not both at once.

By this time, Planck had accepted, although reluctantly, the atomic theory. He knew that all matter was made up of individual atoms, at that time thought to be the basic building blocks of nature. Energy, on the other hand, was thought to be continuous, radiated in waves; for instance, physicists spoke of heat, sound, or light waves.

In 1900, Planck found that in order to explain black-body radiation, he had to introduce a completely new idea. He suggested that energy, like matter, existed in small units or packets. He called the unit of energy radiation the *quantum* (after the Latin word for "how much?") or, in the plural, quanta.

Analogously, we can consider that the quantum of money in the United States is a penny. We have no smaller denomination of money. A purchase might involve a multiple of pennies, and possibly it might only include just one, but you could never buy anything for a fraction of a cent. Planck showed that energy comes only in fundamental, indivisible units, and these units are adjustable only in sequential steps. When the energy of any type of electromagnetic radiation changes from one value to another, it does so in discrete jumps (quantum jumps), with no possible value in between.

Planck knew how revolutionary his idea was the day he had it. He had taken his young son out for a walk and he said to him on that day,

"I have had a conception today as great as the kind of thought that Newton had."

Planck postulated that radiation can be absorbed only in whole numbers of quanta. He went on to demonstrate that the amount of energy in a quantum depends on the wavelength of the radiation. The shorter the wavelength, the more energetic the quantum. In other words, the energy content of the quantum is inversely proportional to the wavelength.

Planck's work showed that a quantum of violet light (short wavelength, high frequency) would have to contain twice the energy of a quantum of red light (long wavelength, low frequency). Therefore, when a black body radiates, it is not likely to radiate all wavelengths equally. Low frequencies are radiated easily because only a small quantity of energy must be brought together to form a quantum of low-frequency radiation. To radiate higher-frequency radiation requires more energy, and it is less probable that the additional energy can be accumulated. In other words, the higher the frequency, the less probable the radiation. Although the high frequencies are many, their quantum-energy requirements make their radiation improbable, and the result is there is no ultraviolet catastrophe.

Planck's Constant

Equations worked out on the basis of Planck's quantum theory explained the radiation of a black body precisely at both ends of the spectrum. What Planck accomplished was to relate mathematically the energy content of a quantum to the frequency of radiation. If both the frequency and the quantum's energy content were inversely proportional to the wavelength, then the two were directly proportional to each other. Planck expressed this relationship by means of his now famous equation:

$$E = hf$$

A quantum of energy, E, is equal to the frequency, f, of the radiation times Planck's constant, h. This constant, h, is an extremely small number, and it is now recognized as one of the fundamental constants of the universe. To reiterate, the short wavelengths (high frequencies) require more energy. At any given temperature, only so much energy is available. Therefore, the high frequencies are less likely to be emitted.

Not only is Planck's constant small, so is the quantum. The units of radiation are so small that light, for instance, appears continuous, just as ordinary matter appears continuous to us even though we know it is made up of discrete units called atoms.

If the question of black body radiation, which led to the quantum theory, was the only question the theory could answer, then quantum theory would have remained only an oddity. It is the utility that quantum theory has in many different areas of physics that has made it so important.

Despite its importance, quantum theory made little impression on physicists when it was first announced in 1900. Planck himself did not quite believe it, suspecting that his results might be the product of mathematical trickery with no real relationship to nature. In fact, Planck's theory disturbed him. He did not want to see classical physics destroyed. Eventually he conceded. "We have to live with quantum theory," he said. "And believe me, it will expand. It will not be only in optics. It will go into all fields."

By 1918, the importance of the quantum theory had become recognized, and in appreciation of his work, Max Planck was awarded the Nobel Prize in Physics.

The Border Line

Planck's quantum theory of radiation, the basis of quantum physics, was, as I've noted, first published in 1900, and thus preceded Einstein's special theory of relativity. This was a time of upheaval and change in the world of physics. Not just Einstein and Planck but Rutherford, Bohr, and Heisenberg were raising questions and suggesting new answers. To put all this activity into some perspective, we note that physics before quantum theory is called *classical physics* and after quantum theory it is called *modern physics*. Max Planck, then, really marks the transition.

Planck and Einstein

A contemporary of Albert Einstein, Max Planck was the first member of the academic physics establishment to recognize the importance of Einstein's original theories. As I related in the last chapter, Einstein had expected widespread, if controversial, response to the publication of his paper proposing the special theory of relativity in 1905. Instead, he had received one letter. That was from Max Planck at the University of Berlin, asking for more details and some further explanation of Einstein's mathematics. Einstein was overjoyed to have the attention of Planck, who, with his proposal of quanta only a few years earlier, had become one of the most renowned of all physicists. Later, Planck used Einstein's principle of relativity in his own work. And as early as 1909, in a letter of reference for Einstein to the University of Prague, he wrote "If Einstein's theory should prove to be correct, as I expect it will, he will be considered the Copernicus of the twentieth century."

Planck's approval, which led to the gradual approval of other leading physicists, was of the utmost importance to Einstein's self-confidence. The two men initiated a correspondence that lasted a lifetime and lead to an important collaboration on the theory of light.

Einstein's Confirmation of Planck's Theory

Just as Planck had appreciated Einstein's worth, Einstein was one of the first to recognize the implications of quantum theory. In 1905 he applied the quantum theory to an observable phenomenon that had been puzzling physicists for some time, the photoelectric effect. Scientists had discovered that when light struck certain metals, it caused the metal surface to emit electrons just as if the force of the light knocked electrons out of atoms. What puzzled the experimentalists was the lack of effect that resulted from increasing the intensity of the light. They found, to their surprise, that although increasing the intensity of the light did not give the knocked-out electrons any more energy, changing the wavelength (or the color) did affect them. Blue light, for instance, caused electrons to be emitted at greater speeds than yellow light did. Red light, no matter how bright, failed to knock out any electrons at all from some metals. Why should the color of the light have so much more effect than the intensity? There was no answer to this puzzle in classical physics.

Using Planck's quantum theory, Einstein found the answer. If radiation takes the form of packets of energy, as Planck had theorized, and this energy is expended in kicking out electrons, then high-frequency radiation should throw out electrons with more energy than low-

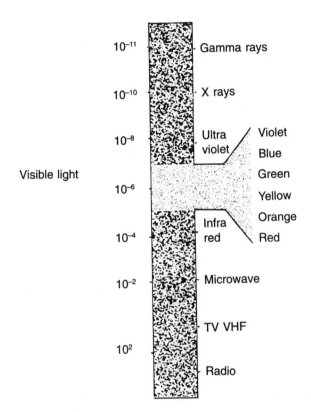

Visible light The portion of the electromagnetic spectrum that is visible to the human eye is called light. Each color—violet, blue, green, yellow, orange, red—has a discrete wavelength measured in microns. The shortest is violet, 0.4 microns; the longest is red, 0.7 microns.

frequency radiation does. Einstein postulated that the more energetic the quantum, the more speed it gives to the electron it has caused to be emitted. Red light, the quanta of which are very small, has no effect, because a certain minimum energy is required just to knock an electron out of an atom. The energy of red quanta is, for most metals, less than this minimum. Violet light drives electrons out with low speed, ultra-violet produces greater speed, and X rays yield very fast electrons. Interestingly, it was for this quantum explanation of the photoelectric effect, not for the theory of relativity, that Einstein was awarded the Nobel Prize in Physics in 1921.

Another important early convert to quantum theory was Niels Bohr. In 1913 he incorporated the quantum theory into his theory of the structure of the atom and explained much of what prequantum physics could not. In three papers published in 1913, Bohr presented his quantum theory of the hydrogen atom. For this work he would win the Nobel Prize in 1922. Three Nobel awards in a five-year period for work in quantum fields marked the acceptance of quantum physics by the world of science.

Irony and Tragedy

Irony, it is said, is a constant companion of history, and so it is in the relationship of Planck and Einstein. They were brought together by physics and forced far apart by political and moral issues. When Planck was elected to the position of rector of Berlin University in 1915, Einstein publicly congratulated the faculty on its choice. Later, Planck helped set up the Kaiser Wilhelm Institute for Physics in Berlin and nominated Albert Einstein as its first director. The function of the Institute was pure research, but in order to receive government funding the potential for military benefits had to be stressed. This was, of course, 1914, and the German government had war on its mind. Just how an institute of pure physics research headed by an avowed pacifist like Einstein would help the German war effort was a hard sell, but Planck managed it.

During this time, the Einstein and Planck families were close. They often dined together. Also, both Planck and Einstein loved music, and they played in the same chamber orchestras. Unlike Einstein, Planck was caught up in the patriotic frenzy of that time and fully supported Germany's position in what he believed to be a defensive and inevitable war against evil opponents. Planck was the father of two boys of military age and the rector of a university soon to be depopulated by the calling up of both students and the younger instructors. Soon Planck's children were all involved in the war. His twin girls, Greta and Emma, had trained with the Red Cross and were awaiting assignment to military hospitals. Planck's oldest son, Karl, was at artillery school, and his youngest son, Erwin, was already at the front. "What a glorious time we are living in," Planck wrote to his sister. "It is a great feeling to be able to call oneself a German." How the Plancks ever tolerated their friend

Einstein passing out antiwar propaganda on street corners is a mystery. Possibly they considered him a hopeless eccentric.

By 1915, the horrors of World War I became personal for Planck. His nephew, a physicist, his brother's only son, was killed. His own son Erwin had been taken prisoner, and Karl was injured and died of his wounds.

In late 1917 defeat was in the air and the German government was near collapse. But even given all of the tragedy visited on his family and the imminent defeat, Planck refused to sign a proclamation calling for the resignation of the Kaiser, as Einstein had. He was loyal to the end. Despite political differences, Planck's relationship with Einstein remained cordial.

Continuing family tragedies caused Planck great grief. In 1917, his daughter Greta, who had married a professor in Heidelberg, died suddenly a week after giving birth. Her twin sister, Emma, came to Heidelberg to care for the infant, and in January 1919 married the widower. By that year's end she too was to die shortly after giving birth. This double tragedy almost destroyed Max Planck. "There are times now," he wrote to his friend Hendrick Lorentz, "when I doubt the value of life itself."

Planck found solace from public and domestic tragedy both in his work and in helping to raise his grandchildren. His quantum principles were becoming more and more acceptable in the world of science and had expanded into virtually every area of physics. Planck's theorized constant h came to be regarded as a fundamental constant of nature, the equal of Einstein's c, the velocity of light.

The Nazis and "Deutsche Physik"

The next period of special note in Planck's life started at the dawn of the Nazi era. In 1930, Planck became president of the Kaiser Wilhelm Society of Berlin, which was then renamed the Max Planck Society. In his seventies at the time, Planck's renown in the world of science was second only to that of Einstein.

The days of Nazi ascendancy in Germany were difficult both for science and for Max Planck personally. The issues were Einstein, because he was a Jew, and the theories of relativity and quantum physics. Anti-Semites identified relativity and quantum theories as the decadent work of Jews. In contrast, the right wing extolled the virtues of applied physics, called "Deutsche Physik," as opposed to contaminated theoretical or Jewish physics. Many German scientists lined up on the Nazi side, and Planck found himself drawn into this ugly fight. The position he took was ambivalent. On the one hand, the major prestigious scientific societies of which he was a dominant member remained silent and did not come to Einstein's defense. Privately Planck condemned the Nazi attacks on Einstein as "scarcely believable filth." Publicly he tried to stay out of what he called "political issues." On the other hand, Planck vigorously defended the theories of relativity. As president of the Society of German Scientists and Physicians, Planck proposed that Einstein be invited to address the annual meeting. Planck hoped that the irrefutable logic of Einstein's science could win the day. Einstein at first accepted the challenge but was forced to withdraw after threats were made on his life. Planck was fighting a losing battle to separate ivory tower science from street politics.

In January of 1933, Adolph Hitler became Reich chancellor and the Nazis were in full power. Max Planck was secretary of the Academy of Science and president of the Kaiser Wilhelm Gesellschaft, key positions in the scientific establishment in two organizations that depended on the Reich for financial support. Planck was faced with the choice of either resigning and leaving the country or staying and attempting to moderate Nazi policies. He chose the latter. His hope was to affect compromises for the sake of science, but compromise was not to be had.

Einstein by this time had decided to emigrate to the United States. Letters between the two physicists revealed their separate states of mind with regard to the advisability of compromise with the Nazis, and they would eventually split on this issue. Planck fought long and hard to protect his Jewish students and colleagues, but in the end his efforts could do no more than delay their persecution. Although he never lent his voice and prestige to the Nazi regime in any way, he never stood up firmly or publicly against it. When the Nazis barred all Jewish faculty and students from the universities and Planck remained silent, Einstein broke off their long relationship and never spoke to him again.

Despite the fact that Planck never publicly opposed the Nazi regime, the regime had mixed feelings about Planck. On the one hand, he was a world-renowned scientist, and he and his fame were used in Nazi propaganda efforts. On the other hand, he continued to espouse relativity (even though he ceased using Einstein's name in connection with the theories). This was a typical Planck compromise, for which his reputation suffered abroad. On Planck's eightieth birthday Hitler sent him good wishes, while at the same time Joseph Goebbels was trying to prove that he was one-sixteenth Jewish and therefore not fit to lead German science.

Despite his age, Planck continued his heavy schedule of lectures during the war years. By 1943 the content of his lectures had turned from physics to philosophy and religion. The son and grandson of pastors had returned to theology. He was to need heavy amounts of both philosophy and religion for solace in the year to come.

Early in 1944, a large Allied air raid against Berlin resulted in the obliteration of the suburb of Grunewald where the Planck family had lived for many years. Nothing was saved from Planck's house. He lost his library, his files, his diaries, and all the memorabilia of a long, productive life in science. He was still in good physical and mental condition. Just the year before, he had climbed a 3,000-meter mountain. Even after the air raid cost him all his worldly possessions he remained optimistic, and at the age of eighty-six he started work on a new lecture series.

Late in 1944, Max Planck's last living child, his beloved son Erwin, was arrested in connection with the plot to kill Hitler. A Nazi court quickly found him guilty, and he was condemned to death. Erwin might not actually have been involved with the assassination attempt, but he did know many of the plotters and there is no doubt that he sympathized with their cause. It is possible that Planck himself was aware of the coup attempt. He and his son were very close, and both were members of the club where the plotters congregated.

Planck used every political means at his command to save his son. According to one account of what followed, a high Nazi official contacted Planck with a proposed bargain: Planck would at last join the Nazi party, adding his still-considerable international prestige to their cause. In appreciation, Planck was told, they would seek to commute Erwin's sentence to a prison term. The old man refused. On February 23, 1945, Erwin was executed.

Planck was devastated by this loss. To a niece and nephew he wrote,

"He was a precious part of my being. He was my sunshine, my pride, my hope. No words can describe what I have lost with him."

The last year of the war in Europe was extraordinarily difficult for the old scientist. He and his second wife were again bombed out of the house in which they had taken refuge and had to hide in the woods and sleep in haystacks. Eventually the old couple were rescued by American troops advancing through the area.

After the war, Planck attempted to reestablish German science. First, he accepted an invitation from the Royal Society of London to participate in a war-delayed commemoration of the 300th birthday of Isaac Newton. Planck was the only German invited, and he felt it was his duty to attend. He was also heavily involved in trying to reconstitute the Kaiser Wilhelm Gesellschaft as a physics research center. In this effort he was successful, staffing the center largely with non-Nazi physicists who had long been out of favor and renaming the organization the Max Planck Institute. He was named president until Werner Heisenberg took over as his successor. Planck then returned to Gottingen, where he spent the last two years of his life, honored and respected.

Could Planck have done more in opposition to the Nazi regime? Einstein, for one, found it difficult to forgive him for his silence and for his compliance, however reluctant, in the destruction of the Jewish professorate. Where Einstein had seen a moral imperative to resist, Planck had attempted to compromise and to work within the system. Seen in retrospect, Planck's choice was a tragic failure, but at the time he might have thought he was doing the best he could both for his country and for science. Ultimately, he was a well-meaning man caught between good science and bad politics. Even Einstein acknowledged Planck's importance as a scientist. In 1948, he wrote the following touching homage, titled " A Tribute to Max Planck."

Many kinds of men devote themselves to science, and not all for the sake of science herself. There are some who come into her temple because it offers opportunity to display their particular talents. To this class of men science is a kind of sport in the practice of which they exult, just as an athlete exults in the exercise of his muscular prowess. There is another class of men who come into the temple to make an offering of their brain pulp in the hope of securing a profitable return. These men are scientists only by the chance of some circumstance which offered itself when making a choice of career. If the attending circumstances had been different, they might have become politicians or captains of business. Should an angel of God descend and drive from the temple of science all those who belong to the categories I have mentioned, I fear the temple would be nearly emptied. But a few worshippers would still remain—some from former times and some from ours. To these latter belongs our Planck. And that is why we love him.

His contribution to science made Max Planck a "scientist's scientist," respected by colleagues in all fields and of all nationalities. When he was awarded the Nobel Prize for Physics in 1918, the occasion was marked by unanimous affirmation from Albert Einstein, Niels Bohr, Ernest Rutherford, and Werner Heisenberg—each of whom might have deserved the honor, but who all unconditionally agreed that it belonged most to Planck.

On October 4, 1947, Planck died from a stroke at the age of ninety. History will remember him for his two major discoveries: quantum physics and Albert Einstein.

Planck's Legacy

Planck certainly did not foresee the long-range implications of his conceptual discovery. In the chapters on Newton and Einstein, I spoke of their predecessors, the giants on whose shoulders they stood. In Planck's case, it is his intellectual descendents who are of importance. In the period between 1900 and 1930, scientists such as Louis de Broglie, Erwin Schrödinger, Niels Bohr, and Werner Heisenberg took Planck's original concept and developed it into what we now call *quantum mechanics*. Neither Planck nor Einstein were eager to accept the logical evolutions of their original ideas, in particular the three founding principles of quantum mechanics: wave–particle duality, the probabilistic nature of physical reality, and the resulting uncertainties inherent in all physical measurements. All three are important signposts guiding our way through the realm of the very small. Because it is through this strange land that we will be traveling for the remainder of our journey, the following general introduction to these fundamentals will serve as our passport to "Quantum Country."

Fundamentals of Quantum Mechanics

Strange phenomena occur in the world of the very small. One of the most difficult to understand is wave–particle duality. Classical physics makes a clear distinction between a wave and a particle. But in the realm of the very small, these distinctions become blurred. Numerous experiments have shown that in the strange world of atoms, a physical entity somehow manages to possess a dual characteristic, sometimes appearing as a particle and sometimes behaving like a wave. A pinpoint particle and a spread-out wave seem to be two quite distinct concepts, but in the subatomic world the two seem to merge.

Planck and Einstein established the wave–particle duality of light, but they did not realize that this concept could be extended to all subatomic particles. Louis de Broglie of France first suggested this novel idea in 1920. He made the speculative and "preposterous" suggestion in his doctoral dissertation, and at first it was not well received. He speculated that if a wave of light energy could behave like a bunch of particles (photons), then, if nature was truly symmetrical, as some said, electrons and photons might possess wave–like properties. The idea was at first rejected by de Broglie's faculty advisors, and if it had not been for the favorable reaction of Einstein himself, de Broglie might never have received his doctoral degree. As we now know, de Broglie was right, and his hypothesis was confirmed by experiments just three years after he proposed it.

Quantum physics forces us into the world of philosophy. Does a tree falling in the forest make any sound if there is no one there to hear it? If we define *sound* as the sensation produced by stimulation of the hearing organs by vibrations transmitted through the air, then without the presence of an ear there is no sound. Another example: When we observe a star in the night sky we are not really looking at the star but at its light, which might have taken a million years to reach our eyes (the star might not even be there anymore). If we define light as electromagnetic radiation to which the organs of sight react, then without the presence of eyes there is no light (and no star).

The point of this excursion into philosophy is to demonstrate that the observer plays a role in the observed, which is precisely what quantum physics reveals.

If this first tenet of quantum physics is fairly readily understood, the second tenet, which has to do with the probabilistic nature of physical reality, is another story. This tenet asserts that the wave characteristics of an object yield mathematical information on the probability with which the object would be observed, detected, or measured at a particular position. This concept implies that chance plays an important role in physical reality. For 300 years, classical physics had assumed precise accuracy and determinability. Now this basic assumption was under question.

What do we mean by *determinability?* Newtonian physics describes a deterministic world. If you fired a shell from a cannon, launched a rocket into space, or discovered a new comet in the solar system, you could predict its path with total certainty. In theory, if you knew the forces and the initial conditions, all this would be predictable. Quantum theory argues against this certainty. It states that the initial conditions are inherently uncertain. As to predicting a particle's location, its energy, or velocity, you would have to settle for probabilities.

Einstein found this theory of reality completely intolerable. He wrote to his friend, Max Born, that if this was the way the world worked, "I would rather be a cobbler, or even an employee in a gaming-house, than a physicist." For the two old-line defenders of the faith, it soon got even worse.

But quantum theory gets even weirder than this. Wave–particle duality and its probabilistic interpretation led to the next logical step: the inherent uncertainty in the measurement of the position of a particle. The uncertainty principle, postulated by Werner Heisenberg in 1927, states that particles cannot have both a well-defined position and a well-defined velocity. The more precisely you measure the position of a particle, the less precisely you can measure its velocity, and vice versa. In the quantum world, Heisenberg argued, a particle—undisturbed by any attempt to observe it—can be in diverse places at the same time. Physicists tell us that a single photon traveling through a crystal simultaneously follows all possible optical paths through the material. In other words, the photon behaves like an array of waves, and how it emerges from the crystal depends on the manner in which the waves along these different paths reinforce and/or cancel one another.

If you find all this mysterious, you are in good company. One of Niels Bohr's students in Copenhagen once complained to him that quantum physics made him giddy. Bohr replied that if anybody says that he can think about quantum physics without feeling giddy, it only shows that he has not understood the first thing about it.

We have seen that the revolution Max Planck set in motion with his original concept of energy coming in small packets led to principles of which he did not conceive nor totally accept in his lifetime: duality, probability, and uncertainty. However, these principles form the currently accepted foundation of quantum mechanics. In the chapters that follow, we will see that it is on this foundation that the structure of modern physics is built.

Quantum mechanics is crazier than the theory of relativity, and even its practitioners, the physicists themselves, don't fully understand what is going on inside the world of the incredibly small. Just as we had to stretch our imaginations to the limit to comprehend the immensity of the universe, so too do we now have to exercise our imaginary powers in the opposite direction to comprehend the mindbogglingly small. Our first step will be to turn our attention to the atom, to its nuclei, and to the men who defined its structure for us.

Chapter Four

Ernest Rutherford

"All science is either physics or stamp collecting."

Ernest Rutherford

Outspoken and uninhibited, not caring whose toes he stepped on, Ernest Rutherford barged onto the physics scene at the turn of the twentieth century and held center stage for thirty years. His work marks the beginning of the era of nuclear physics, but ironically one of his major contributions to science was in geology, a field about which he knew very little. The age of the Earth was the specific issue in question. According to Rutherford's biographer A. S. Eve, Rutherford was walking on the Cambridge campus one day carrying a small black rock when he met a geologist acquaintance. "Tell me," he asked his colleague, "how old is the Earth supposed to be?" The answer was that various methods led to an estimate of 100 million years. "Adams," he said to the professor, "I know beyond any doubt that this piece of pitchblende in my hand is seven hundred million years old." One can imagine the geologist's surprise.

The reason Rutherford could make his startling claim is that in 1905 he had helped pioneer the science of radioactive dating of materials. This procedure dramatically changed the field of geology. And it was not just geology that was changed but paleontology, anthropology, archaeology, in fact all of the scientific disciplines involved in determining the date of origin of a rock, specimen, or fossil. The age of the Earth is one such case in point. By the 1920s, thanks to radiometric dating, geologists, physicists, and astronomers generally accepted that the Earth was billions of years old (current estimate is 4.5 billion years old).

A word or two is in order here on the terms *radiation* and *radioactivity*. *Radiation* is the broader term and means anything that is emitted from a source. In atomic physics, *radiation* refers to electromagnetic radiation (X rays, ultraviolet radiation, visible light, infrared radiation, microwaves, radio waves). In nuclear physics, besides electromagnetic waves (gamma rays), it includes alpha rays (helium nuclei) and beta rays (electrons). *Radioactivity* refers to the phenomenon of spontaneous emission of various radiations (alpha, beta, or gamma rays) from unstable nuclei.

Rutherford's key breakthrough was to originate the concept of determining the half-life of substances and thus their precise age. *Half-life* refers to the time it takes for half of a given quantity of radioactive material to decay, that is, to release energy. An atom decays when it disintegrates, in other words, when it changes from instability to stability. All radioactive substances tend to form stable substances in time, and in that process they emit radiation. Half-lives can vary from less than one-millionth of a second to millions of years. The half-life of any particular substance is constant and unaffected by physical conditions such as pressure or temperature. Therefore, the process of radioactivity can be used to estimate the passage of time by measuring the fraction of nuclei that have already decayed. As is often the case in science, Rutherford had made this discovery almost by accident while working on the more general phenomenon of radiation.

Ernest Rutherford presents a very interesting contrast to Albert Einstein. Whereas Einstein was the model theoretician, working alone and dependent upon thought experiments, Rutherford was the ultimate experimentalist. In this regard, he is often compared to Michael Faraday, who did not accept a concept until he could demonstrate it under laboratory conditions. Where Einstein sat in solitude and thought deeply about questions in physics, Rutherford led teams of colleagues, whom he called his "boys," in carrying out complex experiments in the realm of subatomic physics. A big, gruff New Zealander with a walrus mustache and a loud booming voice, Rutherford was well known for his deeply held belief that swearing at an experiment made it work better, and considering his results he might have been right. In this regard, Rutherford was a disciple of Mark Twain who said, "In times of stress, swearing affords a relief denied even to prayer."

Science recruits its heroes from diverse backgrounds and sometimes remote geographical locations. The case of Rutherford, the man who has been called the father of nuclear energy, well demonstrates this point.

The Rutherfords of Nelson

Ernest Rutherford was born at Brightwater, near Nelson, on the north coast of South Island, New Zealand, on August 30, 1871. He was the fourth of the twelve children of James and Martha Rutherford, first-generation New Zealanders, who had been brought there as children from Scotland. Nelson in those days was a pioneering town of wooden buildings. Many years later when, in recognition of his scientific achievements, Rutherford was ennobled, he became "Baron Rutherford of Nelson," certainly that little community's first peer.

In the early 1870s Nelson was an isolated rural community, populated mostly by hard-working Scottish immigrants out to make a new life in a new world. Their society, though, was fashioned along the lines of the Victorian communities they had left behind. Education was highly respected in this society. Ernest's father, James, was a wheelwright, a self-taught construction engineer, and a farmer. His mother, Martha, was a schoolteacher. They made many sacrifices so that their children might be well educated.

The Rutherford family was large—there were twelve children—and everyone took part in household chores. According to the picture of the family provided by Rutherford's brothers and sisters in their old age, the Rutherfords were a serious, church-going, happy family. They were also cultured. Mrs. Rutherford's most prized possession was her piano, and her husband, James, played the violin. Everyone read, and listening to others read aloud was a popular evening's entertainment. Ernest developed a taste for Dickens as well as for pulp-magazine thrillers and crime novels, which he continued to read throughout his life.

Rutherford's interest extended to science early on. When he was ten he had a copy of a popular book called *Primer of Physics*, written by a teacher named Balfour Stewart. Stewart's book was similar to the teach-yourself-physics books of today in that it called for the use of simple materials such as coins, weights, candles, and household utensils in demonstrating the actions of the basic principles of physics. The young Rutherford evidently found this book fascinating, and it must have contributed significantly to his interest in experimental physics. We also know that when he was a boy, Rutherford was noted for his facility with his hands. He tinkered with clocks and made models of the waterwheels that his father used in mills.

In 1887, sixteen-year-old Ernest won the first of his many scholarships, this one to Nelson College, a private "public" secondary school similar to its misnamed counterparts in England. There he was an outstanding scholar, a popular student, and an enthusiastic rugby player. He won prizes in history, languages, and mathematics.

A second scholarship allowed Rutherford to enroll in Canterbury College, Christchurch, an institution founded the year Rutherford was born. At Canterbury Rutherford majored in science and mathematics, and he was fortunate to come under the influence of very good teachers in both subjects. At the conclusion of his three-year course Rutherford was awarded his Bachelor's degree, and he received a mathematical scholarship that enabled him to remain at Canterbury for another year doing postgraduate work. He received his Master's degree in 1893, with first-class honors in mathematics and mathematical physics and in physical science.

Supporting himself with part-time teaching, Rutherford stayed at Canterbury for still another year doing research in physics and studying the properties of electromagnetic waves—wireless waves—newly discovered by the German physicist Heinrich Hertz. Rutherford found that by using a device of his own design, he could detect these waves even after they had passed through brick walls. It is interesting to note that this was before Marconi began his experiments on wireless communication.

It is fascinating sometimes to look back at scientists' predictions about their discoveries and see how wrong they were. Neither Marconi nor Rutherford foresaw the remarkable range of uses to which these waves would be put. Marconi expected the users of radio to be steamship companies, newspapers, and naval services that needed directional, point-to-point communications. Rutherford thought that the commercial possibilities of his wireless communication device would be limited to communication between lighthouses on the shore and passing ships. Still another early radio-industry leader could not imagine a purpose for broadcasting, except possibly to aid preachers in delivering Sunday sermons. In any event, Rutherford concentrated his work not on wireless communication but rather on the phenomenon of radioactivity. This was to be his field of endeavor for the next forty years.

As for his personal life at the time, when he lived in Christchurch, Rutherford met and fell in love with Mary Newton, his landlady's daughter. It is also noteworthy that during this time, his first extended period away from his home, he initiated the habit of writing to his mother at least twice a month. He carried out this correspondence over her entire lifetime, and she lived until she was ninety-two. She was without doubt a dominant influence in his life, and it seems that it was her approval of his accomplishments in science and in life that he valued most.

In 1895, as a result of two significant scientific papers on radioactivity, Rutherford won an important scholarship, although he had been second choice. The first choice was another New Zealand protégé named J. C. Maclaurin. Only because Maclaurin withdrew his candidacy—he decided to stay in New Zealand and get married—was Rutherford offered the prize. The scholarship had been established with the profits from the famous 1851 Exhibition in London, and the terms of this award permitted the winner to attend an institution of his choice. Rutherford chose Cambridge University's Cavendish Laboratory, directed at that time by J. J. Thomson, the world's leading authority on electromagnetic phenomena. Cambridge had only recently altered its rules to admit graduates of other schools, and Ernest Rutherford became the laboratory's first research assistant.

According to an oft-told story, Rutherford was at home digging potatoes when his mother brought him the news that he had won the fellowship to Cambridge. On hearing this news, Rutherford continued digging until he had unearthed a tuber. Then, tossing his shovel aside and holding the potato high in the air, he shouted, "There, that is the last potato I will ever dig!" And he was right.

A new chapter in humankind's understanding of the structure of matter started at this time—at the end of the nineteenth century—and Rutherford was destined to play a major role in its writing. But the new chapter really began with two accidental discoveries, one in Germany and the other in France.

Radioactivity

You may remember the story of the princes of Serendip who never achieved what they set out to accomplish but always discovered something more desirable along the way. The history of science is replete with examples of serendipity, a notable one being the discovery of X rays in 1895.

In a laboratory of the University of Wurzburg in southern Germany, physicist Wilhelm Conrad Roentgen was experimenting with electricity in a semivacuum tube. He was attempting to study the luminescence produced by cathode rays. The laboratory was dark, and he happened to notice that a screen across the room, which he knew to be coated with barium, platinum, and cyanide, glowed in the dark whenever he turned on the power to the tube, as if light from the tube was reaching the screen. He knew this could not be possible because the tube was enclosed in a black cardboard box and light could not escape. Still, when Roentgen turned off the cathode-ray tube, the glow ceased. When he turned it on again, the glow returned. He took the coated paper into the next room and it still glowed when the cathode-ray tube was turned on. Roentgen concluded that the cathode-ray tube was producing some form of radiation that could penetrate cardboard and even the walls of the laboratory. When Roentgen placed his hand between the tube and the screen, he was startled to see the image of the bones in his hand exposed, as if the flesh had become translucent.

With this accidental experiment, Roentgen had discovered what he called X rays. X rays are very short wavelength (high-frequency) radiation, in fact the shortest wavelength radiation known at that time.

A few years later, Rutherford would go on to show that gamma rays, associated with radioactivity, have even shorter wavelengths.

Roentgen eventually told the world about his discovery in a paper published in December of 1895. X rays were greeted not only with surprise but with shock. Lord Kelvin, England's leading scientist at the time, at first pronounced them an elaborate hoax. For a time the newly discovered X rays were called Roentgen rays, but most people who did not speak German found the name difficult to pronounce, and X rays became the more popular term. Lord Kelvin's doubts notwithstanding, the medical use of X rays was not long in developing. In fact, only four days after the news of Roentgen's discovery reached the United States, X rays were used to locate a bullet lodged in a patient's leg. X rays became a wonderful way to explore the interior of the human body because they pass easily through the soft tissues and tend to be stopped by bones, which are composed of heavier calcium and phosphorus atoms. When a photographic plate is placed behind the body, bones show up white, in contrast to the darker images of the softer tissues. Bone fractures suddenly became easy to detect, as did foreign objects in the body and cavities in teeth. Scientists also discovered that X rays could be used to kill cancer cells that were beyond the reach of a surgeon's knife. Unfortunately, they also discovered that high-energy radiation could *cause* cancer. Tragically, the harmful properties of X rays were not known for some time, and at least 100 of the first people to work with X rays and radioactive materials died of cancer before these effects were understood.

When X rays were first discovered, many in the public found them mysterious. Several firms made a lot of money by exploiting this bewilderment and selling "X-ray-proof underclothes" for women. There was even a bill introduced in the state legislature of New Jersey prohibiting the use of X-ray opera glasses at the theater. These mysterious X rays were viewed by many as a threat to public morals. The scientific community, of course, took a different view. In 1901, William K. Roentgen received the first Nobel Prize to be awarded in the field of physics.

The Radioactive Elements

The other important discovery that led up to Rutherford's work was made by Henri Becquerel in France in 1898. Again chance played a

role. Henri Becquerel discovered that a uranium oxide ore, called pitchblende, somehow darkened a wrapped and unexposed photographic plate
in his laboratory. *Becquerel rays,* as they came to be known, pierced
objects opaque to light. They attracted the attention of the young Marie
Sklodowska Curie and her husband Pierre, and the Curies made them
the focus of their work. Marie Curie believed that the low-level radioactivity of uranium-bearing minerals resulted from very small amounts
of some highly radioactive substances. Her husband, Pierre, put aside
his own research to help in the enormous task of separating an elusive
trace amount of radioactive matter from an immense amount of raw
material. The research necessitated that each of the radioactive elements be isolated and that their atomic weights be determined, a task
that was accomplished only by processing tons of pitchblende ore.
Because they lacked space in the laboratory, the Curies had to set up a
larger, makeshift laboratory in an abandoned wooden shed. In this shed,
stifling hot in the summer and freezing in the winter, the Curies dog-
gedly carried out their breakthrough efforts to isolate the radioactive
elements and determine their atomic weights. The result was the discovery of two new elements, both highly radioactive, which they named
polonium and *radium.* For this work in radioactivity, the Curies jointly
won the Nobel Prize in Physics in 1903. Instead of exploiting their
discovery commercially, the Curies made the formula for radium available freely to the scientific community so that the nature of radioactivity could be studied further.

After Pierre Curie was killed in a street accident, struck by a
horse-drawn wagon, Marie Curie carried on the research alone. (In
1910, the Radiology Congress in Belgium honored the memory of
Pierre Curie by defining the *curie* as the unit of measure of radioactivity.) Despite widespread prejudice against women in the physical sciences, Marie Curie was chosen by a unanimous vote of the Sorbonne
Faculty Council to succeed to Pierre's chair at the college. Thus she
became the first woman to teach at the Sorbonne, and in 1911 she was
awarded the Nobel Prize for Chemistry, becoming the first person to
win two Nobel prizes.

Although Marie did not realize it at the time, her consistent ill
health and physical exhaustion were due in a large part to her constant
exposure to the debilitating effects of radiation, which eventually lead
to her death in 1934.

Cambridge

When Rutherford first arrived in Cambridge in 1895, he worked under the direction of Joseph John (J. J.) Thomson, a professor of experimental physics who had actively recruited Rutherford. Like Rutherford, the renowned Thomson was a workaholic, so devoted to his research that he made little time for anything else. There is a story that one day Thomson bought a new pair of trousers on his way home to lunch, having been persuaded by an associate that his old pants were too baggy and worn. At home, he changed into his new trousers and returned to the laboratory. His wife, returning from a shopping trip, found his old pair on the bed. She immediately telephoned the laboratory in alarm, convinced that her somewhat absent-minded husband had gone back to work without any trousers on.

In a short time, Rutherford made a name for himself at Cambridge. He had brought with him his wireless wave detector and had quickly set it up to receive signals from sources up to half a mile away. This work immediately impressed the Cambridge dons.

Thomson and his wife did what they could to help Rutherford adjust to the somewhat peculiar, stuffy social and academic life of Cambridge. Rutherford was self-conscious and somewhat defensive at first about his "colonial" background, and he had aroused some petty jealousy among the members of the Cavendish fraternity with his displays of brilliance. His relationship with Thomson was important, and it is clear from their letters that both men held each other in high regard.

Thomson asked Rutherford to assist him in the study of what the effects would be of passing a beam of X rays through a gas. Rutherford might well have hesitated to join in this work, because to undertake this assignment meant he would have to put aside his work on the wireless receiver. (Worth noting is the fact that Rutherford at this time was anxious to earn enough money to marry Mary Newton, to whom he had proposed two years earlier, and he did see some limited commercial possibilities for his receiver.) His respect for Thomson, as well as his desire to work on breakthrough science, however, carried the day. About ten years later, the fame and fortune that were to be had by demonstrating the commercial potential of wireless telegraphy went to Guglielmo Marconi. But Rutherford's decision paid off in its own way. Thomson and Rutherford discovered that the X rays produced large quantities of electrically charged particles, or carriers of ionized atoms, that recombined to form neutral molecules. Learning more about atoms had become the greatest scientific challenge of the day and Thomson's and Rutherford's discovery was the first breakthrough.

The next major step was Thomson's. Atoms had been conceived to be simple elementary bodies of various geometrical shapes. Thomson was able to show that on the contrary, atoms were complex mechanisms with a large number of moving parts. Specifically, he was able to demonstrate that atoms of various chemical elements consist of positively and negatively charged parts, held together by the forces of electrical attraction. Thomson conceived of an atom as having a more or less uniformly distributed positive electric charge with a large number of negatively charged particles floating in its interior. The combined electric charge of negative particles—*electrons*, as he called them—equaled the total positive charge, so that the atom on the whole was electrically neutral. For his work in identifying the electron, Thomson won the Nobel Prize for Physics in 1906.

Rutherford's Contribution

Early in his research, Rutherford conceived an experiment that was to identify two distinct types of radiation. The experiment involved studying the manner in which radioactive radiations penetrated sheets of aluminum. He found that some of the radiation could be stopped by a sheet of aluminum $1/500$ of a centimeter thick, while the rest required a considerably thicker sheet to be stopped. He named the first, or positively charged, radiation *alpha rays*, which were highly powerful in producing ionization but easily absorbed. The second, or negatively charged, radiation he called *beta rays*, which produced less radiation but had more penetrating ability. (*Alpha* is, of course, the first letter of the Greek alphabet, and *beta* is the second letter.) A third type of radiation, similar to X rays, was discovered in 1900 by the French physicist Paul Urich Villard. It was of extremely high frequency and short wavelength and was, thus, the most penetrating of all. It was called *gamma rays* (from the third letter of the Greek alphabet). Although Rutherford called the phenomena he had discovered "rays," he thought they must be composed of extremely minute particles of matter. He was right, and

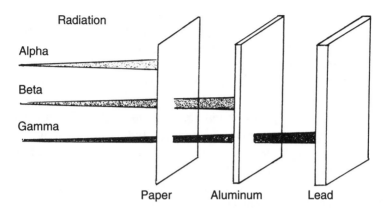

Radiation

Alpha

Beta

Gamma

Paper   Aluminum   Lead

Radiation   Paper is sufficient to stop alpha radiation; aluminum will stop beta radiation, lead is required to stop gamma radiation.

although the term *rays* is still sometimes used, alpha, beta, and gamma radiation is now known to consist of speeding particles.

Rutherford went on from this early work to become the leader in the fast-moving field of radioactivity. He and his colleagues discovered that naturally occurring radioactivity in uranium consists of a uranium atom emitting a particle that becomes an atom of the element helium, and that what is left behind is no longer a uranium atom but a slightly lighter atom of a different element. Additional research showed that this transmutation was one of a series ending with a stable isotope of lead. This finding led to the conclusion that radium was just one element in the radioactive series. The term *isotope* (from the Greek word meaning "same position") refers to the members of a family of substances sharing the same position in the periodic table but differing from each other in the number of neutrons they contain. Isotopes are, in effect, varieties of a specific element—substances that are identical with one another in chemical properties but are different in radioactivity.

Although Rutherford's professional career was off to a good start by this time, he felt that the snobbery at Cambridge toward those who had been undergraduates at other colleges, especially in the colonies, prevented his advancement. And advancement was what he needed if he was to marry Mary Newton. He sought an academic position elsewhere, and armed with a strong letter of recommendation from J. J. Thomson, he was appointed to the chair of physics at McGill University in Montreal, Canada. In the summer of 1900, he traveled to New Zealand to visit his parents and get married. The young couple took up residence in Montreal, where Rutherford joined arguably the best physics laboratory in the western hemisphere and resumed his research in radioactivity.

Working with a young chemist named Frederick Soddy, Rutherford set to investigating three groups of radioactive elements: radium, thorium, and actinium. He soon discovered that thorium or its compounds disintegrated into a gas that in turn disintegrated into an unknown deposit, which was also radioactive. He concluded that radioactivity was a process in which atoms of one element spontaneously disintegrated into atoms of an entirely different element, which also remained radioactive. Rutherford's paper with Soddy on this subject was opposed by many chemists who believed in the indestructibility of matter. The postulated theory that atoms could tear themselves apart to form entirely different kinds of matter was perceived by some as akin to medieval alchemy. But before long, the quality of the work was recognized, and the theory was generally accepted. This discovery revolutionized chemistry because it altered the basic view of matter as something immutable by showing that all radioactive elements undergo spontaneous transformation into other elements, ultimately forming stable substances.

Rutherford, ever the hard worker, quickly moved on. In his experiments, he discovered that radiation from an active substance decreased with time, and he set about trying to understand this phenomenon and if possible to devise a formula that could predict the process. Working with thorium, Rutherford discovered that radiation decreased in a geometrical progression with time. In the case of thorium, radioactivity is reduced to one-half its original value in one minute. It then decreased by one-half that value in the next minute, so that there was only one-quarter of the original value after two minutes and only one-eighth after three minutes. Such a rate of change (increase or decrease) is termed *exponential* because the mathematical equations describing the process involve the "exponential function," which is expressed as the symbol e. To describe this process, Rutherford introduced the term, *half-life*. The half-life, for example, of radium-226 (the isotope isolated from pitchblende by the Curies), is 1,620 years. The half-life of uranium-238 is 4.51 billion years.

The procedure of carbon dating incorporates the phenomenon of half-life in a very useful way. Because every living thing on Earth contains carbon, and because the half-life of carbon-14, for example, is 5,570 years, this radioactive substance is particularly useful in establishing the age of artifacts and samples of many other kinds. After 5,570 years, half of the carbon-14 atoms in any given sample will have decayed into atoms of nitrogen-14. By comparing the amount of carbon-14 to nitrogen-14 in a sample, it is possible to age-date the sample. For instance, if three-quarters of the carbon-14 has decayed into nitrogen-14, then the material under examination is 11,140 years old (5,570 for half of the carbon to decay and 5,570 for the next quarter to decay—one-half of the remaining one-half—5,570 + 5,570 = 11,140). Radiometric age-dating has a wide range of applications in fields extending from archaeology and paleontology to geology and geophysics, to astrophysics and cosmology.

Though Rutherford was producing remarkable discoveries in his lab, he was less successful with his teaching responsibilities. His duties at McGill included lecturing, and some students found him dull. He mumbled and fumbled, getting lost in his own mathematical formulas on the blackboard, and quite often he lectured over the heads of the students. Some students even organized a petition demanding that Rutherford bring his presentations down to a level that they could understand. On the other hand, there emerged from McGill (and later from Cambridge) a number of distinguished physicists who stated later that the direction of their lives and careers were changed by the inspirational nature of Rutherford's lectures. It seems that opinions on the quality of his teaching depended on the quality of his students.

During his nine years at McGill, Rutherford wrote eighty scientific papers and made many public appearances. In 1903 he was elected to the Royal Society of London, and in 1904 he published his first book, *Radio-Activity*, which is recognized as the classic in this field. Also in 1904, Rutherford proposed that the amount of helium produced by the radioactive decay of minerals in rocks could be employed to measure the age of the Earth, which was an issue of considerable importance and curiosity at that time.

Darwin's then controversial *The Origin of Species*, published in 1859, required an Earth several billion years old for the various species to have evolved as they have. Lord Kelvin, one of England's great scientists of the latter half of the nineteenth century, had estimated the age of Earth to be only 500 million years old. Clearly, Darwin and Kelvin could not both be correct. Kelvin's specialty was thermodynamics. He had formulated the first and second laws of thermodynamics: (1) Energy is conserved; that is, energy is neither created nor destroyed, it merely changes form; and (2) Some usable energy is always lost in the process. The Kelvin scale of absolute temperature is named after him. He had calculated the approximate age of Earth by estimating the age of the Sun based upon the release of heat. To his credit, though, Kelvin allowed that some unknown factor might be missing from his calculations.

On the basis of his findings about radioactive decay, Rutherford had come up with his own answer to the riddle of Earth's age, and he spoke on the subject to a meeting of the Royal Society in London. He maintained that the Earth stayed warm because it is heated by radioactive elements in rocks and its molten core, and that the rate of decay of these elements testified to the antiquity of Earth and provided a means of accurately measuring it. Rutherford faced his scientific audience with some trepidation, noting that Lord Kelvin was in the room. To Rutherford's relief, Kelvin fell fast asleep and missed most of his argument. But, just as he reached the end of his presentation, he saw that Kelvin had awakened and was glaring at him. In a moment of inspiration, Rutherford thought of a way to praise Kelvin for his contribution to the issue. Rutherford pointed out that Kelvin had indicated that the Earth could be only 500 million years old, *unless some new source of energy was discovered.* "That prophetic utterance," Rutherford went on, "refers to what we are now considering tonight, radium." With that stroke of diplomacy Rutherford won over the elder statesman of English science and tipped the scales in favor of a much older Earth and to the views of Charles Darwin.

Rutherford's growing reputation in the scientific community led to the offer of chairs at other universities. While he was happy at McGill, Rutherford desired to return to England where he thought he would be closer to the world's leading scientific centers. When the director of the physics research facilities at Manchester resigned his position on the condition that Rutherford succeed him, the post and the laboratory were too attractive to refuse. In 1907, he returned to England to accept the position at the University of Manchester, where he would accomplish some of his greatest work.

Manchester

If Cambridge's Cavendish under J. J. Thomson was the premier physics laboratory in the world, Manchester under Rutherford was easily the second. Rutherford's growing fame attracted to Manchester an extraordinarily talented group of research students who made significant contributions to physics and chemistry.

The Rutherford family found a house that suited them, just a few minutes' tram ride from the university, and soon settled in to what Rutherford's biographer, David Wilson, calls the happiest period of Rutherford's life. He enjoyed Manchester and its people, and he threw himself into his work with characteristic vigor.

At Manchester, Rutherford led a group that rapidly developed new ideas about atomic structure. It was the most productive period of his academic life. Manchester itself was a cultural and intellectual center at that time, and the university boasted a particularly brilliant faculty. Rutherford enjoyed the atmosphere of academic challenge and mixed well with the historians, philosophers, and writers of the campus. He would have scoffed at being called a highbrow himself, but the warmth of his character and his unbounded enthusiasm won him friends among men of many different backgrounds.

Chaim Weizmann, who was at that time a lecturer in the chemistry department at Manchester but who was already heavily involved in the Zionist cause, became a lifelong friend. Weizmann described Rutherford this way: "Youthful, energetic, boisterous, he suggested anything but the scientist. He talked readily and vigorously on any subject under the sun, often without knowing anything about it. Going down to the refectory for lunch, I would hear the loud, friendly voice rolling up the corridor. He was quite devoid of any political knowledge or feelings, being entirely taken up with his epoch-making scientific work. He was a kindly person but did not suffer fools gladly."

Weizmann was also a good friend of Albert Einstein, and he wrote of the two scientists: "I have retained the distinct impression that Rutherford was not impressed by Einstein's work, while Einstein on the other hand always spoke to me of Rutherford in the highest terms, calling him a second Newton." As scientists, the two men were strongly contrasting types—Einstein, all calculation; Rutherford, all experiment. Never in awe of anybody, least of all theoreticians, Rutherford famously stated, "They play games with their symbols, but we turn out the real facts of Nature." He is also reported to have said, "Oh, that relativity stuff. We never bother with that in our work." Indeed one story is that it was at an international conference of the world's top scientists in Brussels, a European colleague of Rutherford's, Wilhelm Wien, attempted to explain the theory of relativity to him. Rutherford resisted, and Wien declared in frustration, "But no Anglo-Saxon can understand relativity." Rutherford's shouted response was, "No! They have too much sense."

But whatever he said in jest, Rutherford treated the work of Albert Einstein and Max Planck with professional respect. It seemed to him that whereas Planck's quantum theory had an impact on his own work, relativity did not seem to have a direct bearing on atomic physics. Rutherford's science and Einstein's science were so different in style that little real understanding between them was possible. Einstein simply did not care about alpha particles, and Rutherford did not care about time-dilation or curved space.

Rutherford received many awards for his efforts at Manchester, culminating in 1908 with the Nobel Prize in Chemistry. This honor was really in recognition of his work on radioactivity, which had been accomplished while he was in Canada. Because Rutherford considered himself a physicist and did not have a reverent attitude toward chemists, the Nobel award was somewhat puzzling to him. He joked, in fact, about his "instantaneous transmutation" from a physicist to a chemist. There was, however, a delicious irony about the award. When Rutherford had discovered the transmutation of the elements, he had crossed the line between chemistry and physics and went on to lead physics in the intellectual and academic domination of chemistry. His chief opponents in the academic world were chemists and that he should receive the Nobel Prize for Chemistry must have afforded him amusement.

The award of the Nobel prize was important to Rutherford, not yet forty years old, in several ways. In addition to placing him among the scientific giants of the day, it carried with it a cash award of 7,000 pounds. This was a considerable sum of money in those days, equivalent to more than five year's salary to Rutherford. He was, for the first time in his life, reasonably wealthy. He sent cash presents to his brothers and sisters and to his parents back in New Zealand and, for the first time, bought a motor car, which he had a fine time learning to drive. He and Mary thereafter took frequent holiday trips about the English countryside.

Rutherford was knighted in 1914, and he wrote to a friend that "he was pleased that his work had been recognized by the powers that be but he found the form of that recognition a little embarrassing for a relatively youthful (he was not yet forty-five) and impecunious Professor." Interestingly enough, what most historians of science consider to be Rutherford's most important contribution to physics was yet to come.

Inside the Atom

The concept that all matter consisted of collections of tiny fragments so small as to be unbreakable was a controversial one. It was the Greek philosopher Democritus (460–370 B.C.) who first called these fragments *atomos* (Greek for "unbreakable"), now called *atoms* in English. The concept was resisted for centuries, both intellectually and sometimes by fiat. In seventeenth-century France, for example, the punishment for believing in the existence of atoms was death. Although it sometimes takes a long time, science usually wins out over ignorance, and eventually atomic theory prevailed as the accepted way to explain various experimental phenomena. What did these mysterious atoms look like, how small were they, and were they indeed unbreakable building blocks of nature? These were leading questions in science in the early twentieth century.

Rutherford had been an atomicist from the early days of the scientific debate, and developing an accurate picture of what the atom looked like became the focus of his research. Rutherford's mentor, J. J. Thomson, discovered the fact that there are separate parts of an atom. He showed that atoms consisted of both positively and negatively charged parts, held together by the forces of electrical attraction. As discussed earlier, Thomson conceived of the atom as a more or less uniformly distributed positive electric charge with a large number of negatively charged particles floating about its interior. This was what Thomson called his "plum pudding" model of atomic structure. It was a reasonable enough model for the time, but it failed to explain much in the way of experimental data. A better model was needed, and Rutherford would show the way.

Rutherford was not entirely dissatisfied with Thomson's model. It

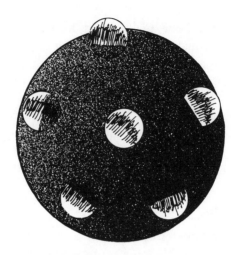

Plum pudding atom   J. J. Thomson postulated that atoms consisted of a number of negatively charged electrons imbedded in a positively charged atmosphere, like plums in a plum pudding.

had its shortcomings, he knew, but he thought that it was basically correct. Over the years, starting in Montreal and continuing at Manchester, Rutherford had developed various experimental techniques and tools. Among these was what might be called the first particle accelerator. Using this device, he was able to direct a beam of alpha particles (helium nuclei) from a radioactive source toward a target, usually some metal foil.

Rutherford had observed in Montreal that fast-moving alpha particles, when passing through thin plates of metal, produced diffuse images on photographic plates, whereas a sharp image was produced when there was no obstruction to the passage of the particles. He had concluded that the alpha particles might be deflected by passing close to atoms of the metal foil, but there was no proof of this and later calculations cast doubt on the conjecture. The phenomenon of diffuse images became a long-standing subject for Rutherford-designed experiments.

One of the professors working under Rutherford at Manchester in 1909 was Hans Geiger (the developer of the "Geiger" counter). He mentioned to Rutherford that a student named Ernest Marsden was in need of a thesis project. Rutherford suggested that Geiger and Marsden work together on a scattering experiment. He wanted them to bombard

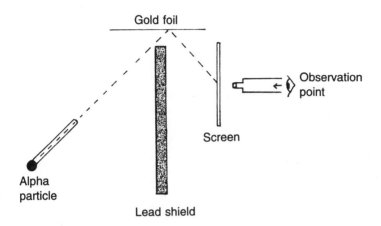

Rutherford's experiment proving the existence of the atomic nucleus Some alpha particles fired at thin gold foil are deflected to the screen rather than passing through the foil.

thin sheets of gold with alpha particles and look for large deflections. He was pretty sure no such large deflections would occur because (assuming Thomson's model of the atom was correct) the only thing that could deflect the alphas would be the electrons in the gold atoms. Because the electrons were several thousand times lighter than the alphas, deflecting them would be like trying to deflect a fast-moving cannonball with a small marble. It was, Rutherford thought, altogether unlikely.

The gold-foil target in Rutherford's apparatus was surrounded on all sides by zinc sulfide screens. When a zinc sulfide molecule is struck by an alpha particle, it emits a flash of light. Researchers can then measure the angle of deflection, if any. This was a difficult experiment to carry out, however, and Marsden and Geiger had to sit in a dark room for several hours to adapt their eyesight to see the flashes. They then had to accurately spot and record the number and positions of the flashes. Rutherford, being the designer of the experiment and the director of the laboratory, delegated this detail work to the two junior scientists, but he did come by from time to time to check on the work and suggest variations to be tried. One of Rutherford's suggestions was to see if any particles were scattered backward, in other words, deflected through an angle of more than ninety degrees. He wanted to see if any of the alphas hit the gold foil and bounced back toward the source.

Geiger and Marsden might have thought that Rutherford had gone round the bend with this request, but he was the boss so they followed his orders. To everyone's amazement, numerous alpha particles were indeed reflected backward from the gold-foil screen. Marsden reported the news to Rutherford, whose now famous reaction to this information was: "It was quite the most incredible event that ever happened to me in my life. It was as if you fired a fifteen-inch artillery shell at a piece of tissue paper, and it came back and hit you." There had to be something inside the atom to account for this incredible back scattering, something larger than the alpha particles hitting it.

Here, it is interesting to follow Rutherford's way of thinking. The results of the experiment were inconsistent with the prevailing theory of what the inside of an atom looked like. Either the experiment had a flaw, or the theory of the atom had to be revised. The experiment had been performed in 1909, and it took until early 1911 for Rutherford to propose an explanation. He finally arrived at the conclusion that there obviously had to be something comparable in mass to the alpha particle inside the atom, something thousands of times heavier than the electron. Rutherford referred to this "something" as the *nucleus*.

In May of that year, his paper declaring the existence of the nuclear atom was published, and it spelled the end of Thomson's plum pudding model and the beginning of the era of nuclear physics.

Rutherford went on to postulate that the atomic nucleus contained positively charged particles that he called *protons* (Greek for "first things"). He demonstrated their existence in 1919 by knocking them out of nitrogen nuclei using alpha particles. Later, he suggested that there was probably another constituent to heavier nuclei, that is, an electrically neutral particle about as massive as the proton. He called this hypothetical particle the *neutron*. He came to this conclusion by noting that most atoms seemed to weigh about twice as much as one would expect them to if one added up the masses of the protons and electrons in them. Also, something had to be holding the positive protons together in the nucleus. Rutherford's postulated neutron was eventually discovered in 1932. Rutherford was a much better theorist than he let on. When experimental data did not match the prevailing theory, he was inventive and original in coming up with new theories that did match the data.

How small were atoms? Using the work of Maxwell and the mathematical formula devised by Albert Einstein, the French physicist Jean Baptiste Perrin (1870–1942) estimated the size of water molecules, as well as the size of the atoms that made them up. Perrin published his results in 1913. Atoms, he calculated, were roughly one hundred-millionth of a centimeter across. To put it another way, 100 million atoms placed side by side would stretch across a centimeter; 250 million atoms placed side by side would stretch across an inch. If atoms could be measured, and if the effect of their collisions could be seen, then they must exist. Atomic theory had become atomic fact. Today, thanks to a device called a *scanning tunneling microscope*, atoms can actually be seen with the eye and photographed.

Rutherford's greatest achievement at Manchester—in fact, of his entire career—was his discovery of the nuclear structure of the atom. With this discovery, he became the Copernicus of the atomic system. It is interesting that his chief scientific accomplishments occurred after his Nobel award and after his knighthood. The history of science does not contain many other examples of such continuing industry and creativity in a scientist's career. And Rutherford did not stop there.

During World War I, Rutherford worked on the problems of subma-

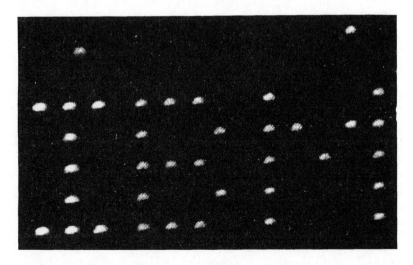

Atoms arranged by IBM scientists to form company logo Using a scanning tunneling microscope, individual atoms were used to spell out letters. The letters are about 500,000 times smaller than the letters on this page.

rine detection by underwater acoustics. Apparently he threw himself into this work in characteristic fashion. In only a few months he produced three secret reports that drew the map of underwater warfare for that time. His influence was needed to set the Royal Navy to serious work on the problems of underwater detection and to guide these efforts once started. Although Rutherford himself never claimed it, some scientific historians acknowledge that he was in effect the co-inventor of sonar.

Cambridge II

In 1919, J. J. Thomson moved on to become Master at Trinity College, and Rutherford took his place at Cavendish. Although Rutherford's experimental contributions from then on were not as numerous as in earlier years, his influence on research students was still important. In a lecture to the Royal Society in 1920, he speculated on the existence of the neutron and of isotopes of hydrogen and helium; all three speculations were eventually proven by workers in the Cavendish Laboratory.

Between 1925 and 1930 Rutherford was president of the Royal Society, and following this he became chairman of the advisory council to the British Government on Science and Technology. Both posts involved many public appearances and ceremonial activities, which he seemed to enjoy. Generally speaking, he stayed out of politics, yet he felt he could not remain idle when Nazi Germany expelled hundreds of Jewish scholars. During this period he headed the Academic Assistance Council, which sought to obtain financial aid and positions for these refugees.

More than any other man, Rutherford formed the views now held concerning the nature of matter. He was clearly the greatest experimental physicist of his day and the greatest since Michael Faraday. Dozens of scientific societies and universities awarded him memberships and honorary degrees. King George V personally honored him in 1925 with the Order of Merit, an honor limited to a few of the most distinguished living Englishmen. For bringing honor to British science he was made a peer (Baron Rutherford of Nelson) in 1931 and sat in the House of Lords. Rutherford hugely enjoyed his fame, titles, access to world leaders, and all of the accoutrements of worldly success. He told the following story in a speech: "I was standing in the drawing room at Trinity. A clergyman came in, and I said to him: 'I'm Lord Rutherford.' And he said to me: 'I'm the Archbishop of York.' And I don't suppose either of us believed the other."

He did, however, insist on informality among his scientific peers. At a Royal Society dinner shortly after Rutherford had been raised to the peerage, he overheard Niels Bohr refer to him in the third person as Lord Rutherford. As Bohr tells it, Rutherford furiously turned on him and shouted, "Did you Lord me?" Chastised, Bohr said he never did it again. Indeed, his many public duties did not keep him away from his laboratory, and he made frequent rounds to "ginger up" his team, as he put it.

In 1937, Rutherford died suddenly of an undetected strangulated hernia. He was sixty-six and still a vigorous man. The English writer and scientist C. P. Snow recalls that on a quiet October morning in Cambridge, when he and a few other researchers were working in the old Cavendish laboratory, someone put his head round the door and said: "The Professor's dead." They were stunned, and there was no need for anyone to ask whom he meant.

Prior to Rutherford, the atom was, to use his words, "a nice hard fellow, red or grey according to taste." Now it was a miniature solar system of innumerable particles and suspected of containing more unsolved mysteries. Rutherford had given the world a new model of the atom. Planck had introduced the idea of *quanta*. What was needed now was someone to bring these ideas together. And, indeed, they were soon brought together by the brilliant Danish physicist, and most famous of Rutherford's students, Niels Bohr.

Chapter Five

Niels Henrik David Bohr

If one forgets the occasional employment of a pair of skis, the bicycle was Bohr's favorite mode of locomotion. Its relatively slow progress, based upon a balance of dynamic variables that one cannot explain adequately in a few words, is, I think, a good introduction to the character of Niels Bohr.

Edward Teller, "Niels Bohr
and the Idea of Complementarity," 1969

Two scientist friends, Abraham Pais and an unnamed colleague, were discussing Niels Bohr one day in 1962, shortly after Bohr died. Pais's associate confessed that he really did not understand the essence of the Danish physicist's work. "You knew him well," he said to Pais. "Just what did he do?" If a scientist was not clear about Bohr's work, you might well ask what can be expected of a nonscientist. But, in truth, Bohr's accomplishments can be fairly easily described.

One of the most important things Bohr did was to show that one could not describe the structure of the atom solely according to classical physics; one had to make use of quantum theory. Simply put, Bohr took Rutherford's image of the atom in one hand and Planck's quantum theory in the other, and, in 1913, at the age of twenty-seven, he put them together to form the modern image of an atom. For this he received the Nobel Prize for Physics in 1922.

The Man

Bohr's upbringing was almost too good to be true, with no stories of childhood neglect or hardships of any kind. Bohr was born in Copenhagen in 1885. His father was Christian Bohr, a professor of physiology at the University of Copenhagen. His mother, Ellen Adler Bohr, came from a wealthy Jewish family, prominent in Danish banking and parliamentary circles. The Bohr household included older sister Jenny, Niels, and his younger brother Harald. By all accounts, the Bohr home was intellectually stimulating and provided a comfortable and loving family atmosphere.

The Bohrs entertained a procession of visitors, some of whom were colleagues of Christian Bohr at the university. As a young boy, Niels listened to many animated debates on subjects ranging from philosophy and physics to theology and politics. This verbal give and take must have stimulated Niels and his siblings and encouraged them to learn to express their own thoughts.

The Bohrs were not churchgoers. Although Bohr's mother came from a Jewish family, she had agreed that her children would be brought up Christians. Accordingly, Niels, his sister Jenny, and his brother Harald were baptized shortly after their birth, but the family attended church only on Christmas Eve, and then only because everybody they knew did.

Niels and Harald were always extraordinarily close. They played together, fought together, studied together in their school years, and were in frequent correspondence later in life. In 1891, Niels was enrolled in the Gammelholms Latin-og Realskole in Copenhagen where both he and Harald would stay until they were ready to take their college entrance examinations. Schoolmates remember Niels as tall, rather coarse of limb, and strong as a bear. He was also remembered as a bit wild and short tempered and as having been involved in schoolyard fights from time to time. But he was also a conscientious pupil. He did well at school and, although never first, was usually ranked third or fourth in the class of twenty. He was interested in all subjects, but mathematics and physics were favorites. Sports were also a major interest, and both Niels and Harald were on the school soccer team. Both Niels and Harald passed the final examination, called the Studenterexamen, which allowed pupils to enter the university with honors.

In 1903, Bohr enrolled in the University of Copenhagen, where he studied physics and was also noted as a first rate soccer player. (His younger brother was even better, and made the 1908 Danish Olympic Soccer team.) Academically, Niels distinguished himself at the university, winning a gold medal from the Royal Danish Academy of Sciences and Letters for his theoretical analyses and experiments in determining the surface tension of water. In 1911, he received his doctorate for his thesis on the electron theory of metals, which stressed the inadequacies of classical physics for treating the behavior of matter at the atomic level. (In this paper, he was beginning to focus on what would be his life work.)

Bohr then journeyed to England for postgraduate work under the direction of the celebrated J. J. Thomson at Cambridge. Bohr knew little English when he arrived at Cambridge, and to make up for the deficiency he read *The Pickwick Papers* by Charles Dickens with a dictionary in hand. Dickens became one of his favorite authors. Language, however, was only one of his problems at Cambridge. All did not go well at the Cavendish Laboratory. Thomson showed little interest in Bohr's work. Bohr had given him a copy of his doctoral thesis upon arrival, hoping for some comment or encouragement; but Thomson left it unread on his desk. This may have been for the better, because it contained a number of critical comments regarding Thomson's theory of the atom. At any rate, Bohr became disenchanted under Thomson's indifference. Because Bohr was intrigued with Rutherford's theory of the atom, he decided to arrange for a transfer to Manchester. There things went very differently.

Bohr's relationship with Rutherford set a standard for the whole of his later scientific life. The two men became friends from their first meeting and remained close for the rest of their lives. When one considers that Rutherford was the ultimate experimentalist with little regard for theorists, and Bohr was the ultimate intellectual theorist with little need for any tools other than a blackboard, it seems odd that these two should have hit it off as well as they did.

To his great credit, Rutherford recognized Bohr's brilliance right away, and from the first, encouraged Bohr in every way he could. Bohr's first stay at Manchester was a relatively short one, March to July 1912, but it was pivotal in shaping his approach to physics and to the management of physics research projects. Rutherford's method of combining his own active research program with leadership in guiding younger physicists made a powerful impression on Bohr and influenced his own style. (When Bohr, in his middle years, headed up a physics research center in Copenhagen, he patterned his collegial method of management on what he had experienced at Manchester.) In sum, it was Rutherford who brought Bohr into the top level of world physics.

In 1912, Bohr returned to Denmark, where he was appointed assistant professor at the University of Copenhagen. With his career starting to take shape, he married Margrethe Norlund. They had met, according to her recollection, at a dinner party—he had sat next to her but did not say a word. Bohr then visited her and her brother, who was a friend of his, at their country home. Later she visited the Bohr home in Copenhagen, and by 1910 they were engaged. Her influence on and assistance to Niels is evident early in their relationship. The manuscript for his doctoral thesis defense, for instance, is in her handwriting. The marriage turned out to be a strong and happy one, a lifelong source of harmony and strength to Niels, who was the quintessential family man. The Bohrs had six sons, four of whom survived to adulthood.

The Bohr Atom

Once settled in Copenhagen, Bohr continued to think about the theoretical implications of the Rutherford nuclear model of the atom. Rutherford had proposed the idea of the nuclear atom, a sort of miniature solar system with the electrons orbiting around the sun-like nucleus. This was a neat model that answered many questions, and it was generally accepted by physicists. There was, however, one big problem with the model, which was what scientists call an anomaly. The anomalous issue was: What kept the electrons in place in the nuclear atom? If electrons are negatively charged and the nucleus is positively charged, and if opposite charges attract, then the electrons should fall into the nucleus.

The electromagnetic theory shows that when an electrically charged object revolves in the fashion of the electron around the nucleus, it gives off electromagnetic radiation, losing energy in the process. As the electron loses energy, according to the theory, it should spiral inward and eventually fall into the nucleus. But such is not the case. Electrons do not collapse as theory says they should. Atoms remain stable for indefinite periods, and therein lies the anomaly.

One of many physicists losing sleep over this problem was Niels Bohr, and he took a fresh approach to finding an explanation. He de-

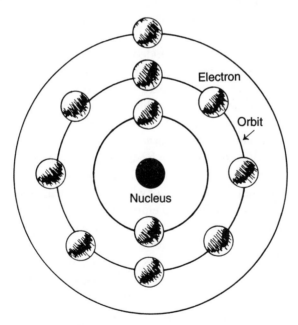

Bohr's atom Electrons further out from the nucleus have a higher energy than those closer in, and electrons can move from one orbit to another.

cided that, theory or no theory, the electron did not radiate energy while it was in orbit. On the other hand, both theory and experimental evidence showed that hydrogen, for instance, did radiate energy when heated—energy that many physicists believed came from the electrons. Where was this energy really coming from? This is the question Bohr decided he must answer.

Colleagues said of Bohr that his greatest strength was his ability to identify, and to exploit, failures in theory. He developed this ability into a rigorous scientific methodology. He would collect instances of failure, examine each minutely, and identify those that seemed to embody the same flaw. He then conceived a hypothesis to correct the flaw, keeping as much of the original flawed theory as he could. By continually pushing and pulling theory and experimental results until a new theory emerged, Bohr regularly ended up with success. This was a torturous method that required not only creative genius but also the ability to withstand ambiguity, uncertainty, and apparent contradiction.

In 1913, using this method, Bohr conceived a model of the atom that was a variation of Rutherford's model but that explained the mysterious anomaly of the electrons. Bohr asked himself how a hydrogen atom could radiate energy when heated and, when cooled, absorb it and still not collapse. He concluded that as long as the electron in the hydrogen atom remained in the same orbit, it did *not* radiate energy. Bohr suggested instead that the electron could take a stable position on any of a number of different orbits at different distances from the nucleus. Whenever an electron was in a particular orbit, it did not gain or lose energy. When it changed orbits, however, it would either absorb or emit energy. Electrons that are farther out from the nucleus have higher energy, and an electron can jump to a higher level by absorbing energy. This would happen at high temperatures or when photons with enough energy hit the atom. Conversely, it would emit energy in the form of radiation when it dropped down to a level closer to the nucleus. This would happen when there was a gap at a lower level.

Why did Bohr conceive of "steps" of orbits? Why was an electron never in an orbit half way between levels? Bohr was drawing on Planck's quantum theory. He proposed that an atom can only absorb or radiate quanta—energy of fixed amounts—and that these amounts of energy are just enough to send electrons to the next orbit.

Bohr went on to explain why an electron acts this way by making

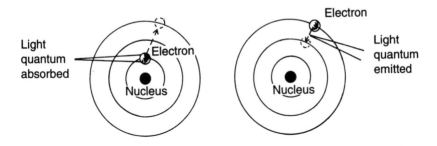

Electron movement in Bohr's atom Electrons that absorb energy jump to higher orbit. Electrons emit energy when they jump down to a lower orbit.

a new connection between matter and light. He suggested that, when electrons move from one energy level to another, they give out or absorb "packets" of radiation in the form of light. These packets are called *photons*, or quanta. The shorter the radiation's wavelength, the higher the photon's energy. He then worked out the precise energies involved in an electron jumping from one permissible orbit to another.

Bohr's theory is easier to understand if one looks at the fascinating evidence he used to support it. This evidence comes from the field of study known as *spectroscopy*, which is the study of spectrums of light that are emitted by atoms of different elements. The inside of the atom is invisible to the human eye, but spectroscopy provides a window (some writers have likened it to a stained glass window), which is comprised of the spectrum of light. Any object warmer than absolute zero emits radiation; the hotter the object, the higher is the frequency of this radiation. The important attribute of this radiation that permits chemical analysis is that different atoms and molecules emit distinctive radiation fingerprints. Each fingerprint, or spectrum, is marked by peaks and valleys at places characteristic of the chemicals emitting the radiation.

In 1859, the German physicist Gustaf Kirchhoff found a connection between spectral lines and chemical elements. He discovered that when various elements were heated, they emitted spectra of light that is different for each of the various elements. Kirchhoff and his colleague Robert Bunsen (developer of the Bunsen burner) were able to finger-print elements by their spectral lines. Science now had a tool to examine the chemical composition of any object that gives off light. In fact, it is by this means that astronomers today analyze the elemental composition of distant stars.

But what has all this to do with determining the structure of the atom? In his analysis of the electron problem, Bohr had selected the hydrogen atom for detailed study because of its simplicity (one electron in orbit around one proton). Heated hydrogen, like any other element, emits a distinctive series of spectral lines. In contemplation of hydrogen's spectral lines, Bohr postulated that radiation occurs when an electron jumps from one energy level to a lower one and that the energy of the radiating photon is the difference of the two energy levels. An electron would jump from one orbit to another when it either absorbed energy or emitted energy. Assuming that this energy was converted into light, he calculated the corresponding wavelengths. He compared these to the known, but not understood, spectrum of hydrogen, and the match was exact.

Hydrogen has three rather vivid lines in its visible spectrum: a red line, a blue-green line, and a blue line. Bohr explained that the emissions of atoms are what are seen as a characteristic hydrogen spectral line. The red line is when the electron jumps from the third orbit to the second; the blue-green line when the electron jumps from the fourth orbit to the second.

The nineteenth century had seen the accumulation of beautifully observed spectra of many elements, but they had been little understood until Bohr. When Albert Einstein heard of how the theory matched so strongly with the data of spectrum lines, he called Bohr's finding one of the great discoveries of physics.

Bohr's theory represented the first application of quantum theory in a field that classical physics had always regarded as its own—the physics of matter. From that point on, physicists knew the limits of classical physics on the very small scale—Einstein had already taught them the limits of classical physics in the domain of ultrahigh speeds. Bohr's scheme was also the first successful attempt to make the internal structure of the atom explain spectroscopy and to use spectroscopic data to explain the internal structure of the atom.

Bohr's Atom

At first, many of the old guard of physics, including J. J. Thomson, were skeptical of Bohr's theory; but Rutherford was a strong Bohr supporter, and the new theory was eventually accepted.

In 1913, Bohr published three papers on the physics of atoms, including *On the Constitution of Atoms and Molecules*, which became a classic in a short time. He spent the years from 1914 to 1916 in Manchester, once again working under the auspices of his mentor, Rutherford. Then in 1916, he was offered an appointment to a professorship in his native city of Copenhagen at the University of Denmark. In the summer of 1916, he returned to Denmark.

It was the custom in those days for a new professor to present himself at a public audience to the king or queen shortly after being appointed. Formal dress—morning coat and white gloves—were required. Accordingly, Bohr called on King Christian X. When Bohr was introduced, the King said that he was pleased to meet the famous soccer player, which put Bohr in an awkward position. He knew the King had confused him with his younger brother Harald. On the other hand, protocol forbade correcting the monarch during a public audience. Bohr managed to mutter something about the fact that he did play soccer, but that his brother (a member of the Danish Olympic soccer team) was the *famous* soccer player. The annoyed King then terminated the audience, and Bohr took his leave, walking backward, as the custom demands.

But if Bohr ran into difficulty with the monarch, at the university he was very much appreciated. The university created for Bohr a new Institute of Theoretical Physics, which opened its doors in 1921. Niels Bohr served as director for the rest of his life.

The Nobel Prize

In November of 1922, the Royal Swedish Academy of Sciences awarded Niels Bohr the Nobel Prize in Physics. He became the sixth Dane and the first Danish physicist to be so honored. In these days of mass media, the award of a Nobel Prize is headline news throughout the world. This was not the case in 1922. A one-paragraph news item on page four of the *New York Times* carried the news of Bohr's award to the United States, and his name was misspelled. Moreover, the headline of the news item featured Einstein's name, not Bohr's—Einstein had been awarded the prize in physics for the previous year, and it was belatedly being announced at the same time as Bohr's.

Kopenhgagener Geist

Bohr drew to the Copenhagen Institute for Theoretical Physics many of the most respected theoretical physicists in the world. Under his leadership, they substantially developed the ideas of quantum mechanics. Bohr's international group included Oskar Klein, Werner Heisenberg, Wolfgang Pauli, George Gamow, Lev Landau, and Hendrik Kramers. The center of balance for the study of nature's secrets had clearly shifted to Copenhagen, where the most famous scientists of the world gathered to consult, debate, argue, and just talk physics. For theoreticians worldwide, visiting the Institute to listen to Bohr talk and to exchange ideas with him was both a duty and a pleasure. Bohr's technique was Socratic, in that he answered questions with questions in a slow, probing, but patient search for truth.

A Bohr lecture on physics has been likened to a one-man tennis match. Bohr, it is said, hit the ball from one side of the court, and then ran to the other side fast enough to hit it back. The more times the subject at issue went back and forth like a tennis ball, the more enjoyable the game. From time to time, to lighten the atmosphere, Bohr would tell a joke. He had a set repertory of jokes, most of which were well known and loved by his students. One of his favorites was his definition of a "great truth": a truth whose opposite is also a great truth.

As a public speaker, however, Bohr was spectacularly bad. His low voice did not carry far, and his accent was an added problem. He often switched from language to language without warning. In addition to Danish, he spoke both English and German, and, in the words of one of his colleagues, he somehow had the idea that he also spoke French. On one occasion he greeted a puzzled French Ambassador with a cordial "Aujourd'hui (Today)." More perplexing, however, were his intricately evolved, convoluted sentences that often omitted phrases because Bohr, deep in thought, would forget to articulate them. Listening to Bohr was reputedly not unlike reading James Joyce's *Ulysses*. If your attention slipped for a moment, you were lost.

Bohr gave a welcoming address to each new group of research students and their spouses arriving at the Copenhagen Institute. The wife of one of these eager newcomers related how she sat through the welcoming talk by Bohr, noted the enthusiastic applause from the audience, and then turned to her neighbor at the lecture to tell him how eager she was to hear the English translation. He looked at her a moment and then gave her the bad news: "That was the English translation."

Bohr's colleagues forgave him his inability to communicate well because they recognized the profundity and originality of his thoughts. They probably would have forgiven his shortcomings anyway because of his immensely likable personality. Unlike most other top scientists of his day, he did not possess a flamboyant ego, was never sarcastic or unkind in the give and take of scientific debate, and generally projected an air of calm, brooding wisdom.

Bohr and Einstein

Albert Einstein played a singularly important part in Bohr's life. They met for the first time in 1920 on the occasion of Bohr's first visit to Berlin. Einstein, at that time the world's most famous scientist, was much impressed with the younger Bohr. They were, of course, familiar with each other's work, and their first meeting was a success. They held long talks while walking in the Berlin suburbs near Einstein's home, and they began an exchange of letters that lasted through their lifetimes. Later in 1920, Einstein visited the Bohr family home while returning from a trip to Norway. Einstein wrote to a friend that the hours he spent with Bohr in Copenhagen were the highlight of his trip to Scandinavia.

Both scientists were famous, in some cases notorious, for their ability to concentrate on a particular problem to the exclusion of any and all outside distractions, and the following story demonstrates just how intense their concentration could be. As the story goes, Einstein was returning home from a trip to Sweden in 1923 when he stopped off in Copenhagen. Because Bohr's automobile was not available that afternoon, he took the streetcar to the train station to meet Einstein. The two scientists boarded a streetcar to return to Bohr's home and became so engrossed in conversation that they missed their stop. They got off, caught a returning streetcar and became so immediately preoccupied again with their ongoing debate that they missed the stop a second time.

According to Bohr, this reoccurred so many times that people began to look at the two physicists strangely. Bohr and Einstein held opposing views on the philosophy of quantum physics and their famous debate on the subject carried on over thirty-five years.

Principle of Complementarity

One particular point of contention between Bohr and Einstein was Bohr's principle of complementarity, which has become an essential part of the way physicists today think about nature. *Complementarity* can be defined as the coexistence of two different descriptions of a physical phenomenon, seemingly incompatible descriptions, but both needed for a complete description of the system. A case in point is wave–particle duality—the phenomenon by which, in the atomic domain, objects exhibit the properties of both particles and waves. In classical, macroscopic physics, particles and waves are considered mutually exclusive categories. Bohr considered the particle concept and the wave concept to be two complementary descriptions of the same reality, each of them being only partly correct and having a limited range of applications. Each concept was needed to give a full description of atomic reality.

Bohr pointed out that for many experiments, it is more convenient to think about radiation as waves. Wave frequencies and intensities, for instance, provide information about the atom. Bohr thought that in this case, the wave picture came much nearer the truth than the particle picture. Therefore, Bohr advocated the use of both pictures, which he called "complementary" to each other.

The two pictures are, of course, mutually exclusive because a certain thing cannot at the same time be a particle and a wave, but the two concepts can complement each other. By playing with both pictures, by going from one picture to the other and back again, Bohr pointed out, the right impression of the strange kind of reality behind atomic experiments is finally achieved. Bohr used the concept of complementarity in his interpretation of quantum theory.

Bohr maintained, "Evidence obtained under different experimental conditions cannot be comprehended within a single picture, but must be regarded as complementary in the sense that only the totality of the phenomena exhausts the possible information about the objects." The foregoing, it must be pointed out, are Bohr's words—Bohr's own explanation of complementarity. Just what Bohr meant was always the subject of lively discourse among his colleagues and students. In fact, interpreting Bohr became something of a cottage industry. One of those having trouble with Bohr's concept was his star pupil and protege, Werner Heisenberg.

In 1927, Heisenberg was living in an attic at Bohr's Institute, and Bohr often came to his room at night to argue new ideas in atomic theory. The two theorists found little common ground, and eventually their discussions became more heated. According to Heisenberg's account of these events, it was during a walk one night behind the Institute that it occurred to him that the central difficulty in quantum measurements lay in the impossibility of establishing, at any given instant, both the momentum and the location of a particle. Bohr was away on a skiing vacation in Norway, and, while he was away, Heisenberg drafted a paper demonstrating what has come to be known as his *uncertainty principle*. (The implications of this brilliant insight will be discussed in the next chapter.)

Bohr thought that his complementarity principle was a better explanation of reality than the uncertainty principle, and, when he returned from the vacation, the two men fought over their different approaches. After several angry exchanges, they decided to keep their distance for a few days. Eventually, they both relented and managed to find a way beyond the impasse. They decided to agree that complementarity and Heisenberg's uncertainty relations amounted to the same thing, and their joint concepts became known as *the Copenhagen interpretation*.

The Copenhagen interpretation implies the division of the physical world into an observed system (referred to by both Bohr and Heisenberg as the "object") and an observing system. The object can be an atom, a subatomic particle, or an atomic process. The observing system consists of the experimental apparatus (a microscope or a telescope, for instance) and one or several human observers. Bohr and Heisenberg asserted that the two systems function according to different sets of physical laws. The observing system follows the laws of classical physics, but the observed systems (the "objects") follow those of quantum theory. This means that the question of where a subatomic particle will be at a certain time or how an atomic process will occur can never be predicted with certainty, because at the quantum level, the position and momentum of a particle cannot be determined with certainty. They can only be calculated in terms of probabilities. All that can be done is to predict the odds.

Most subatomic particles known today are unstable; that is, they disintegrate or decay into other particles after a certain time. The Copenhagen interpretation says that it is not possible to predict this time exactly. Rather, it is only possible to predict the probability of the amount of decay after a certain time. In the same way, the specific process of decay cannot be predicted with absolute accuracy. An unstable particle can decay into various combinations of other particles, but all that can be predicted are statistical averages. For instance, out of a large number of particles, x percent will decay in one way, y percent will decay in another way, and z percent in a third way. Such statistical predictions require many measurements to be verified. In fact, in high-energy physics today, tens of thousands of particle collisions are recorded and analyzed to determine the probability of any particular process.

Quantum theory requires that probability be recognized as a fundamental feature of atomic reality that governs all processes, and even the existence of matter. In quantum theory, subatomic particles do not exist with certainty at definite places but rather show "probabilities to exist." And atomic events do not occur with certainty at definite times and in definite ways but rather show "probabilities to occur."

The Bohr/Heisenberg interpretation of the meaning of *quantum*, which implied an altered view of the meaning of *physical explanation*, was gradually accepted by most physicists. The most famous and most outspoken dissenter, however, was Albert Einstein. (I have touched on the subject of this long-standing debate in Chapter Two.) The crux of Einstein's disagreement lay in the fact that Bohr believed in a "probabilistic" universe in which chance plays an important role in the occurrence of events. This deeply offended Einstein's sense of order and contradicted his belief in a "deterministic" universe, as evidenced by his much-quoted remark that "God does not play dice with the universe." Although, as I have said, most physicists today agree with Bohr, Einstein remained unconvinced to his dying day.

During the 1930s, Bohr continued to work on problems raised by quantum theory and also contributed to the new field of nuclear physics. His concept of the atomic nucleus, which he likened to a liquid droplet, was an important step in understanding many nuclear processes. In particular, it played a key part in 1939 in the understanding of nuclear fission.

Splitting the Atom

In 1939, Otto Hahn and Lise Meitner had studied the disintegration of uranium nuclei by neutrons. Working together, they found that bombarding certain atoms with particles from radioactive materials could fracture the nuclei of those atoms, releasing energy. At first, they did not fully understand what they had done.

In Stockholm, Meitner and her nephew, the physicist Otto Frisch, analyzed the data and concluded that what had occurred was the fission (splitting) of uranium. Together, Meitner and Frisch prepared a letter announcing this accomplishment and submitted it to the British journal *Nature*. Frisch, who was working in Bohr's laboratory in Copenhagen, told Bohr about the letter before it was published. Bohr at once saw the implications of nuclear fission, and on a trip to the United States, he spread the word among those assembled for a physics conference in Washington, D.C.

The implications of the Meitner/Hahn/Frisch discovery were astounding. Einstein had explained that mass and energy were convertible back in 1905, but that was theory and this news was fact. If a neutron that split a uranium nucleus could start a chain reaction whereby released neutrons could break up other nuclei, thus liberating more and more energy nearly instantaneously, then this process could result in an explosion of stupendous power. But Hahn's laboratory in Berlin had not exploded nor had Meitner's facility in Sweden.

Bohr and a young Princeton colleague named John Wheeler got to work trying to solve this paradox at once. The Bohr/Wheeler paper published in 1939 explained the process of nuclear fission and why Hahn's laboratory was still standing. Bohr and Wheeler showed that most of the uranium nuclei were not being split. Only a small portion were. These, they explained, must belong to a particularly susceptible uranium isotope. Nuclear fission happened not in the stable, common nucleus of uranium (uranium-238), but in that of the much rarer isotope, uranium-235. (Recall that *isotopes* refer to the members of a family of elements sharing the same position in the periodic scale but differing from each other in the number of neutrons they contain.) In the case in question here, both U-235 and U-238 have 92 protons, but their neutrons number 143 and 146, respectively. In their now famous paper, Bohr and Wheeler explained how and why the nuclei of U-235 is less stable, or fissile.

Fission and Fusion

If, as in Bohr's analogy, atomic nuclei are considered as tiny droplets of nuclear fluid, then it must be assumed that these droplets are electrically charged because about one half of the particles forming the nucleus

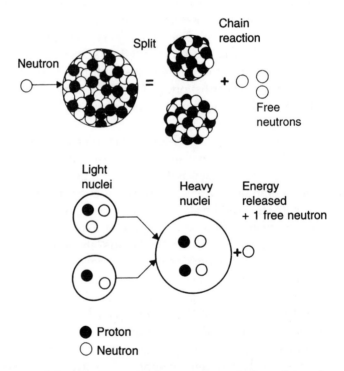

Nuclear fission and fusion   Fission is the process in which nuclei are bombarded by neutrons and split into two parts, releasing energy and several additional neutrons. Fusion results when light nuclei combine (under high-heat conditions) to form a heavier nucleus, releasing energy and extra neutrons.

are protons. The forces of electric repulsion between nuclear constituents trying to disrupt the nucleus into two or more parts are counteracted by surface-tension forces that tend to keep the nucleus in one piece. This is the basis of nuclear stability. If the electric forces of repulsion are made stronger, the nucleus will have a tendency to fly apart at high speed; this breaking-up process is designated by the term *fission*.

Bohr and Wheeler worked out the mathematical balance between the so-called surface-tension and electric repulsive forces in the nuclei of different elements and showed that whereas the surface-tension forces were dominant in the nuclei of all the elements in the first half of the periodic system (approximately up to silver), the electric repulsive forces prevail for all heavier nuclei. In other words, the nuclei of all elements heavier than silver have a tendency to be unstable and, under sufficiently strong particle bombardment, would break up into two or more parts, with the consequent liberation of a considerable amount of internal nuclear energy. On the other hand, a spontaneous fusion process should be expected whenever two light nuclei with a combined atomic weight less than that of silver are combined. The Bohr/Wheeler paper was a seminal breakthrough in the understanding of the atomic nucleus and the potential for the release of energy from atoms, slowly and controlled in the case of an atomic power plant, and rapidly and uncontrolled in the case of an atomic weapon.

When a neutron hits a uranium nucleus, the nucleus fissions (or splits) into two smaller nuclei of approximately half the size. Several neutrons are also emitted, together with high-energy radiation. These free neutrons can go on to cause further fissions in a chain reaction. But neutrons can be slowed down by graphite or heavy water mixed with uranium, and, thus, a chain reaction can be controlled.

The Atomic Bomb

About this same time, the eccentric Hungarian physicist Leo Szilard—who, like Meitner, had fled Nazi Germany because he was Jewish—was also thinking about the possibility of an atomic bomb. H. G. Wells had first used the term *atomic bomb* in a work of science fiction that Szilard had read and not forgotten. Szilard knew that nuclear fission alone would not produce a weapon; but, if some trigger to produce a nuclear chain reaction could be invented, then a bomb might be possible. Szilard also knew that German physicists, particularly Werner Heisenberg, must be just as much aware of this potential as he was. Szilard was profoundly concerned, and he made his distress known. First, he worked hard to persuade American physicists to establish self-censorship about their investigations into nuclear fission. Second, with the help of Eugene Wigner, he persuaded Albert Einstein to sign a letter to President Roosevelt, which in time resulted in the Manhattan Project. The irony in Szilard's efforts was that he was later so little trusted by the U.S. military that he was kept under almost continuous FBI surveillance.

As previously explained, it was Bohr and Wheeler who pointed out that on theoretical grounds, it was uranium-235 that should set off a chain reaction. Uranium-235 is less stable than uranium-238, and even a slow neutron can cause uranium-235 to undergo fission. One of the main technological tasks in developing the fission bomb was separating uranium-235 from uranium-238 because ordinary uranium found in nature does not have enough uranium-235 in it to support a nuclear chain reaction. Concentrated amounts would have to be extracted.

Years before, Rutherford had joked about what was at that time only a remote theory: "Some fool in a laboratory might blow up the universe unawares." Now the idea was no longer a joke.

War Years

In 1940, Germany occupied Denmark, and a period of severe moral trial began for the Danes. Despite many opportunities to escape, Niels Bohr chose to remain in Denmark. He was by this time a high-ranking member of the Danish establishment. His King had chosen to stay with his people, and Bohr thought that he should do the same. Throughout the first two years, the Nazi occupation was relatively benign. The Germans permitted the Danes the semblance of self-rule through their own parliament and King. The German ruler, Werner Best, was even referred to as an ambassador. Bohr hoped to continue his work in theoretical physics at the Institute with little Nazi interference. He also thought he could protect his colleagues better by remaining at the head of the Institute. Such was not to be.

Bohr's uneasy situation and the fragile fiction of an independent Denmark came to an end in August 1943 when Hitler's government decided to round up and "deport to the East," meaning send to death camps, Denmark's 8,000 Jews. The Danish government resigned rather than carry out Nazi directives, and the Germans declared martial law. Bohr's life, like that of every other Danish Jew, was now in immediate danger. The Bohr family was not religious, but because his mother was Jewish, Bohr was Jewish by Nazi decree.

One of the most heroic and extraordinary events of World War II then took place. Over the next few weeks, almost the entire Jewish population of Denmark disappeared. By means of boats of every size and description, from skiffs to fishing trawlers, they proceeded to cross the Kattegat Strait to sanctuary in Sweden. This sanctuary was arranged in part by Niels Bohr, who had personally arranged to see King Gustav of Sweden and secure a safe haven for all Jewish people of Denmark who could reach Sweden. On the night when the Nazis had expected to round up the Danish Jewish population, they could arrest fewer than 300. These were largely the elderly or infirm or a few who lived in small villages that were too remote to receive warning or too slow to react when they did. In total, about 450 Danish Jews were sent to the Nazi death camps. The credit for the Danish feat of bravery must go to the Danish underground, who, with the courageous support of their King and key government officials, managed to save the lives of over 7,000 men, women, and children.

The British government, and in particular the English scientific community, had been secretly in touch with Bohr for some time and had urged him to escape to England. After the declaration of martial law in Denmark, Winston Churchill's scientific advisor, Lord Cherwell, issued another invitation to Bohr, and he accepted. Cherwell wanted Bohr for Britain's atomic bomb project, called Tube Alloys at that time. Equally important, he wanted Bohr kept away from the German atomic bomb project he knew to be underway under the direction of Werner Heisenberg.

While the Danish refugees, including the Bohr family, were finding safety in Sweden, Bohr accepted England's offer on behalf of himself and his son Aage, then twenty-one and a recent graduate in physics. Mrs. Bohr and the rest of the family were left in Sweden.

The English concluded that they had to work fast to keep Bohr out of the hands of the Nazis, even though he was in neutral Sweden. Only a day or two after his arrival in Sweden, he was instructed to report to the airport at Stockholm where he would be flown out of that country in the empty bomb bay of a British Mosquito bomber. This was a dangerous flight over the North Sea that also passed over several enemy airfields in Norway. Bohr was helped into a heavy flying suit, a parachute was strapped to his back, and he was given a helmet equipped with a headset for communication with the pilot. The pilot told Bohr that to avoid Luftwaffe interceptors he would have to fly at very high altitude for part of the trip and that he would tell Bohr when to turn on his oxygen. However, the aviator's helmet given to Bohr rode so high on Bohr's large head that the earphones did not cover his ears. The result was Bohr did not hear the pilot's instructions and never did turn on his oxygen. He passed out from lack of oxygen and made much of the trip to Scotland unconscious. Alarmed by the absence of response from his passenger, the pilot came down to lower altitude as soon as he could, and upon landing rushed back to see what had happened. Bohr had regained consciousness, and none the worse for the experience, was flown on to London where a high-ranking group of English scientists greeted him warmly.

Although Bohr suspected that work on atomic weapons was underway, he had been largely out of touch with the outside world for over two years due to the war. He was surprised at how much progress had been made toward the development of a nuclear weapon, and he immediately became part of the British team participating in the huge Manhattan Project in the United States. Niels and son Aage journeyed to Los Alamos, where Bohr found many of his former students at work under the direction of Robert Oppenheimer, whom Bohr held in high esteem as a physicist and as a leader.

At Los Alamos, Bohr functioned as a sort of senior advisor and helped clear up several unanswered questions. In particular, he contributed to the design of the bomb assembly and the initiator device. He later recalled how he was fascinated by the vast Manhattan Project. He could see that under Oppenheimer's direction, the work was going well and that a nuclear bomb would surely be developed in the near future. With this realization, Bohr became more interested in the worldwide political implications of the bomb than in the technical details of its construction, and he spent much of his time thinking about the postwar implications of the weapon and writing political memoranda.

Bohr feared that an arms race would evolve between the Western powers and the Soviet Union, and he proposed that the Soviets should be informed about the bomb before its use. He knew, as the politicians and military did not, that the physics of the bomb could not be kept secret anyway and that the Soviets had the technical and industrial capability to build an atomic weapon on their own within a few years. He did not know that the Klaus Fuchs/David Greenglass spy network was, in fact, sharing secrets with the Soviets. Nor did he know then that Stalin had decided to take a tough confrontational political stance against the West after the war. Therefore, the "Open Nuclear World" Bohr proposed would not have prevented a cold war in any case.

In May of 1944, Bohr succeeded in arranging a meeting with Winston Churchill to discuss his proposal. The meeting was a disaster. The Prime Minister had not wanted to see Bohr to begin with, and Bohr's whispered philosophical ramblings fell on deaf ears. Churchill later told his science advisor, Lord Cherwell, "I did not like the man when you showed him to me, with his hair all over his head."

Undeterred by this setback, Bohr continued to plead for international control of the atomic bomb. He went back to the United States where Justice Frankfurter and presidential science advisors Vannevar Bush and J. B. Conant, all of whom supported his position, arranged for Bohr to see President Franklin Roosevelt. Bohr got an entirely different response at the White House than he had received from Churchill. Roosevelt was impressed by Bohr and heard him out with sympathy and understanding. However, when Roosevelt and Churchill met at their second Quebec conference, Churchill was adamant in his opposition to international control of atomic weapons. Nothing about the Manhattan Project was to be shared, not with the Russians and not even with the French. Churchill was so angry that Bohr had managed to influence Roosevelt that at one time he demanded that Bohr be arrested. He grumpily settled for keeping Bohr, and anyone under his influence, under surveillance.

Bohr's campaign for a scientifically open society, however, did not end with World War II. In June of 1950, Niels Bohr issued a public statement entitled "Open Letter to the United Nations." In this document, he made a long plea for an "open society." With the cold war now well underway, however, there was little taste for such "liberal" views in the international community.

Later Years

In his last years, Bohr was more of a spectator than a participant in the world of physics, but he still asserted an important moral spirit. He attempted to point out ways in which the idea of complementarity could throw light on many aspects of human life and thought. Throughout his career, he exerted a major influence on two generations of physicists, shaping their approach to science as well as providing a model of how a scientist should conduct his life. Bohr died in Copenhagen on November 18, 1962. He was seventy-seven years old. He had been a much-loved man of science, and his death was mourned throughout the civilized world.

Bohr began his career at a time when the structure of the atom was still unknown. By the time his career ended, atomic physics had reached maturity. The energy in the atomic nucleus had been put to industrial use for the production of electric power, to medical use in the treatment of cancer, and also, regrettably, to military and political use in the most destructive weapon ever conceived.

Throughout his distinguished public career, Bohr was always profoundly international and humanitarian in spirit. It must have been a bitter pill for him to accept that his star pupil and much loved brilliant apprentice chose in the end to serve a dishonorable cause. The dark career of Werner Heisenberg provides a sharp contrast to that of Bohr and, when one considers the kind of man Bohr was, represents an almost unfathomable betrayal.

Chapter Six

Werner Karl Heisenberg

"All my attempts to adapt the theoretical foundation of physics to this knowledge failed completely. It was as if the ground had been pulled out from under one, with no firm foundation to be seen anywhere upon which one could have built."

Albert Einstein, in regard to the implications
of the Uncertainty Principle

The irony of Einstein's plea is that at the time he made it, only a few years had passed since he himself had so profoundly challenged accepted scientific assumptions. Thanks to Einstein, three-dimensional space and undimensional time had become relative aspects of a four-dimensional space–time continuum. Time flowed at different rates for observers moving at different speeds. Time slowed down near heavy objects, and under certain circumstances it could stop altogether. The planets moved in their orbits not, as Newton had taught, because they were pulled toward the Sun by an attractive force acting at a distance, but because the very space in which they moved was curved. Nobody had shaken the world of science more than Einstein, and now here was this new young upstart from Germany with still another attack on classical physics.

Who was this man who so radically undermined the long-established certainties of classical modern science—and, by implication, all human attempts to understand the natural world with any confidence? He was a multidimensional man and a study in contradictions. And he provoked many perplexing questions. Was he a "reticent hero who may have saved humanity from an unimaginable catastrophe," as Thomas Powers claims in *Heisenberg's War*? Or was he a liar and a hypocrite who bungled Germany's attempt to build an atomic bomb and then concocted what C. P. Snow called "a sweet romantic story" in which he had deliberately held back the development of a Nazi nuclear weapon on moral grounds? There are, it seems, only two adjectives upon which both Heisenberg's admirers and his detractors can agree to describe him: *brilliant* and *controversial*.

Werner Heisenberg was one of the pioneers leading the way into the weird quantum world. Is *weird* a proper term to describe the quantum? Consider two of the main conceptual problems of quantum physics: (1) the *nonlocality effect*, which means that different parts of a quantum system appear to influence each other even when they are a long distance apart and even though there is no evident connection between them; and (2) the so-called *measurement problem*, which arises from the idea that quantum systems must possess measurable properties although there is apparently nothing outside quantum physics that can make those measurements. Quantum physics challenges the conventional views of the physical world, and its implications are far-reaching and mind-stretching. Heisenberg is one of the most important guides in trying to understand those implications.

Early Life

Heisenberg was born on December 5, 1901, in Würzburg, Germany, the youngest son of August and Anna Heisenberg. His father was a professor who specialized in Byzantine history, and young Werner was brought up in an atmosphere of genteel upper-middle-class academia. Heisenberg attended primary school first in Würzburg and later in Munich, when his family moved there. As a student, he began piano lessons, and, by the age of thirteen, was playing master compositions. He remained an excellent pianist throughout his life.

In 1911, Heisenberg entered the Maximilians-Gymnasium, where his maternal grandfather was rector. His extraordinary talents in the field of mathematics were recognized there for the first time. By the time of his final examinations, he had taught himself calculus, had worked on the properties of elliptic functions, and, at the age of eighteen, had attempted to publish a paper on number theory.

Heisenberg's life was not all academics, however. The post-World War I time was a period of upheaval in Germany, and the streets of Munich were the scene of much political turmoil. Germany's defeat in the war and the abdication of the Kaiser provoked unrest throughout Germany. In Bavaria, a socialist republic came to power in 1918, followed in 1919 by a Bolshevik-oriented republic that was ousted by troops from Berlin. The young Heisenberg supported the nationalist movement represented by the army, and he took part in several street fights against communist groups.

Many young German men belonged to youth organizations such as the German Pathfinders, which was founded to inspire nationalism and military preparedness, or the state-supported Young Bavarian League, against which some of the teenagers at the Maximilians-Gymnasium rebelled and started a new organization. In their search for a leader, they found seventeen-year-old Werner Heisenberg. He was ideal for the role: an older student, disillusioned with the established order, well liked at the school, and endowed with intellectual self-confidence and good looks. Gruppe Heisenberg, as the new organization became known, broke off from the Young Bavarian League, though it remained part of the Pathfinders, and met for a time in the Heisenberg home. Yet Heisenberg's involvement was focused more on athletic activities than on political issues. His main focus was on mountain climbing, skiing, and camping. During their excursions into the mountain country, Heisenberg and his followers often engaged in philosophical debates or played chess. Heisenberg was an outstanding chess player. From a young age, he was legendary and was known for holding chess matches under his desk at school during a lecture. He would often play without his queen to give his opponent a fighting chance to win. It is said that he and his older brother Kurt would sometimes even play chess in their heads while hiking.

Rather than embrace the extremist politics encouraged by the youth movement, Heisenberg instead became increasingly apolitical and academically elitist. He believed that science and politics did not mix, and science was becoming his obsession.

Heisenberg entered the University of Munich in 1920. He intended to study pure mathematics, but for some reason the eminent mathematics professor Ferdinand von Lindemann refused to admit Heisenberg to his seminar for advanced students. According to Heisenberg's own account of his interview with von Lindemann, the Professor kept a barking dog on his lap the whole time and hardly heard a word the applicant said. Heisenberg's father then arranged an interview with the professor of physics Arnold Sommerfeld, who not only accepted the young student but became his mentor and guide into the esoterics of theoretical physics. This was a fortuitous course of events: Sommerfeld's institute was then the only German institute emphasizing the quantum theory of atomic physics.

In addition to physics, Heisenberg studied the classics, in particular the scientific works of the early Greek philosophers from Plato and Aristotle to Democritus and Thales. Heisenberg's interest in the relationship of philosophy and science continued throughout his life. During his undergraduate years with Sommerfeld, Heisenberg made the acquaintance of a remarkable fellow physics student named Wolfgang Pauli, who became his closest friend, sometimes collaborator, and often his severest critic.

While still a student, Heisenberg revealed evidence of his supreme self-confidence, even audacity. There was a problem bothering researchers in atomic physics. It was known as the *Zeeman effect* and concerned the unexplainable reactions of an atom while in a magnetic field.

Specifically, the spectral lines of an atom split into more than the three components expected if the atom was in a magnetic field. In his first published paper, Heisenberg presented a model for the Zeeman effect that explained the phenomenon. The model had its flaws and was later superseded by other theories. However, Heisenberg's paper did serve as the basis for most of the subsequent work on the Zeeman effect and, of course, brought the student to the attention of established theoreticians.

In 1922, Professor Sommerfeld brought his protégé to Göttingen for a series of lectures on quantum atomic physics presented by Niels Bohr. At the first session, young Heisenberg had the nerve to criticize one of Bohr's assertions. The subsequent debate between the brash student and the established world leader of atomic physics resulted in mutual admiration and marked the beginning of their long-term collaboration, which was to be as important to Heisenberg as his lifelong collaboration with Wolfgang Pauli. Heisenberg was only twenty years old at the time of this first meeting with Bohr, who was ever alert for bright students who were not afraid to argue with him. At the conclusion of his talk, Bohr sought out Heisenberg and invited him for a walk that afternoon. Many years later, in his biography, Heisenberg said, "My real scientific career only began that afternoon." Bohr suggested that after his graduation Heisenberg should find his way to Copenhagen so they could work together.

Not all was easy going for Heisenberg at the University of Munich. For one thing, Sommerfeld ordered him to give up chess, claiming it was taking up too much of his time. Pauli, a year ahead of him, was always there to deflate his ego with sharp criticism of his papers. And finally, there was the problem of his doctoral thesis. During his oral examination, Heisenberg antagonized one of his examiners, the eminent professor of experimental physics, Wilhelm Wein, by his inability to explain how a battery works or how a telescope magnifies images. Practical experimental physics had never been Heisenberg's forte, and, as one of his later critics claimed, he could not even solder two wires together. Wein was shocked by Heisenberg's lack of knowledge about such simple subjects, and it took special pleading by Sommerfeld to persuade Wein to pass Heisenberg. In the end, Heisenberg passed with the lowest possible mark that would let him get out the door with a doctoral degree. Thereafter, he followed Pauli to the University of Göttingen in Germany, and he studied there under the mathematician Max Born.

As a result of his meeting with Niels Bohr in 1922, Heisenberg and Bohr started a collaboration by means of correspondence. Heisenberg started by questioning Bohr's picture of the inside of an atom. He thought it fanciful and inaccurate, and he decided that although Bohr's concept had pictorial appeal, there was no real proof that it depicted reality. No one, after all, had ever observed an electron circulating in an atomic orbit. Bohr had just made a theoretical assertion that electrons orbited. Heisenberg decided to pursue his own path in discovering the yet unknown rules governing the physics of the atom.

In 1925, suffering a hay fever attack, Heisenberg took a two weeks' leave of absence and journeyed to Helgoland off the coast of Germany. There he recalls that swimming in the cold sea and long walks on the beach cleared his mind for a fresh attack on the mathematics of the atom. After only a few days into this trip, he made a major breakthrough. With a strange mathematics he devised for the purpose, Heisenberg began to see a way of constructing a mathematical framework for describing atomic behavior. This mathematical approach required a strange algebra where numbers multiplied in one direction often produced different products from the same numbers multiplied in the opposite direction. Heisenberg returned to Göttingen elated with his nascent discoveries and eager to talk them over with Max Born. Born recognized Heisenberg's strange mathematics as matrix algebra, a system that had been invented in the 1850s, but which Heisenberg had not been taught.

A *matrix* is a two-dimensional table of numbers. In matrix algebra, rules had been devised by which two matrices can be multiplied together to give another matrix, and, in doing so, the matrices obey unconventional multiplication laws. In matrix algebra, the product of A and B is not the same as the product of B and A, whereas in ordinary multiplication with numbers, the product of, for example, 5 and 4 is the same as the product of 4 and 5—they both equal 20. In Heisenberg's concept, each atom would be represented by a matrix, and the motion of the electrons within the atom could be represented by another matrix. In three months of intensive work, Born, Heisenberg, and their colleague Pascual Jordan used Heisenberg's idea to devise a coherent mathematical framework that seemed to embrace all the multifarious aspects of atomic physics. The Born/Heisenberg/Jordan mathematical legerdemain permitted the highly accurate prediction of experimental results concerning atomic radiation.

Copenhagen

In 1926, Heisenberg accepted an invitation from Niels Bohr to move to the Institute for Theoretical Physics in Copenhagen and work as his assistant. It was a fateful decision and marked the beginning of the most scientifically creative period in Heisenberg's life, as well as the beginning of a long and close collaboration with Bohr. Heisenberg was twenty-four years old at the time, sixteen years younger than his world-renowned mentor. Their professional relationship soon grew into a close personal one as well. Heisenberg not only became Bohr's favorite at the Institute but also was invited into the intimate circle of the Bohr household. He played with the Bohr children, joined the family for musical evenings during which he played the piano, and was often a guest at the Bohrs' summer home on the Danish coast. Only Bohr's wife, Margrethe, was a holdout to Heisenberg's charm. She found him difficult, defensive, and closed.

Heisenberg for his part was impressed with the intellectually challenging atmosphere of the Institute and with the warmth of the Bohr household. At first, he was intimidated by the other young men gathered at the Institute. They seemed to him more worldly and much more knowledgeable about physics than he was. Living alone in a boarding house, Heisenberg spent his spare time learning both Danish and English. Languages came easily to him, and he was soon literate in both.

As for the physics, the collaboration between Heisenberg and Bohr was devoted to determining a more complete picture of the atom: a theory that would be mathematically provable and one that would answer all the questions raised about the observable qualities of atoms. The Born/Heisenberg/Jordan paper had made significant progress toward that goal, and for a short period, matrix mechanics ruled the scene of atomic physics. Physicists worldwide both struggled with the arcane mathematics and hailed its originators. But before long, Prince Louis de Broglie and

Erwin Schrödinger posed a serious challenge to Heisenberg's predominance by offering a completely new theory.

Wave/Particle Duality

Prince Louis de Broglie (pronounced "de Broy") was descended from a noble French family. His great-great-grandfather was executed on the guillotine during the French Revolution. The Prince had initially obtained a degree in history but turned to science while serving in the French army during World War I. While still a graduate student in 1924, he involved himself in the study of the nature of light. At this time, the traditional concept of light as a wave motion had been challenged by Max Planck and Albert Einstein. They had postulated that light could be more easily understood if it was thought of as a stream of individual particles called *photons*. Not all physicists agreed with this conception, and sometimes both the wave and the particle concept were taught. In an original insight, de Broglie suggested that all matter, even objects usually thought of as particles (such as electrons), should display wave-like behavior. De Broglie made this revolutionary idea part of his doctoral thesis, and at first his examining committee in Paris was not sure how to assess this puzzling concept. They could not judge it because they really did not understand it. They were apparently on the verge of rejecting de Broglie's thesis when they heard from Einstein on the subject. One of the examining committee members had sent Einstein a copy of the paper, seeking his opinion. Einstein's reply was enthusiastic; not only was it an acceptable thesis, but it was brilliant. With such enthusiastic approval from the great man, de Broglie was readily awarded his doctorate.

In this work, de Broglie had used a combination of Einstein's formula, which related mass and energy, and Planck's formula, which related frequency and energy, and showed that with any particle there ought to be an associated wave. Further, he showed that the wavelength of such waves is inversely related to the momentum of the particle, and the momentum, in turn, depends on the particle's mass and velocity. The greater the mass and velocity of the particle, the greater its momentum and the shorter its wavelength.

Einstein's original contention that matter was but a form of energy and that the two were interconvertible ($E = mc^2$) made more common sense when it was realized that particles were always wavelike and waves always particlelike. So important was de Broglie's achievement in his 1924 paper that he was awarded the 1929 Nobel Prize in Physics for it and its central concept of wave/particle dualism.

The Austrian physicist Erwin Schrödinger, at that time a professor at the University of Stuttgart, first read about de Broglie's particle waves in a footnote in one of Einstein's papers, and it occurred to him that the picture of the atom as built up by Bohr should be modified to take waves into account. Consequently, he set out to refine and improve the Bohr atom and came up with his own conception.

Schrödinger decided that the electron does not circle around the nucleus as a planet circles the Sun but constitutes a wave that curves all around the nucleus, so that it is in all parts of its orbit at once. On

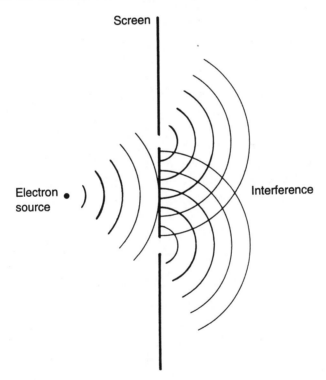

Two-slit experiment Electromagnetic radiation acts both like particles and like waves. Interference patterns, as shown here, can be explained only by assuming light is propagated as waves.

the basis of the wavelength predicted by de Broglie for an electron, a whole number of electron waves would exactly fit the orbits outlined by Bohr. As in Bohr's picture, as long as the electron remained in its orbit, it would not radiate light. Also, any orbit between two permissible orbits for which a fractional number of wavelengths would be required is not permissible. Schrödinger's concept explains the existence of discrete orbits, with nothing possible in between, as a necessary consequence of the properties of the electron, specifically the wave properties proposed by de Broglie. Until this suggestion, the existence of discrete orbits had been proven by Bohr's evidence of the spectral

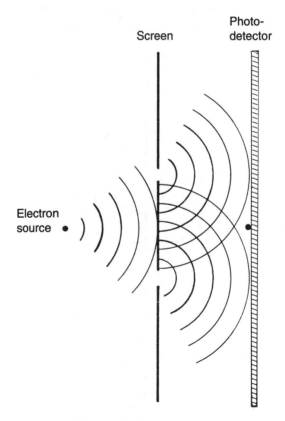

Two-slit experiment with particle detector   Placing a photodetector opposite the two slits will indicate individual photons striking the screen, showing that electromagnetic radiation acts both like particles and like waves.

lines—but not really explained. Working with his colleagues P.A.M. Dirac and Max Born, Schrödinger worked out the mathematics involved in this concept. The relationships they derived, now known as *quantum mechanics*, put Planck's quantum theory on firm mathematical ground twenty-five years after it was first promulgated.

Schrödinger's work was published in 1926 and was immediately attacked by both Bohr and Heisenberg, who saw Schrödinger's explanation as a threat to the matrix mechanics of Heisenberg. Bohr invited Schrödinger to Copenhagen to discuss the issue, and a heated debate between them began at the railroad station and continued for days, morning and night. Schrödinger soon came down with a cold and took to his bed, and, unfortunately for him, he was staying in the Bohr house. Mrs. Bohr nursed him with tea and sympathy, but Niels Bohr reportedly sat on the edge of Schrödinger's bed and continued to harangue him about his theories. In desperation, Schrödinger exclaimed that he was sorry he ever got into atomic physics. "But the rest of us are so grateful that you did," Bohr replied, "for you have thus brought atomic physics a decisive step forward."

Eventually, it was shown that matrix mechanics and Schrödinger's wave mechanics were equivalent because everything explained by one was also explained by the other. In some ways, wave mechanics was more attractive to physicists because it offered the mind a picture of the atom that was easier to visualize than Heisenberg's version.

The Uncertainty Principle

In the Spring of 1927, Werner Heisenberg, then only twenty-six years old, submitted a short paper to the *Zeitschrift fur Physik* entitled "On the Perceptual Content of Quantum Theoretical Kinematics and Mechanics." This twenty-seven-page document, forwarded to the journal from Denmark, contained Heisenberg's formulation of the famous Uncertainty Principle in quantum mechanics (also known as the principle of indeterminacy) and assured Heisenberg's place in the history of science. This is because the Uncertainty Principle involves far-reaching implications not only for subatomic physics but for all human knowledge.

The realization at the heart of the Uncertainty Principle arose from theoretical attempts to determine the exact orbit of electrons in an atom. In order to detect the position of a circling electron in an atom, it is necessary to illuminate the electron in some way; that is, a beam of some short-wavelength electromagnetic radiation must be focused on the electron. However, this illuminating radiation behaves like so many particles, and, when these particles—or even just one particle—impact the electron, they alter the electron's position. This is similar to the way one billiard ball hits and moves another. Therefore, the very act of illuminating the electron in order to observe it and to measure its position changes the motion of the electron, and therefore the electron's position cannot be measured with certainty.

A simple analogy that helps explain the principle can be made regarding a classroom full of students. It is impossible for the principal of the school to find out by direct observation how the students behave normally because the mere fact of his coming into the classroom makes them behave abnormally. For another example, in attempting to measure the temperature of hot water in a pot on the stove, the very insertion of a thermometer into the water changes the temperature of the water—not by much, of course, but by enough to preclude exactitude. The same thing is true with all physical quantities. The act of observation always alters the observed in such a way that a definite measurement cannot be made.

The Uncertainty Principle is easiest to understand on the microscopic level, because it is not hard to imagine how exceedingly small particles such as electrons can be effected by something so slight as a light beam. But it is most important to understand that Heisenberg and his colleagues showed that uncertainty is not confined to the microworld. Heisenberg showed that, in fact, uncertainty is imbedded throughout nature; it is not just an anomalous side effect of working with very minute experimental variables. Uncertainty is always there, inescapable. The mathematics worked out by Heisenberg shows that the product—meaning the ultimate effect—of the uncertainties of, for example, position and velocity, or position and momentum, or time and frequency, is often far from minute and is always greater than a very small physical quantity.

The position and the momentum of an elementary particle cannot both be known simultaneously. The reason for this is that if an electron could be held still long enough for its position to be determined, then its momentum could no longer be determined. A special point is that the product of the two uncertainties (or spreads of possible values) is always at least a certain minimum number. The frustrated researcher seeking certainty must always make a compromise; knowledge gained about time, for instance, is paid for in uncertainty about frequency, and vice versa.

What difference does this inexactitude make to those of us who live in the larger world, the macrocosm? The answer is that although all measurements involve some degree of uncertainty, this degree of uncertainty is not meaningful on the macroscopic scale. We can still fly from San Francisco to New York with confidence that we will not miss our final destination. We will not be exactly on target, but we will be close enough. We can even launch satellites into deep space with the confidence that even though we will be a little off in our calculations, the error will be so small as to be undetectable by any measuring instrument.

Still it might be philosophically disturbing to realize that there is an inherent inaccuracy in everything we do, in every measurement we make. Some mathematicians, for example, would like to believe that when they have made all their calculations as accurately as possible, the result will be absolutely predictable. But not so, according to Heisenberg's principle. The very attempt to know with complete precision any physical fact is fundamentally intrusive. Are we therefore to give up scientific research? Obviously not. Scientific research goes on, but with a new understanding of our limitations.

With time, the full implications of Heisenberg's Uncertainty Principle began to emerge. First quantum physicists accepted Heisenberg's ideas, then other scientists, and finally even a few of the knowledgeable general public. With this acceptance came the disturbing realization that uncertainty was not confined to the laboratory.

Analogies to quantum mechanical uncertainty were soon discovered in many other fields, and disquieting questions began to be asked about knowledge itself. Was there any area of human investigation where knowledge could be thought of as absolutely certain and correct? Even in the field of mathematics, long thought of as the citadel of certainty, doubts arose. The Austrian mathematician Kurt Gödel showed in the early 1930s that within any logical system, no matter how rigidly structured, there are always questions that cannot be answered with certainty, contradictions that may be discovered, and inaccuracies that may sneak in.

Another important implication of uncertainty that is worthy of comment is its effect upon causality—the relationship of cause to effect. Cause produces an effect. In classical physics if we understand fully the nature of a particular cause, we can then predict the effect. Cause and effect and predictability were cornerstones of classical physics, and now they were under question. If it is impossible to measure precisely both the position and velocity of an electron (or any other particle) at the same moment, then it is also impossible to predict exactly where that electron will be at any given time afterward. An experimenter could send off two electrons in the same direction, at the same speed, and they would not necessarily end up in the same place. In the language of physics, the same cause could produce different effects.

We have seen in Chapter One how Newton invented a new math, the calculus, to replace the plane geometry of Euclid, which Newton found inadequate to describe the system of the universe. But even with Newton's improved technique, our ability to describe that system was limited. No differential equation of calculus can ever be solved with perfect exactitude. Well before Heisenberg, scientists had to come to terms with making their best approximations, as opposed to expecting perfect precision. But Heisenberg's theory made what had long been suspected undisputably obvious: Humankind's knowledge of the natural world is not, and never has been, perfectly accurate.

So pervasive has Heisenberg's influence been, that it can even be spotted in the world of fiction. One critic writing in the *New York Times Book Review* said of a novelist that "she knows enough about Heisenberg to realize that the act of observation alters the object being observed; or in literary terms, telling the story alters the story being told."

Herr Professor and the Nobel Prize

In 1927, as Heisenberg, Bohr, and others were presenting and arguing the Copenhagen interpretation, Heisenberg accepted an appointment at the University of Leipzig as a professor of theoretical physics. At age twenty-five, he was Germany's youngest full professor. At Leipzig, Heisenberg helped to elevate the Physics Institute to a leading center for research on atomic and quantum physics. Among his early students were Rudolf Peierls, Edward Teller, and Carl Friedrich von Weizsäcker, all of whom would achieve fame in the world of physics.

In recognition of his many contributions to quantum mechanics, Heisenberg was awarded the Nobel Prize for Physics in 1933 (the award was actually for 1932, but the Nobel committees sometimes fell behind in its awards, as it had done with Einstein). Heisenberg and his mother traveled by train to Stockholm to receive the prize from the reigning Swedish king. They stopped in Copenhagen on the way to thank Niels Bohr personally for his collaboration, which played such an important role in Heisenberg's discoveries. When Heisenberg and his mother arrived at the Stockholm train station, they were greeted by two other physicists, P.A.M. Dirac and Erwin Schrödinger, who were there to share the 1933 Nobel prize for physics. For the first time, three physicists were chosen primarily for their contributions to theoretical physics.

Something else happened in 1933 that was to have a greater impact on Heisenberg's life than even the Nobel prize: Adolph Hitler was appointed Reich Chancellor, and the Nazis came to power. Heisenberg and other academics must have seen this coming because the takeover by Nazi students of German student bodies, such as that at Leipzig, preceded the Nazi control of German society. During the Nazi period, science in Germany was to become subservient to the state.

Although Heisenberg was appalled by the street violence, the crudity and anti-Semitism of the Nazis, and the excesses of their new regime, he sympathized with the Party's goal of national revival. "Much that is good is now also being tried," he wrote, "and one should recognize good intentions." He never joined the Nazi party, but in 1935 he signed the solemn oath of personal allegiance to Hitler that was required of all civil servants and soldiers.

Also in 1935, there were several challenges to the Bohr-Heisenberg Copenhagen interpretation of quantum physics. These challenges lead to much debate in physics circles—debate that must have seemed to nonscientists to be similar to medieval theologians arguing about how many angels could dance on the head of a pin. However, the attacks on the Copenhagen interpretation were taken seriously. A brief discussion of two of the more famous problems, the apparent E.P.R. paradox and Schrödinger's alive/dead cat will, I suggest, add to our understanding of quantum reality.

E.P.R. Paradox

Despite the general acceptance of quantum theory, as we have seen there were aspects of quantum mechanics as described by Bohr and Heisenberg that bothered a number of physicists, and none more than Albert Einstein. Einstein took particular exception to one of the strangest assertions of quantum theory: that the path that a particle will follow in moving from one point to another—from A to B—is unknowable. The path cannot be definitely determined. And not only that, but all paths are possible, and each of those paths has a probability associated with it. The best we can do, according to the theory, is to calculate those probabilities and predict the path on that basis. Einstein, on the contrary, maintained that if an electron starts at point A and is seen to arrive at point B, it is common sense to assume it took a particular path from A to B.

Also, Einstein did not accept the assertions of quantum theory regarding the problem of measurement. To reveal what he thought were the inconsistencies of quantum mechanics, he worked with his two young assistants at Princeton, Boris Podolsky and Nathan Rosen, and proposed a thought experiment now known as the E.P.R. experiment, after the initials of the last names of its inventors. Before turning to the explanation of this hypothetical experiment, let us first consider two fore-runner examples by the Irish physicist John Bell.

Dr. Bell introduced one of his examples in an essay entitled "Bertlmann's Socks and the Nature of Reality" in his book *Speakable and Unspeakable in Quantum Mechanics*. Bell tells of a certain Dr. Bertlmann who liked to wear pairs of socks of different colors, that is, unmatched pairs of socks. Which color socks he would wear on any given day was unpredictable. However, when one saw him striding down the street and noticed that his left sock was pink, one at once knew that the other sock was not pink. Observation of the first foot and knowledge of Bertlmann's unvarying habit provided immediate information about the second foot. This seems simple enough.

Bell's second example was equally simple. Suppose a coin has been sliced down the middle so that the head and tail are completely separated. Without anyone looking at the two pieces, they are sent off to different parts of the world in the pockets of two different people. The first person to look at the coin in his pocket will find either a head or tail and will know at once what the other person will find when he looks.

Einstein, Podolsky, and Rosen used this same logic in their assault on the fundamental precepts of quantum mechanics. The basic idea behind their hypothetical experiment was to use experimental information about one particle to deduce the properties, such as position and momentum, of a second particle. Einstein, Podolsky, and Rosen imagined two particles that interact with one another and then fly apart, not interacting with anything else until an experimenter investigates one of them. Each particle has its own momentum, and each is located at some position in space. In accordance with the rules that the E.P.R. trio set up, the hypothetical experimenter is permitted to measure precisely the total (that is, added together) momentum of the two particles, as well as the distance between them when they are close together. When, at a later time, the experimenter measures the momentum of one of the particles, he should know, automatically, what the momentum of the other one must be because the total would be unchanged. Likewise, the experimenter could have measured the precise position of the first particle and, in the same manner, deduced the position of the second particle. On the other hand, the Uncertainty Principle argues that the physical measurement of momentum of particle A prevents precise knowledge of its position. Similarly, the physical measurement of the position of particle A disturbs its momentum, which remains unknown. What bothered Einstein and his colleagues was the assertion, inherent in the Bohr/Heisenberg interpretation of quantum physics, that the state of particle B depended on which of the two measurements the experimenter had chosen to make on particle A. How can particle B "know" whether it should have a precisely defined momentum or a precisely defined position? It seemed to the writers of the E.P.R. paper that in the quantum world, measurements made on a particle at one point in space somehow affected its partner at some distant point in space.

If one accepted the Copenhagen interpretation, the E.P.R. paper points out, it makes the reality of position and momentum in the second system depend upon the process of measurement carried out on the first system, which did not disturb the second system at all. The E.P.R.

team concluded that "no reasonable definition of reality could be expected to permit this." The E.P.R. paper argued that the Copenhagen interpretation was flawed.

The essence of the difference between the E.P.R. team and the Bohr/ Heisenberg team lies in what constitutes a "reasonable" definition of *reality*. In the Copenhagen interpretation of reality, the position and momentum of the second particle have no objective meaning until they are measured, regardless of what one did to the first particle. Remember that according to strict rules of quantum mechanics, there is no definite reality until it is observed.

Eventually Bohr and company did point out a logical discrepancy in the E.P.R. paper: Even if the E.P.R. measurement device did exactly what its three inventors said it would—first measure the exact position of a distant particle and then, after some modification, measure the exact momentum of the distant particle—it was still true that two separate and distinct measurements were required. In no single measurement could one measure both the position and momentum with precision. Thus, the central precepts of quantum mechanics remained inviolate. Einstein, however, remained unconvinced.

The arguments I have described here have been presented, of course, in much simplified language. They were actually made in the more powerful language of higher mathematics. A significant contribution in this regard was made in 1964 by John Bell (of Bartlmann's socks and the split coins). Bell wrote a paper titled "On the E.P.R. Paradox," which explained the experiment in mathematical terms. It was subsequently discovered that using what by then was called Bell's theorem, the hypothetical E.P.R. experiment could actually be carried out in the laboratory, and physicists have done so many times since. In every case tested, Einstein, Podolsky, and Rosen have been proved wrong.

Well before these overwhelmingly supportive experimental results confirmed the theory, quantum physics had been gathering speed as a practical success. By the 1930s, Linus Pauling, and others explained chemical bonding using quantum mechanics. Also by this time, Heisenberg, Enrico Fermi, and others had shown experimentally that the theory was valid at the subatomic level. As P.A.M. Dirac put it, quantum theory explained "most of physics and all of chemistry."

Schrödinger's Cat

But with the general acceptance of quantum physics, an important new question arose: Where does the quantum world leave off and the classical world begin? Daily human experience is conducted in the macroworld, and none of the bizarre effects described by the "spooky" quantum theory are actually experienced. How big does an object have to be before the quantum theory does not seem to apply? In 1935, Erwin Schrödinger proposed what has become a famous thought experiment, one that illustrates that the quantum theory perhaps might not apply outside the microworld.

Anyone who has read any of the many popular books on quantum mechanics will have already encountered Schrödinger's poor, misused feline. However, because this shabby tabby has generated so much speculation and controversy, the paradoxical implications of her fate are worth a brief review.

Schrödinger's alive/dead quantum cat Theorists who accept the pure version of quantum mechanics say that the cat exists in some intermittent state, neither alive nor dead, until an observer looks into the box.

Schrödinger proposes that a cat, along with a weak radioactive source and a detector of radioactive particles, is sealed into a steel box. Also in the box is a small vial of poisonous gas and a hammer hooked up to a triggering mechanism. If the hammer is released, it will shatter the vial and release the gas. The detector in the box is turned on only once and only for one minute. The radioactive material in Schrödinger's box has a 50-percent chance of emitting a particle during this minute and therefore a 50-percent chance of not emitting a particle. If a particle is detected, the lethal device is triggered, the gas is released, and the cat is killed. It is important to note that no one can see into the box.

According to the strict Copenhagen interpretation of quantum physics, after the minute has passed and before the box is opened, we cannot speak of the cat as *either* alive or dead because we cannot observe at that moment whether it is alive or dead. To those who believe quantum mechanics apply also in the macroworld, the cat is in an indeterminate state, a sort of suspended animation, *neither* alive nor dead. Only after the box is opened can a state of aliveness be conferred on the animal.

I believe that Schrödinger's intent in this hypothetical experiment was to show the limitations of the Copenhagen interpretation of quantum mechanics—that quantum theory cannot simply be applied to all reality. However, it has often been translated otherwise. To many observers, it is obvious that the cat cannot be both alive and dead at the same time. But to those who adhere to the strict Copenhagen interpretation, the alive/dead cat is no different than the electron that can be both a wave and a particle at the same time.

The debate, which continues today, turns largely on semantics, specifically on the definition of "observing," and on the borderline between the observer and the phenomenon being observed. Analysis of Schrödinger's paradox focuses on this borderline, and the main point of this analysis is, as I understand it, that once information about the quantum world (obtained by observation) is in the macroworld, it becomes objective and irreversible—in other words, it cannot fall back into the weird world of quantum physics.

Schrödinger's cat comes up so often in popular science books that it drives some physicists to distraction. "When I hear about Schrödinger's cat," Stephen Hawking once said, "I reach for my gun."

The Attack on "Jewish Physics"

While Bohr and others were engaged with the debates over various aspects of quantum theory in the scientific community, Heisenberg was more involved in defending the theory from an attack of a different type. Theoretical physics and physicists fell into increasing disfavor in Germany with the rise of Hitler, and Heisenberg's job as the foremost spokesperson for German theoretical physics became his major preoccupation. Early in 1936, the Nobel Prize-winning physicist Johannes Stark and his followers unleashed a newspaper assault in Germany against "Jewish physics," by which he meant all theoretical physics, which he contrasted with "German" or experimental physics. Heisenberg led the opposition to this attack, although his opposition had little effect on the course of the Nazi regime's policies. Heisenberg himself was accused of being a "White Jew," and his patriotism was questioned. It was only because his mother was a personal friend of the mother of Heinrich Himmler, chief of the Nazi Secret Service (SS), that the SS was persuaded to review the issue of Heisenberg's loyalty. Otherwise his disloyalty might have just been assumed. After a lengthy investigation, the Nazis finally gave Heisenberg clearance to work on German military projects.

Heisenberg's life during these prewar years in Leipzig was difficult in other ways, too. He was professionally successful, but he had few friends. He did have a brief romance with the sister of his closest acquaintance, his laboratory assistant Carl Friedrich von Weizsäcker; but the charming Adelheid was only a teenager, and her disapproving father soon brought the relationship to an abrupt end. Then, early in 1937, Heisenberg participated in an evening of chamber music at the home of a friend. There he met a young woman who caught his eye. She was a tall and slender book dealer with a warm smile. The hostess at the social evening noticed an attraction between the two and asked the young professor to please accompany Miss Elisabeth Schumacher home. The professor was pleased to comply. A week later, he invited her to his Bavarian ski cabin (with a chaperon), and only two weeks after that the couple was engaged. Less than three months later, they were married in Berlin. Heisenberg was thirty-five years old, and his bride was twenty-two.

In early 1938, the new Mrs. Heisenberg gave birth to fraternal twins,

Wolfgang and Maria, the former named for Heisenberg's onetime class-mate and colleague Wolfgang Pauli. The Heisenberg marriage was, by most accounts, a good one. Mrs. Heisenberg bore five more children over the next twelve years and provided a stable home life for her driven and ambitious husband. Heisenberg, however, always put his career first and his family life second.

Applied Nuclear Fission

The outbreak of World War II and the interest of German Army Ord-nance in the military opportunities of nuclear fission offered Heisenberg and other German atomic physicists an opportunity, as they saw it, to serve their country and advance science at the same time. Heisenberg began dividing his time between his academic post at Leipzig and Ber-lin, where nuclear fission research was then underway. He soon became the chief technical consultant on fission research. He had been excused from military service for medical reasons (he suffered from anemia).

Heisenberg's involvement in the German effort to build an atomic weapon is the most controversial aspect of his life. After the war, Heisenberg claimed he had tried to thwart the German efforts, but other accounts told a different story. One of these accounts came from none other than Heisenberg's closest professional associate, Niels Bohr.

In 1941, Heisenberg visited the Copenhagen Institute in what was by then German-occupied Denmark. At several luncheon meetings at the Institute, Heisenberg stressed the importance of Germany winning the war and how Danish science could help. His overall reception by the Danish scientists ranged from cool to frigid. Over the objections of Bohr's wife Margrethe, Heisenberg was invited to dinner at the Bohr home, where he had been a welcome guest many times in the past. After dinner, the two physicists went for a walk and a talk. All of the facts about that meeting, including where they actually walked, are subject to controversy. Heisenberg's version and Bohr's version of the conversation agreed only on the matter of the subject: the military applications of atomic energy.

Heisenberg claimed, after the war, that he had proposed to Bohr a secret agreement between the German and American physicists whereby both sides would use their influence to dissuade their respective govern-ments from proceeding with a bomb project. Heisenberg reasoned that about twelve of these scientists, by coming to a mutual agreement, might prevent the construction of an atomic bomb. As part of his argument, Heisenberg explained that he knew how a bomb could be made and to prove his point he gave Bohr a sketch of some sort. Heisenberg claimed that proposing this agreement was the reason he went to see Bohr in the first place.

Bohr's version of the conversation differed entirely. He recalled that Heisenberg had been trying to pump him about what he knew about fission and that Heisenberg was trying to use him in an attempt to prevent the Allied bomb project from proceeding. Bohr's anger at Heisenberg and his distrust following the meeting were evident in everything he said and did in regards to Heisenberg from that evening onward. Bohr returned home after the walk and told his family that either Heisenberg was not being honest or he was being used by the Nazi government. The next day at the Institute, he told his fellow scientists the same thing. They all remembered that Bohr was very upset. And with good reason. For one thing, he was convinced that Germany was then at work trying to develop an atomic weapon and that Heisenberg was a key member of the project. Bohr wasted little time in conveying his concerns, by means of the Danish underground, to the British.

Bohr and Heisenberg had been close friends and colleagues for nearly twenty years, but their walk in the woods marked the end of their intellectual partnership. They would not see each other again until after the war was over, and Bohr remained aloof to Heisenberg for the rest of his life.

The Morris Berg Story

Bohr's concerns about what Heisenberg was doing in Germany and how close the Nazis were to developing an atomic bomb were shared by a number of scientists in the United States, including J. Robert Oppenheimer. When advised of the danger posed by Heisenberg, General Leslie Groves, director of the Manhattan Project, was willing to entertain some pretty wild suggestions as to what to do about the German scientist. In Los Alamos, physicists Hans Bethe and Victor Weisskopf proposed either kidnapping or assassinating Heisenberg and actually volunteered to carry out the mission. It must be remembered that these two scientists were both refugees from Hitler. General Groves needed these two nuclear theorists where they were, and he did not take them up on their offer.

Groves turned instead to the U.S. Office of Strategic Services (OSS), precursor of the CIA. The agent chosen to deal with the Heisenberg threat was Morris (Moe) Berg, a former third-string catcher for the Boston Red Sox. The story of this mission, one of the strangest episodes in the history of espionage, is well told in *The Catcher Was a Spy: The Mysterious Life of Moe Berg*, by Nicholas Dawidoff. Berg was a colorful character. In addition to being a major-league ballplayer, the six-foot, 195-pound, Princeton graduate was a polymath, linguist, ladies' man, raconteur, lawyer, one-time contestant on the radio show "Information Please," and a spy. Berg was chosen by General Bill Donovan, head of the OSS, to sneak into Europe, determine the likelihood of a Nazi A-bomb, and assassinate Heisenberg if he judged that necessary. How he was supposed to determine this necessity is a bit vague. He was, after all, not a physicist. From Donovan and Groves' point of view, there was one big advantage in using Berg as their agent, despite his lack of knowledge about physics: If captured and tortured, he could tell the Germans nothing about the technical details of the American Manhattan Project.

On June 5, 1944, the American Fifth Army marched into Rome, the first major European capital liberated from Nazi occupation. A short time later, Moe Berg arrived in Rome to interrogate Italian nuclear scientists and find out what they could tell him about the German atomic bomb project. The Italians could tell him very little, but he did learn that Werner Heisenberg was going to Switzerland for a lecture at a technical college in Zurich. Heisenberg was due to address a weekly colloquium on December 18, 1944, at the invitation of Swiss physicist Paul Scheerer. Scheerer was well known to Heisenberg because the two had worked together before the war. What Heisenberg did not know was that Scheerer was a heartfelt anti-Nazi and a friend of the Allied cause. He was in fact Allen Dulles's prime source of information regarding German science as well as the whereabouts and activities of German scientists. Dulles at that time headed up OSS activities in neutral Switzerland. Between them, Dulles and Scheerer arranged for Moe Berg to attend the high-level scientific collegium, armed with a .45 caliber pistol.

On the day of the lecture, Berg and another OSS officer found seats in the second row of the hall. Berg estimated later that there were only about twenty people in the room. There was no screening of attendees and in fact no security whatsoever. Berg did his best to take notes throughout the lecture, which, as it turned out, was not about nuclear fission at all but rather a talk about something called S-matrix theory, a difficult and abstruse subject that had nothing to do with the bomb.

After the formal part of Heisenberg's talk, Berg mingled with the scientists and somehow got invited to a private dinner for Heisenberg a week or so later. At that private dinner, he not only sat next to Heisenberg but later accompanied him as he walked back to his hotel. Heisenberg had no idea who Berg was, but he later told his son that he thought Berg was Swiss. Whatever else he was, Berg was a good listener. He had listened carefully to various Italian, Swiss, and German refugee scientists argue that Heisenberg was no real threat. The Zurich physics lecture and the later personal contact without any bodyguard in evidence reinforced Berg's impression that the Nazis did not regard Heisenberg as an important national asset. In the end, Berg kept his finger off the trigger.

Project ALSOS and Goudsmit

General Groves, however, was still not convinced that there was no significant German atomic bomb project underway, and to be prepared for the possibility, however remote, he authorized the formation of a paramilitary organization that advanced into areas of Europe then being liberated by the rapidly advancing Allied forces. The unit was given the code named ALSOS (Greek for "grove"). To head ALSOS Grove picked Lieutenant Colonel Boris T. Pash. As science advisor, he appointed the Dutch-born theoretical physicist Samuel A. Goudsmit, in part because he had not worked on the Manhattan Project and so if he were taken prisoner he could reveal nothing about the Allied bomb effort. Ironically, Goudsmit had known Heisenberg well prior to the war. In fact, he considered Heisenberg a friend. When Heisenberg visited the United States just prior to the beginning of the war he stayed at the Goudsmit home. In the early days of World War II, Goudsmit's mother and father found themselves trapped in occupied Holland. Fearing for their safety, Goudsmit wrote to Heisenberg soliciting his help. For whatever reason, Heisenberg chose not to intervene. The couple were subsequently shipped to a German death camp and murdered. It is quite possible that Heisenberg did not have the authority to assist the senior Goudsmits, but, at any rate, he did not try.

The mission with which ALSOS was charged was threefold: (1) ascertain the status of the Nazi atomic bomb project; (2) capture, secure, and ship to the United States all the uranium known to be in the possession of the Germans; and (3) make sure no German atomic scientists evaded capture or fell into the hands of the Soviet Union. Following close behind occupying Allied units, the ALSOS unit carried out all three parts of their assignment with dispatch. From captured papers found at the German physics laboratory in Strasbourg, they determined that although Germany did have an atom bomb project, it was relatively small scale and had made little significant progress. Colonel Pash considered this to be the single most important accomplishment of ALSOS. They also captured most of the 1,200 tons of uranium ore that Germany had obtained from the Belgium Congo. They arranged for this material to be shipped back to the United States for use by the Manhattan Project. Lastly, they succeeded in locating the key German atomic scientists.

Papers uncovered by ALSOS placed Werner Heisenberg, Otto Hahn, Carl von Weizsäcker, Max von Laue, and others in their nuclear-fission organization in the Black Forest region of southwestern Germany in the resort town of Haigerloch. Pash and his forces raced to that area ahead of the oncoming French army (the Russians were coming from the other direction). On the way, they took and returned fire from the retreating German army. At Haigerloch, they found that the hidden Nazi "uranium machine" was actually an atomic pile somewhat similar to what Enrico Fermi had developed two years previously in Chicago. Fermi had directed efforts to construct the first self-sustaining fission reaction at a secret laboratory beneath Stagg Field at the University of Chicago. In 1942, Fermi's atomic pile went critical and sustained a chain reaction. The atomic pile the ALSOS unit found at Haigerloch was on the edge of criticality; that is, a chain reaction had not been started, but one more shipment of uranium would have been all that was necessary to bring this about.

Heisenberg was not there when the ALSOS forces arrived, but Pash and Goudsmit found him a few days later with his family at a lake cottage in Bavaria. What Goudsmit said to Heisenberg during interrogation is not known, but what Goudsmit thought about Heisenberg's later claim of deliberately trying to discourage the German bomb effort is known. In his book about the ALSOS project published after the war, Goudsmit calls Heisenberg a "liar" and a "hypocrite." Heisenberg and Goudsmit were to fight this battle out in print, particularly in the pages of the *New York Times*, where Heisenberg defenders were harshly taken to task by Goudsmit, who clearly did not buy what he and other Heisenberg critics called the "fairy tale."

Heisenberg and the other German atomic physicists were taken into custody and shipped off for temporary safekeeping to England. The English security establishment had conceived a brilliant deception. Rather than try to question the German scientists about their war-time research into atomic fission, they proposed housing them all at a rural estate called Farm Hall. There the Germans could take lessons in English, while away time in the music room, or roam the gardens of the estate. Of course, they could also talk physics. Talk physics is what the English hoped they would do, as they had bugged every room in the house.

The Farm Hall Verdict

Interned at the Farm Hall estate near Cambridge were the ten German physicists who had been in charge of Germany's attempt to develop and build an atomic weapon. They were confined there for almost six months—between July and December of 1945. It was not a particularly arduous confinement. They dined on English officer's mess rations, played tennis on the estate courts, and talked politics and physics, with their conversations secretly recorded for the entire period. The transcripts of the recordings, for many years highly classified, were finally released by British Intelligence in 1992.

In addition to Heisenberg, the Farm Hall captives included Walter Gerlach, Otto Hahn, Max von Laue, Carl Friederich von Weizsäcker, Paul Harteck, Karl Wirtz, Ernst Bagge, Horst Karsching, and Kurt Diebner. The transcripts of their discussions presented the most accurate picture available of just where Germany was on its path to a nuclear weapon; and, in effect, they delivered the final verdict on whether Heisenberg and company were "deliberately" trying to divert the project away from weapons research for what they later called humanitarian reasons.

After a month of gentlemanly captivity at Farm Hall came the news of Hiroshima and a few days later, Nagasaki. These reports were a shock to the Germans, and at first they did not believe them. They thought the reports were a scheme to make them reveal hidden knowledge. As the truth became apparent, they fought among themselves as to whose fault it was that Germany had not developed the bomb first. Just how close were the German scientists to achieving a nuclear bomb for their Nazi masters? In general terms, they were, by the end of the European war, about where Enrico Fermi had been in Chicago two years previously (Fermi and his team had developed the world's first nuclear reactor in December 1942). As is now known, the German research would have culminated in a reactor that could have gone critical with only one more small shipment of uranium. Had it not been for the heavy bombing of Berlin, which forced the project to relocate and move the reactor to Haigerloch, and for the disruption of supplies of its heavy-water moderator from Norway, the Germans might well have had a working reactor in 1943 or 1944.

Developing a reactor and developing a nuclear weapon are not, however, the same thing. While Fermi worked in Chicago, the Los Alamos research and design effort had already gotten well underway on the assumption that Fermi would achieve a nuclear reaction. Also, other elements of the huge Manhattan Project were in operation, specifically uranium and plutonium separation plants. The Germans had not undertaken these other crucial efforts. The Farm Hall tapes also made it clear that with one or two exceptions, not including Heisenberg, the captured scientists were clearly sorry Germany had lost the war.

The status of the German effort is now quite clear: In the period of 1941 and 1942 when the United States and Britain launched their efforts to develop a fission bomb, the Germans concluded that isotope separation on the required scale was simply not feasible and that extensive development of reactors would be needed before the expected fissionable isotope of element 94 could be bred in adequate amounts. They were led to this erroneous conclusion by their crude and pessimistic estimate of the size required for a critical mass.

The German scientists and, in particular, Werner Heisenberg, estimated that the critical mass needed for a bomb would be several tons. The American and British team, using a different approach to the problem, arrived at a significantly smaller figure for critical mass. In point of fact, the true figure is only a few pounds, and the atomic weapon dropped on Hiroshima consisted of 15 kilograms, or 33 pounds, of uranium. From the recorded conversations among the German scientists at Farm Hall, including Heisenberg, it is apparent that if they had made a more realistic estimate of the critical mass and if they had known how feverishly the U.S. scientists were working on the project, most of them would have had few, if any, compunctions about building the bomb for Hitler. Heisenberg's "sweet story" was just what Goudsmit said it was: a fairy tale.

Postwar and the "World Formula"

Whatever his actions during World War II, Heisenberg's influence in postwar Germany was significant. He became the leading spokesman for German science in the international arena. He participated in the decision to locate the European research center for high-energy physics (CERN) in Geneva and later served as chairman of its scientific policy committee. In the area of West German nuclear policy, Heisenberg directed his influence in support of nuclear energy and in opposition to the development of nuclear weapons. In 1955, the Western Allies granted the Federal Republic of Germany full sovereignty and membership in the NATO alliance. All postwar restrictions upon West German research were lifted. Heisenberg and a group of colleagues immediately launched a public campaign for a crash program in nuclear energy development. At the same time, they energetically opposed Chancellor Adenauer's plan to equip the German army with so-called tactical nuclear weapons. Heisenberg's political campaign against nuclear weapons culminated in 1957 in a public declaration formulated by Heisenberg and Weizsäcker and signed by numerous nuclear scientists opposing possession of nuclear weapons by West Germany. The campaign was successful, and the West German army remained nonnuclear.

In addition to his political involvement, Heisenberg continued to pursue his search for a consistent quantum field theory. In 1958, he published with Wofgang Pauli a so-called preprint of his proposed unified field theory of elementary particles, which was later repudiated by Pauli. Three days before the preprint was to be distributed, Heisenberg announced his new theory in a lecture at the University of Göttingen. A journalist in the audience, looking for a headline, reported a sensational new "world formula," which was picked up by newspapers around the world. One headline proclaimed, "Professor Heisenberg and his assistant, W. Pauli, have discovered the basic equation of the cosmos."

The hype became even more sensational when Heisenberg, in a radio address on his new "theory of everything," stated that, "except for a few details to be worked out later," this was indeed the master key to the universe.

Wolfgang Pauli was furious. He sent Heisenberg a crude drawing of two blank squares and said that "except for a few details to be worked out later, they were masterpieces of art the equal of Michelangelo." He also distributed a letter of renunciation to the leading physicists in the world. This did not stop Heisenberg from continuing to proclaim his formula to large audiences all over West and East Germany. The clash came to a head at a conference on elementary particles at CERN in Geneva where Pauli attacked Heisenberg, calling his work mathematically objectionable and his ideas "only a substitute for fundamental ideas." Once again, Heisenberg had bitterly alienated one of his closest associates, a man with whom he had worked closely throughout his career and who had greatly influenced his contributions to physics. Most physicists were already highly doubtful of Heisenberg's work and did not give Heisenberg's "theory to end all theories" much serious consideration. This disreputable affair was, in effect, Heisenberg's last hurrah.

Heisenberg returned to Munich in 1958, at the age of fifty-six, and took over the directorship of the Max Planck Institute. He continued to lecture throughout the world, but the content of his lectures became more philosophical than scientific. In the middle of 1973, he fell seriously ill with cancer. The cancer went into remission, and Heisenberg appeared for a while to have fully recovered. But in July 1975, he suffered a severe relapse and died six months later.

Summing up Quantum Mechanics

The ideas of de Broglie, Schrödinger, and Heisenberg, once thought to be "absurd," have led to whole new technologies, the very existence of which depend on the discoveries of these pioneers. Today's electronics industry, with its silicon-chip technology, is based in part on the quantum theory of materials called semiconductors. The multitude of laser applications are possible today only because of the understanding, at the fundamental quantum level, of a mechanism for radiation of light from atoms. Furthermore, understanding how large numbers of quantum objects behave when packed tightly together leads to an understanding of many different types of matter, ranging from superconductors to neutron stars. While it is true that much of quantum mechanics is difficult to comprehend, it seems to work just fine. On the basis of the experimental data and practical applications, the indeterminate nature of unmeasured physical properties must be accepted at face value.

In his book The *End of Physics*, David Lindley suggested that "The way to understand quantum mechanics, if it can be understood at all, is to concern oneself only with what is measured in a specific experiment, and to ignore resolutely all else." Quantum mechanics provides lots of good answers for specific measurements, and maybe it is better not to worry about how. Remember Niels Bohr's famous remark that anyone who claims that quantum theory is clear doesn't really understand it.

And what about the verdict on Heisenberg himself? His contribution to physics, in particular quantum mechanics, was a major one. But there is considerable doubt about his character. There are those who have reviewed the facts in detail, such as Thomas Powers in his book *Heisenberg's War*, and who find him a misunderstood and innocent man. Others, including C. P. Snow and Samuel A. Goudsmit, to name only two, are highly critical of him.

It is supremely ironic that the history of physics now takes us chronologically from Heisenberg the Inscrutable to the man who was his opposite in almost every way discernable, the colorful, witty, and completely charming American physicist and folk hero Richard Feynman.

Chapter Seven

Richard Phillips Feynman

"You will have to brace yourself for this—not because it is difficult to understand, but because it is absolutely ridiculous: All we do is draw little arrows on a piece of paper—that's all."

*Richard Feynman on
quantum electrodynamics*

When Richard Feynman was notified of his Nobel Prize in Physics on October 21, 1965 (he shared the prize with his old rival from New York, Julian Schwinger, and with Shin'ichiro Tomonago of Japan), he was besieged by reporters at his home in Pasadena, California, all asking variations of the same question: What did you actually do to win this prestigious award? The telegram notifying the winners said the award was "for fundamental work in quantum electrodynamics with deep-ploughing consequences for the physics of elementary particles." But what did that mean?

One journalist is reported to have asked Feynman to please tell him, in no more than two sentences, what he won the prize for. "If I could tell you in two sentences," Feynman replied, "I wouldn't have won the Nobel Prize." It turns out that this story might be apocryphal and that a *Time* magazine reporter might have suggested that he use that answer. Of doubtful authenticity or not, the remark was typical of Feynman: quick, witty, and direct. For the first time in his life, the resolutely unpretentious forty-eight-year-old scientist from Far Rockaway, Queens, New York, would have to outfit himself in white tie and tails and learn how to bow before the King of Sweden. Would he have to walk backward after receiving the award, he worried, and how did one learn to do that? Hearing about these social concerns, one friend sent him a rear-view mirror from an automobile as a joke. Feynman was not sure he was joking and practiced walking backward up and down stairs (in case stairs were involved in the awards ceremony).

Feynman was obviously afraid to make a social gaffe that might become as infamous as did the one he had made in Princeton back in the fall of 1939. The twenty-two-year-old graduate student, not at all at ease in the environment of formal Sunday tea at the Dean's house, was asked by the formidable Dean's wife if he "would like cream or lemon in his tea?" Feynman had blurted, "Both, please." She put the awkward bumpkin in his place with a cold look and said, "Surely you're joking, Mr. Feynman." He never forgot this remark, and he used it forty years later as the title of his first popular book.

Note that Feynman told this story on himself. In fact, much of the Feynman legend can be traced back to stories purveyed by the man himself. He was clearly out to create the image that so many of his readers and students remember so fondly: "half genius, half buffoon," to use his friend Freeman Dyson's description. Dyson, a brilliant young English mathematician and physicist, met Feynman at Cornell University in 1946 and wrote that description of his new friend in a letter to his parents. In his next letter home, he amended the first impression by describing his colleague as "all genius and all buffoon." Still later, he said he regretted both descriptions because he had come to know the real man behind the facade.

The popular image of Feynman the "character" comes principally from two best-selling books, mischievously titled *Surely You're Joking, Mr. Feynman* and *What Do You Care What Other People Think?* Stitched together from interview tapes by his friend Ralph Leighton, these books present many of Feynman's funniest stories about himself, but they are all but devoid of scientific content. They are fun to read, but they present Feynman the celebrity rather than Feynman the scientist, and we are concerned here with both.

Feynman the scientist was esteemed by his colleagues as a theorist of great originality and scope. He invented the Feynman diagrams, a graphical method of depicting particle interactions that is now employed throughout high-energy physics. He developed the "path integral" approach to quantum mechanics, a method of handling quantum probabilities that has shed light on questions ranging from the microworld to the origin of the universe. He contributed to the elegant and accurate theory of quantum electrodynamics (called QED), a blending of special relativity and quantum mechanics applicable to nuclear physics, solid-state and plasma physics, laser technology, and many other fields. It was for this work that he shared the Nobel Prize in Physics in 1965.

As we explore the life and achievements of this charming character, we will try to catch a glimpse of the genuine Richard Feynman inside the image, while at the same time taking a good look at his significant accomplishments in the world of physics.

If It's a Boy, He's Going to Be a Scientist

Melville Arthur Feynman made that statement to his young pregnant wife Lucille in 1918. He was right, of course, but it is interesting to note that the next Feynman baby, Richard's sister Joan, also earned a Ph.D. in physics.

An immigrant from Byelorussia, Melville Feynman had an inquiring mind and a lifelong fascination with science. A sometimes salesman, shirt manufacturer, and operator of dry-cleaning stores, Melville Feynman had stored up a wealth of self-taught knowledge and regularly bombarded his son with questions about the natural world around them. This world centered on Far Rockaway, Queens, a pleasant seaside community. Later in life, Richard Feynman (called Richy or Ritty, never Dick, by his parents) pointed out in many interviews how influential all of those questions were in his development into a scientist. Melville and his son took frequent walks together, during which the father would tell the boy about nature: the way the oceans work, why and how birds fly, what stars were. More importantly, Melville taught his son to think about the "why" of natural events. For instance, the young boy noticed that when he pulled his toy wagon forward, the ball in it rolled to the back of the wagon; and when he was pulling the wagon along and stopped suddenly, the ball rolled to the front of the wagon. When he asked his father about this, the senior Feynman explained the general principles of inertia: Things that are moving try to keep on moving, and things that are standing still tend to stand still unless you push them hard. Feynman was learning physics from his father long before he ever heard of the term.

He was also learning respect for knowledge in general. The Feynman family had a set of the *Encyclopaedia Britannica*, and Melville would sit the boy on his lap and read to him from the encyclopedia. And he would do more than just read the facts about a given subject; he would explain the information in terms the little boy would understand. Later Melville would take his son to the Museum of Natural History in Manhattan. The museum became Ritty's favorite place to visit, and with his father as an informative and inquisitive guide he eagerly explored the world of nature and science.

Feynman would always remain proud to state that he had been trained by his father. "I find him now," he once told his biographer Jagdish Mehra, "when I look back, a very remarkable man, because I have since met many scientists and trained people, and there are only a few, but they are very few, who understand deeply what science is about, so to speak." Early on in their relationship, Richard recognized that his father might not know the facts that well—after all he had no formal training in science—but he did know how to search for the underlying fundamentals, and this his son never forgot.

Religion played only a minimal role in Feynman's youth. The family was Jewish, but Melville was an atheist. For his wife's sake, he went along with sending Richard to the temple on Saturday and to religious school to learn a little Hebrew and maybe something of the Old

Testament; but the teachings did not take. In Feynman's own words, "I gave it up at the age of thirteen. I became an atheist because I didn't believe it."

Feynman loved to tinker with radios, clocks, and chemistry sets, and he built his own crystal and cat-whisker radio on which he could listen to "The Shadow" and other adventure dramas. He even became good enough at radio repair to pick up a little side money from it, and money was hard to come by in those days of the Great Depression. He fixed a clock in his room to run backward, learned to read the correct time from it, and loved to show this to his playmates. He read science fiction for a while, but by the time he went to high school he had given up this genre, never to return to it. Real science, he found, was exciting enough.

Far Rockaway High School

Feynman started high school in 1931, at the age of thirteen. He already knew some of the teachers because he had been spending time in the high school science laboratory. He performed well in all subjects, even though he took only mathematics and science very seriously.

He was well ahead of the other students in science and mathematics and had even taught himself advanced algebra while in elementary school. He quickly became the whiz of the Math Club (as well as an eager member of the Chemistry Club, the Physics Club, and the Chess Club).

Sports, on the other hand, did not interest him at all. Mathematics was his game—one at which he was extremely good and that allowed him to show off a bit. Showing off was to become a characteristic that stayed with him all his life. A number of other lifelong characteristics had already appeared by the time he entered high school. Among these were a rigidly disciplined rationalistic outlook, lack of reverence for authority, disdain for formality and ceremony, respect for intellectual achievement, and a generally cheerful disposition.

He had discovered by reading the encyclopedia that the calculus was important, and he wanted to learn it as soon as possible. So his father bought him a book called *Calculus Made Easy*, and he plunged right in. He was encouraged in the endeavor by a quote (from an ancient Simian proverb) on the flyleaf of the book: "What one fool can do, another can." In many ways, Richard Feynman made this something of a lifelong motto.

Feynman was in many ways what students today would call a nerd, but he was, like any adolescent, extraordinarily conscious of his image and went to great lengths to be like the other guys—not what he called a "sissy." He carried this determination on into college and into his professional career. He always wanted to be one of the boys.

Feynman had the good luck in his last year in high school to be singled out by his physics teacher, Abram Bader, for special attention. Bader was no ordinary high school science teacher. For economic reasons, he had been forced to abandon his own career in physics and take a job teaching, but he had studied under I. I. Rabi at Columbia and had an excellent background in physics. Bader had heard about an unusually bright boy who was coming to his class, which was an honors course. All of the students in this class were expected to be bright, but right away Feynman stood out. He was, Bader remembered, the top student in a class of top students. He was also a problem.

One day, Bader told Feynman to stay after class. "Feynman," he said, "you talk too much, and you make too much noise. I know why. You're bored. So I'm giving you a book." This was a book on advanced calculus. "Study this book," Bader told him, "and when you know everything that's in it, you can talk again." Every day Feynman sat in the back of the class and studied college-level calculus while the rest of the class caught up with what Feynman already knew.

On one occasion when Bader and Feynman were hanging around the laboratory, Bader took Feynman to the blackboard and explained a principle of physics that was to have a profound impact on Feynman; this was the *principle of least action*. Bader explained that there is a number—the kinetic energy minus the potential energy—the action of which, when averaged over the path, is least for the true path. This law of nature is often illustrated by a hypothetical problem. A lifeguard, some distance down the beach, sees a drowning swimmer diagonally ahead, some distance offshore and some distance to one side. How can the lifeguard find the fastest path to the swimmer? The lifeguard travels faster on land than in the water. If the lifeguard takes a straight line to the swimmer, he will spend too much time in the water. If he runs up the beach until he is directly opposite the swimmer, he will spend the least time in the water, but he would have wasted time running up the beach. It turns out that the best compromise is the path of least time, angling up the beach and then turning again for a sharp angle through the water. What the lifeguard must do instinctively, a calculus student can do mathematically. Bader showed Feynman that the same principle holds when light is bent as it travels through water or a glass prism— it always follows the path of least time. Feynman was delighted by this principle, and in some ways it influenced his whole philosophy of science. Much later, as a professor at Caltech, he would be known for insisting on simplicity in his work. "I have a principle in strong interaction theories," he once observed: "If the theory is complicated, it's wrong." In the famous Feynman Lectures on Physics, which he gave to freshman and sophomore students at Caltech in the early 1960s, he devoted a special lecture to the principle of least action and recalled what he had learned from Bader way back in those years at Far Rockaway High School.

In those formative years, Feynman started another important relationship that had long-term effects on his life: He fell in love with the beautiful and popular Arline Greenbaum. Their high school romance was to last for over fourteen years, and it is a tragic story of pain and devotion that reveals a different picture of Richard Feynman than that of the cocky, carefree youth. But before we get into that story, there are Feynman's very happy college years.

College Days

When Feynman graduated from high school in 1935, he thought he would major in mathematics in college because it had been his strongest subject. In his final year at Far Rockaway, he had applied to Columbia University, MIT (Massachusetts Institute of Technology), and CCNY (City College of New York). Even though he passed Columbia's admission examinations with the highest grades, he was turned down because at that time a Jewish quota existed for the freshman class. Feynman had paid fifteen dollars to take the admission test, and, as he told later interviewers, he greatly resented the rejection as well as the loss of the fifteen dollars. MIT, however, accepted Feynman and granted him a very small scholarship, about a hundred dollars per year. MIT was the perfect place for him because it provided both an excellent education and a lively social life. His social life revolved around his fraternity,

Phi Beta Delta. According to Feynman, the fraternity required the better students to tutor any brother having academic problems, and the more socially adept members assisted their less self-assured brothers, teaching them to dance and even getting dates for them if necessary. It is easy to guess into which half of the fraternity Feynman fell.

There was a dance somewhere on campus every weekend, and chasing girls became Feynman's number-one extracurricular activity. The only really important woman in his life, however, was still Arline Greenbaum. He brought her up to MIT for the more important dance weekends, and they carried on an extensive correspondence. Feynman was rapidly building a reputation in the fraternity as a colorful and completely unpredictable character. He was once told by a fraternity brother that if you took aspirin and Coca-Cola together, you would fall over in a dead faint. Feynman said that was ridiculous and demonstrated his point by taking six aspirin and three Cokes while a fraternity brother stood behind him ready to catch his inert body. Except for not sleeping well that night, he recalled no other problems. On another occasion, he and his fraternity brothers got into an argument as to whether urine ran out of the body by gravity alone. Feynman, at that time more the experimentalist than the theorist he was to become, demonstrated that this was not the case by standing on his head and urinating. Regarding academics, he proceeded to follow the same procedure that had worked well for him in high school: Work hard in the science and math courses and fake it in the humanities—or as he called them, "crap courses." Feynman's aversion to the arts did not originate at MIT, but it was certainly nurtured there.

In the courses that he took seriously, he performed extraordinarily well. While still a sophomore, he took a course on theoretical physics designed for seniors and graduate students. At that time, the 1936–1937 academic year, there was no course on quantum mechanics given at MIT, but Feynman and two other students prevailed upon their professor, Philip Morse, to teach them the subject. The four would meet in Morse's office once a week for an hour or so, and Morse would lecture and assign projects in quantum mechanics. Even among such a small group, Morse gave Feynman special attention. Feynman's exceptional talents were demonstrated also by the fact that while he was still an undergraduate, he published two papers in the *Physical Review*.

Upon graduation from MIT, Feynman moved to Princeton for his graduate work. He had chosen Princeton because he had been impressed with the number of papers by its students and faculty in *Physical Review* and because his faculty advisor had recommended it. It was on his first day at Princeton that Feynman attended the faculty tea at which he made his notorious lemon/cream gaffe.

Feynman had been informed that he would work as a research assistant to the famous physicist Eugene Wigner. However, upon his arrival at Princeton, he found that he had been assigned instead to work for twenty-seven-year-old John Archibald Wheeler, who had only recently joined the physics department. As things turned out, Wheeler and Feynman were ideally matched to work together. At their first meeting, Feynman was surprised at how young Wheeler was, but he knew that Wheeler had spent a year with Niels Bohr in Copenhagen and was already making a reputation for himself in the field of quantum physics. Feynman was also somewhat surprised by Wheeler's formality at this meeting. Wheeler gave him a fixed schedule for the days they would get together, with strict times for their sessions, and he took out a large pocketwatch and placed it on the table between them to keep strict time for even this first meeting.

Feynman liked Wheeler right away, but he was not comfortable with such formality. At their second meeting, when Wheeler came in and placed his watch on the table, Feynman took out a large cheap pocketwatch he had purchased and, with a straight face, placed it on the table also. The gesture was a calculated gamble—Wheeler might have taken offense—but it worked. Wheeler broke out in laughter, and the two went on to become close colleagues and lifelong friends.

Wheeler developed a distinguished career as one of the foremost authorities on nuclear physics, making theoretical contributions to the study of the atomic nucleus and black holes. He was in many ways the perfect mentor for Feynman, who was interested in electrodynamics and the fundamental problem of the interaction between charged particles and whether such interaction is best treated as "action at a distance" or the action of a field.

Early in their collaborative work, Wheeler decided that it was time that Feynman learned to give a presentation, and he chose the subject of a joint paper on which they had been working. Feynman was frightened at the prospect of giving this colloquium, but Wheeler assured him that the regular seminar schedule would provide a good audience and that he would be there with Feynman to answer any questions.

A few days before the talk, Feynman ran into Professor Eugene Wigner in the hallway. "Feynman," Wigner said, "I think your work with Wheeler is very interesting, so I've invited Russell to the seminar." Henry Russell was a famous astronomer of the time. Wigner continued with more disconcerting news, "I think Professor von Neumann would be interested, so I've asked him." John von Neumann was the most famous mathematician of the time. "Also Professor Pauli will be visiting from Switzerland, so I've invited him, too." Feynman recalled that by this time he was about ready to faint when Wigner added, "Professor Einstein rarely comes to our weekly seminar, but I've invited him 'specially, so he's coming, too." So doctoral candidate Richard P. Feynman gave his first presentation ever before a group that included what he called "the monster minds." The lecture proceeded well, although Feynman recalled that his hands were shaking as he took his notes out from their envelope and that he was so relieved to be able to sit down at the end that he later had no memory of the questions asked after the talk.

As Feynman worked on the final draft of his doctoral thesis, world events encroached on his career. In November of 1941, just a month before the attack on Pearl Harbor, Feynman was told of concerns about Germany building an atomic weapon. He was soon to be on his way to Los Alamos, a place of which he had never heard in the Sangre de Christo mountains of New Mexico.

After a distinguished college career, he had been recruited into the most impressive group of scientists ever to be assembled. His professional future looked very bright, but not all was to be well in his life. He and Arline Greenbaum had been a couple for almost eleven years. Before Feynman had left for Princeton, they had become engaged. Just as he was finally finishing college and the time was right for them to be married, Arline became seriously ill. Her illness was at first misdiagnosed as typhoid fever and then as Hodgkin's disease, but it was at last correctly identified as tuberculosis of the lymphatic system, which was most likely fatal. Feynman's family and friends tried to dissuade him from marrying Arline, given that she was sure to die in a short time. But he would not abandon her. "We were already married in our minds," he told friends. "To leave her now would be like divorcing her." Right after receiving his Ph.D., on June 29, 1942, Richard picked up Arline, only recently out of the hospital, and they drove to Staten Island, where they were married by a justice of the peace. Arline was so ill by this time that she was now confined to hospital care. Before Feynman moved to Los Alamos, he made an agreement with Robert Oppenheimer that Arline would be admitted to a hospital in Albuquerque. Because he did not own a car, he would hitchhike down to Albuquerque to spend weekends with her.

Los Alamos and the Bomb

At the laboratory on the hill, Feynman met a number of men whose names were familiar to him from their papers in *Physical Review*. This group included, of course, the elite of the world's physicists, and Feynman found a number of outstanding mentors in his days at the lab.

One day early in the project, when most of the top-echelon physicists were away, Hans Bethe wanted to talk over an idea he had had. He found Feynman alone in his office and decided to use the young man as a sounding board. A no-holds-barred argument ensued between them during which Feynman, never one to be impressed by authority, called Bethe's ideas crazy. Bethe responded in like manner, but in the end he found the argument stimulating and shortly thereafter requested that Feynman be assigned to his division. For his part, Feynman was impressed with Bethe's analytical powers, his erudition, his integrity, and, almost as important, his sense of humor. After their initial encounter, Bethe and Feynman got along exceeding well. They both loved to play mathematical games, and whenever they had to calculate anything together they would have a race—races that Feynman tells us Bethe usually won.

For most of his stay at Los Alamos, Feynman worked under Bethe's direction, but Oppenheimer also needed a smart assistant whom he could trust with special assignments. Feynman soon became the director's unofficial trouble-shooter, often sent on fact-finding missions or to investigate when some aspect of the project was not proceeding on schedule. Feynman also made many important contributions to the project. He gave a series of lectures on the central issues of bomb design and assembly; he supervised the critical-mass calculations; and he helped compute the effects of various tamper materials in reflecting neutrons back into the reactions. He also contributed to the design of both the gun method and the implosion method of ignition. In addition, he was sent by Oppenheimer to Oak Ridge, Tennessee, to establish safety procedures when it appeared that the unsophisticated handling of uranium materials there could lead to an unplanned explosion. Feynman was, in short, the technical boy wonder of Los Alamos.

But even as he was doing all of this important work, Feynman was also busy establishing his reputation as the "Peck's Bad Boy" of the Los Alamos theoretical division—later to be described as the most eccentric, temperamental, volatile assortment of thinkers and mathematical whizzes ever collected in one place. Feynman developed an astonishing expertise in picking locks and bedeviled the security people by opening classified filing cabinets and leaving mysterious notes in them. He loved parties and dances, at which he sometimes performed on the drums, flirted with every attractive female, and danced like an Arthur Murray instructor. Always the showoff, he delighted in doing math tricks for any captive audience he could find. He once bet his luncheon companions that he could calculate, within sixty seconds and with at least ninety percent accuracy, any problem that could be stated in ten seconds. He usually won these contests until one day his colleagues came up with a problem that required him to know the value of pi to 100 decimal places.

All in all, Feynman made quite an impression. None other than Robert Oppenheimer described him as "by all odds, the most brilliant young physicist here" and "a man of thoroughly engaging character and personality." When Niels Bohr visited Los Alamos, he sought out Feynman to try out new ideas on him because Feynman was the only person there not in awe of Bohr's reputation and would tell him if his ideas were "lousy."

Feynman, during all of this frantic activity on the hill, was leading something of a double life. At work, he seldom spoke of Arline and his concerns for her. But, whenever he could get away for a day or two, he traveled to Albuquerque to see her and bolster her spirits. Her health was failing rapidly, and Richard knew she would certainly die soon. He also knew that any day he might get a call to come to Albuquerque right away, and his usual hitchhiking would not get him there fast enough. So he made an advance arrangement to borrow his dormitory friend's car when the time came. That friend was Klaus Fuchs, later to be shockingly revealed as a Soviet spy.

When that call did come, Feynman arrived at the hospital in Albuquerque only a few hours before Arline died. She had fought a long, courageous struggle, and he had supported her with heartfelt optimism all along. "Keep hanging on," Richard had written to her, "Nothing is certain. We lead a charmed life."

Feynman did his best to conceal his grief over his wife's death. Back at Los Alamos, he would not talk about it, and, when asked about Arline by people who had not heard the news, he replied curtly, "She's dead. And how's the program going?" As he recalled, he did not cry until a number of months later when, at Oak Ridge, he walked past a department store with dresses in the window and thought to himself that Arline would have liked one of them. Hans Bethe, however, saw that he was hurt and sent him home to Far Rockaway on leave. Not until the Trinity test at Alamogordo was scheduled was he called back.

The first man-made nuclear explosion occurred in the early morning hours of July 16, 1945, at a spot in the desert ominously named *Jornada del Muerta* (Dead Man's Trail). Robert Oppenheimer and his formidable team of physicists had done their job and would soon leave their isolated community on the Los Alamos mesa for postwar lives that, for Feynman and many others, would require some significant adjustments.

The Move to Cornell

When the Los Alamos team dispersed, Feynman chose to follow his mentor, Hans Bethe, and accepted a position at Cornell University in Ithaca, New York. The Manhattan Project had afforded Feynman the opportunity to test himself against the top minds in physics, but it involved mostly engineering and technology rather than theoretical science. Now it was time to get back to science.

While he was still a graduate student at Princeton in the early 1940s, Feynman had begun developing a completely new approach to quantum mechanics. The term *quantum mechanics* refers to the description of the behavior of matter in all its details and, in particular, of the happenings on an atomic scale. This behavior of matter at the atomic and subatomic level is not easy to describe nor is it easy to envision. Feynman's method, at its simplest, was a quantum mechanics version of the classical idea that a particle takes the "path of least resistance" in going from point to point.

At Cornell, Feynman went back to developing his early ideas and method. He explained this method in two papers published in 1949, "The Theory of Positrons" and "Space–Time Approach to Quantum Electrodynamics." In those papers, he introduced simple diagrams that act simultaneously as graphical representations of subatomic-particle collisions and as convenient shorthand for the formidable calculations required in predicting the outcome of such collisions. It should be understood that those now famous diagrams were not created in lieu of the arduous mathematics involved, but rather were the product of the detailed calculations. Those diagrams made an important contribution to the field of quantum electrodynamics.

Quantum Electrodynamics

The world of physics can be divided into three principal domains: the very small, the very large, and the intermediate—everything that falls between the other two.

The *domain of the very small* is the world of short-lived particles that are seen in high-energy collisions brought about by accelerators and inside the nuclei of atoms. In this domain, what are known as the strong nuclear forces are dominant. There is not yet any complete theory that explains all phenomena in this domain. Fragments of theories come and go, describing more or less satisfactorily some of the things that experimenters observe, but there are many aspects of this domain that are not understood. Exploration of this domain is underway at the present time both at CERN in Switzerland and the Stanford Linear Accelerator Center (SLAC) in California.

The *domain of the very large* is the physical world: the planets, stars, galaxies, and universe considered as a whole. In this domain, gravity is the dominant force, and Einstein's general relativity is the triumphantly successful theory. Exploration of this cosmological domain is entering new phases today as a result of the Hubble Space Telescope and other sophisticated satellite-based sensors.

Between the very small and the very large, there is the *domain of the intermediate*, the middle ground of physics. This middle ground is an enormous domain, including everything between an atomic nucleus and a planet. It is the domain of everyday human experience, and it is comprised of atoms and electricity; light and sound; gases, liquids, and solids; chairs, tables, and people. The theory called *quantum electrodynamics*, known as QED, covers this middle ground. Its aim is to give a complete and accurate account of all physical processes in the third domain, excluding only the very large and the very small.

Feynman did not invent or discover quantum electrodynamics. That honor goes principally to Paul Adrien Maurice (usually called P. A. M.) Dirac in 1928. What Feynman (along with Julian Schwinger and Shin'ichiro Tomonago) did was reformulate the understanding of quantum electrodynamics and solve the anomalies that were inhibiting the practical use of QED as a theory to explain phenomena in the third domain. It is a remarkable coincidence that Feynman and Schwinger (and, as they later discovered, Tomonago), working from different points of view, arrived at the same solutions to the QED problems at about the same time.

The theory of quantum electrodynamics is a quantum-mechanical theory of the electron and electromagnetism—in other words, a synthesis of Einstein's relativity theory and quantum mechanics. It has been verified by experiment and observation and is now completely accepted by the physics community.

In his book, QED: *The Strange Theory of Light and Matter*, Feynman described the concept as follows: "The theory of quantum electrodynamics describes nature as absurd from the point of view of common sense. And it agrees fully with experiment. So I hope you can accept Nature as She is—absurd." In the following section, we'll see how Feynman devised some ingenious methods for understanding the absurd ways in which the natural world works.

Feynman Diagrams

"Feynman diagrams," as his graphical representations came to be known, proved to be a major contribution to both nuclear theorists and experimenters alike. They are, in effect, a set of tools for handling the mathematical complexities of particle physics, and they have proved to be as useful to the theoretical physicist as circuit diagrams are to an electronics designer. By using these diagrams, physicists can rapidly calculate almost any sort of complex particle collision and at the same time produce a "picture" of those collisions that serves as a handy summary of pages of mathematics. A skeptical Murray Gell-Mann said that the diagrams "give the illusion of understanding what is going on." But as Nobel laureate Julian Schwinger more enthusiastically remarked in 1980, "It was through the use of the so-called Feynman diagrams that Feynman brought calculations to the masses." Although not exactly of "mass" appeal, these "funny little pictures" have indeed become the accepted shorthand of quantum physics.

Feynman diagrams are a refinement of a more general type of graph called *space–time diagrams*. In space–time diagrams, the vertical direction usually represents time, and the horizontal direction represents one-dimensional space. So, for example, if a particle is at rest in space, it will be represented by a vertical line because even though it does not move in space, it does move through time. If the particle also moves in space, its line will be inclined—the greater the inclination of the line, the faster the particle moves. Note that particles can only move forward in time, but can move backward or forward in space.

Space–Time Diagrams

Essentially, Feynman used space–time diagrams to help visualize the interaction that takes place when two electrons move toward each other. Feynman diagrams reinterpret the basic textbook process of electromagnetic repulsion. Two negative charges, electrons, repel. Feynman diagrams illustrate *how* they repel, specifically by an exchange of energy in the form of a photon.

Space–time diagrams are used in physics to picture the interactions between various particles. For each interaction, a diagram can be drawn with which a mathematical expression can then be associated. The mathematical expression gives the probability for that interaction to occur.

Virtual Particles

The diagram shown in the next section shows the interaction, or repulsion, of two electrons by the transfer of a single virtual photon.

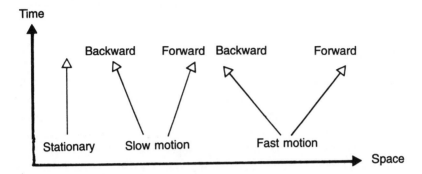

Space–time diagrams Used in relativistic physics to picture interactions be-tween various particles. Note that particles can only move forward (upward) in time, but they can move backward or forward in space. The degree to which the line is inclined toward the horizontal indicates the speed of particle motion.

But what is a *virtual particle*? As mentioned in Chapter Six, Heisenberg showed that there is no way of devising a method of pinpointing the position of a subatomic particle unless one is willing to be quite uncertain about its exact momentum. To calculate both exactly, at the same instant of time, is impossible. In 1930, Einstein took this uncertainty principle one step further when he implied that it is also impossible to reduce the error in measurement of energy without increasing the uncertainty of time during which the measurement can take place.

Although he did not intend it this way, Einstein's version of uncertainty proved useful to quantum physicists because it meant that in subatomic processes, the law of conservation of energy can be violated for extremely brief periods of time, provided all is brought back to the conservational state by the end of those periods. The greater the deviation from conservation, the briefer the time interval allowed. This concept makes it possible to explain certain subatomic phenomena by assuming that particles are produced out of nothing (in defiance of energy-conservation laws) but cease to exist before the time allotted for their detection; so they are only "virtual particles." The theory of virtual particles was worked out independently by Jules Schwinger, Richard Feynman, and the Japanese physicist Shin'ichiro Tomonago. When the three were jointly awarded the Nobel Prize in Physics, it was in part for this contribution.

Feynman Diagrams and Quantum Interaction

Each line in a Feynman diagram corresponds both to a particle and to a specific term in the complex mathematical expression for the probability of this collision. The progress of time is shown upward. One can cover the diagram with a sheet of paper and then draw the paper upward to illustrate the passage of time. A pair of electrons, their paths shown by the solid lines, move toward each other. The electrons are denoted by e– because of their negative charge. At point A, a virtual photon, its path indicated by the wiggly line, is emitted by the left-hand electron, which is then deflected away. At point B, the photon is absorbed by the right-hand electron, which is then deflected away.

Classical physics would say that the electrons exerted a repulsive force upon one another. Quantum physics looks at the interaction in a different way. The concept of force is not used in subatomic physics. In place of the Newtonian idea of force being felt over a distance, there

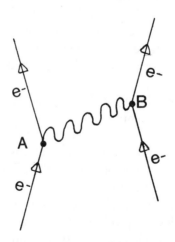

Feynman diagram   The diagram shows two electrons approaching each other, one of them emitting a photon at point A, the other one absorbing it at point B. Both electrons change speed and direction as a result of this exchange.

are instead only interactions between particles, mediated through fields, that is, through other particles. A key feature of this theory is the creation and destruction of particles. In the diagram, for instance, the photon is created in the process of emission at point A and is destroyed when it is absorbed at point B.

This concept is central to understanding QED, and it will help to look at Feynman's contribution in its historical context. You will remember how Einstein used Maxwell's laws of electromagnetism to investigate the properties of a moving body. He found (as shown in Chapter Two) the now well-accepted but peculiar effects of relativity: A moving body becomes shortened; its mass increases; its clocks run slower. But what were the forces involved? Feynman studied the details of electromagnetic force itself. He postulated in QED that the electric repulsion is not caused by some mysterious "action at a distance" as had been supposed. He then concluded that electrical and magnetic forces are the result of charged particles exchanging entities called photons. Photons thus are considered the units of radiation, the quanta that Planck and Einstein had discovered at the turn of the century. In this process, however, photons are not acting as particles of radiation but as units of energy producing an effect. They are exchanged so quickly that, as Heisenberg's uncertainty principle ensures, scientists cannot detect them passing from one body to another.

Feynman developed this concept until the theory could explain all the phenomena of electricity and magnetism. QED, as an example, predicts with accuracy the strength of the electron's magnetic field, a factor that previous theories had invariably gotten wrong.

In quantum physics, all particle interactions can be pictured in space–time diagrams, and each diagram is associated with a mathematical expression that allows one to calculate the probability for the corresponding process to occur. It was Feynman who established the exact correspondence between the diagrams and the mathematical expressions. Similar diagrams can be drawn for other cases in which the electrons swap two or more virtual photons; the mathematical expressions for the probability of these events follow from the diagram.

The arrowhead on the lines is not used, as might be expected, to indicate direction of motion of the particle (which is always forward in time). Instead, the arrowhead is used to distinguish between particles and antiparticles: If it points in the direction of time (upward, in this illustration), it indicates a particle (for example, an electron); if it points in the opposite direction from time (downward in this illustration), it indicates an antiparticle.

Matter and Antimatter

In the early 1930s, the British theorist P. A. M. Dirac postulated the interesting theory that, for each particle, there must exist an *antiparticle*, opposite in electrical charge but equal in mass. Within a few years, his prediction was confirmed by Carl David Anderson's discovery of the electron's antiparticle, called the *positron*, identical to the electron in all respects save that it carries a positive electric charge. Dirac's postulate has since been confirmed for many other types of particles. Therefore, the world of matter is mirrored by a world of antimatter.

Feynman diagrams illustrate two basic concepts of quantum physics: (1) that all interactions involve the creation and destruction of particles, such as the emission and absorption of the virtual photon seen earlier; (2) that there is a basic symmetry between particles and antiparticles—for every particle, there exists an antiparticle with equal mass and opposite charge. In Feynman diagrams, the electron, for example, is usually denoted by *e*–, and its antiparticle, the positron, is usually denoted by *e*+. The photon, having no charge, is its own antiparticle.

It has been shown than a *fundamental particle* such as the electron can be created only if at the same time its own antiparticle is created. Similarly, it can be destroyed only if it encounters one of its own antiparticles.

These rules of quantum physics present something of a problem to cosmologists. For example, if they applied at the time of the Big Bang when the universe was created, what happened to all the antimatter? It is known that the Milky Way consists entirely of matter, except for an occasional antiparticle. Nowhere in the universe is the kind of giant explosion seen that would occur if large amounts of matter and antimatter came together. So far, cosmologists have not been able to explain the disappearance of the antimatter that must have been created during the Big Bang.

Despite its incompleteness, Feynman's interpretation of quantum electrodynamics was a major contribution to understanding electromagnetic interactions in quantum terms. His professional reputation growing, Feynman was ready for new worlds to conquer.

California Institute of Technology

After five years at Cornell, Feynman concluded that he should leave. Bethe would always be number one at Cornell, and Feynman needed fresh fields and a new audience.

He found both in the affluent southern California city of Pasadena—ten Cadillac-convertible miles from downtown Los Angeles—where a relatively new university, California Institute of Technology, was rapidly coming to prominence in the sciences.

The first thing Feynman did after accepting his new appointment to the faculty at Caltech was to a take a year's sabbatical. This was, of course, part of the deal that had lured him away from Cornell, and he took full advantage of it. He went to Brazil, participated in Rio de Janeiro's *Carneval*, drank too much, picked up women on the Copacabana beach, and learned to play samba music on the drums well enough to join a local band. During this trip, he found that he was enjoying drinking too much and swore off alcohol for good.

Despite all of his social activity, he was not out of touch with science during this sabbatical, as his extensive correspondence on *meson theory* with Enrico Fermi at the University of Chicago showed. (*Mesons* are one of the two classes of *hadrons*—the other being *baryons*—that make up the fundamental particles of matter; they are part of quark theory described in Chapter Eight.) During Feynman's sabbatical, an apparently envious Fermi wrote, "I wish I could also refresh my ideas by swimming off Copacabana."

Marriage to Mary Lou

After a ten months' stay in Brazil, Feynman returned to Caltech, where he had decided to stay permanently. He had become tired of the bachelor life, and some of his close friends say that he was never the ladies' man he pretended to be anyway. Shortly after he returned to Pasadena in 1952, he proposed to Mary Lou Bell, his platinum blonde girlfriend from Neodesha, Kansas, whom he had met at Cornell and had dated for some time. Theirs was not to be a happy marriage for either of them. One source of tension was that Mary Lou always wanted Richard to act and dress in a dignified manner, befitting her image of a college professor. Apparently he tried. His friends said that they could always tell if Mary Lou was around because that would be the only time he would be wearing a tie. A more seriously aggravating problem was that Mary Lou apparently was not fond of scientists, physicists in particular. Feynman's colleague at Caltech, Murray Gell-Mann, recalled that when he and his then wife Margaret invited the Feynmans to dinner, Mary Lou claimed that she lost the invitation. On another occasion, as Richard and Mary Lou sat down to dinner, she said, "I forgot to tell you, but you had a telephone call this afternoon. Some old bore is in town and wanted you to join him for dinner." According to Feynman's recollections, she had not got it quite right. The "old bore" she referred to was Niels Bohr, who was visiting, and Feynman missed a chance to talk to him, which he was not at all happy about. After just four years, the marriage was clearly not working, and they were divorced in 1956.

Feynman the Teacher

As a teacher at Caltech, Feynman received mixed reviews. On the one hand, there were those undergraduate students who took his uncredited course called Physics X and who later remembered these unstructured seminars as the most unforgettable intellectual experience of their education. On the other hand, he clearly shirked ordinary teaching duties, avoided graduate students who sought his help on their thesis work, and had little patience for guiding students on their research problems. Even his now famous *Feynman Lectures on Physics* were not totally successful. Starting in 1961 and for the next two years, Feynman presented this notorious introductory physics course at Caltech. Freshmen, sophomores, graduate students, and even fellow faculty members struggled to follow Feynman's thoughts. Some found the course inspiring, but many freshmen and sophomores dropped out. Many college professors who adopted the books made from these lectures (they were edited transcripts of the course) found them too difficult for the intended readers. (Recently, a selection of these lectures was published under the title *Six Easy Pieces*. They are stimulating and inspiring reading, but easy they are not.)

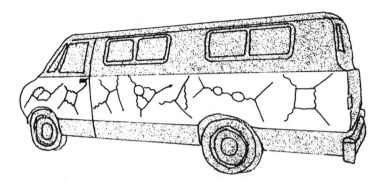

Feynman's van The van, replete with Feynman's diagrams, advertises its owner's presence and was well known on the Caltech campus.

As a lecturer, most students found Feynman fascinating even if difficult to follow. None other than the eminent historian of physics, C. P. Snow, graded Feynman highly as a lecturer, but he did add that with Feynman's New York cab driver's accent, his colloquial language, his gesticulations, and his practice of striding about in front of the blackboard, watching him was not unlike watching Groucho Marx do an imitation of a great scientist.

Despite his sometimes lackadaisical work with graduate students and his antics in class, Feynman did take his responsibilities as a teacher of science quite seriously in a certain sense. "Science," he once said, "is a way to teach how something gets to be known, what is not known, to what extent things are known (for nothing is known, absolutely), how to handle doubt and uncertainty, what rules of evidence are, how to think about things so that judgments can be made, how to distinguish truth from fraud, and from show." This explanation revealed how much he cared about conveying what science is and should be, and it is about as nice a summing up of the subject of teaching science as one could wish for.

Gweneth Howarth

In the summer of 1958, Feynman was in Geneva, Switzerland, to present a joint paper he had written with Murray Gell-Mann, which was a survey of the then current status of elementary particle physics and in some ways provided a basis for Gell-Mann's later definitive work in this area. After presenting the paper, Feynman went to the beach at Lake Geneva to relax. There he spotted an attractive young woman in a polka-dot bikini, and he struck up a conversation with her. She was Gweneth Howarth, she was from a small village in England, and she was working as an *au pair*, taking care of the children of an English family living in Geneva. She had an adventurous turn of mind, and her grand plan was to work her way around the world. Australia was to be the next stop, before returning to England to settle down.

Feynman told her about California and what a great place it was, and eventually he persuaded her to accept his offer of employment as a housekeeper for him in Altadena. It took a bit of doing, but eventually he secured a visa for the young adventure lover, and she took up residence in her own room at the back of Feynman's house. They were romantically involved but they were not living together in the usual sense of that term—they both dated other people, and as Gweneth said later, "I had no intention of marrying him."

Richard, however, had other ideas. He had already told at least one friend that he had met a beautiful English girl in Geneva and that he intended to marry her. And marry they eventually did at an Episcopalian ceremony at the Huntington Hotel in Pasadena on September 24, 1960—about two years after their first meeting.

This turned out to be a much happier marriage. Gweneth was quite content to be the wife of the "great scientist" and was tolerant of his more flamboyant public behavior. Feynman's good friend Richard Davies said that Gweneth gets short shrift in most accounts of Feynman's life—that in fact she was the truly adventurous one of the couple and pushed him into various trips to exotic locales. Davies also stated that on separate occasions Feynman told his sister Joan and Davies himself that, "Gweneth is smarter than I am."

The Nobel Prize

When Feynman first learned that he had been awarded the Nobel Prize, he considered rejecting it—he did not like awards and ceremony—but he was persuaded that in so doing he would attract more attention than if he just accepted it. Feynman's reluctant attitude toward the prize was not due to a lack of pride about the work he had done. Speaking of the insight that lead to the work that earned him the prize, he once remarked, "It was so goddam beautiful, it was gleaming."

A charming indication of just how well-liked Feynman was by his students was shown when, after news of the award got around the campus, a group of students draped the top of the college administration building with a huge banner proclaiming:

"WIN BIG, RPF"

Despite his original reservations, Feynman apparently thoroughly enjoyed the entire Swedish Nobel award ceremony, as did Gweneth. What Feynman enjoyed the most was the students' party held after the king's dinner. It was, of course, less formal and there was dancing, in which, as usual, he delighted.

After the award ceremonies in Stockholm, Feynman went on to Geneva, where he had been invited to give a lecture by his old Los Alamos colleague Victor Weisskopf, then director of CERN. He appeared in a new tailored suit and tie and told the audience that he had learned formality in Sweden. The audience laughed and shouted their disapproval. Weisskopf led a revolt by standing up, tearing off his jacket, and shouting "No, No." Feynman said that this reaction woke him up, and he quickly took off his own jacket and tie and gave the lecture in shirt sleeves the way he usually did, back to being Richard Feynman again.

Challenger Disaster

In his work at Caltech in the years after the prize, Feynman turned his attention to the application of theoretical quantum electrodynamics to nuclear forces and to high-energy particle physics. Working with Murray Gell-Mann, he reformulated the understanding of the interaction between fundamental particles in terms of a general type of interaction that can be applied universally. Toward the end of his career, Feynman also conducted extensive pioneering work in low-temperature physics, with particular emphasis on the properties of liquid helium and superconductivity.

Important as Feynman's work in his later years was, there is another contribution he made that was much more public and that reveals the strength of character and integrity of the man. Feynman was appointed to the Presidential Commission assembled to investigate the tragic explosion of the space shuttle *Challenger* on January 28, 1986, just seconds after liftoff, that killed all seven crew members. A shocked nation, many of whom had witnessed the tragedy on television, wanted an explanation of what had happened. The Commission, headed by William Rogers, a former Secretary of State, was appointed to carry out that task. Most of the Commission members had ties to NASA and were not motivated to be critical of the space agency. Feynman, on the other hand, had no ties to NASA, and he took his role as investigator quite seriously. He was determined to discover what had happened, and he did not care about any official "party line" with which the rest of the commission might come up.

With the reluctant approval of the Commission chairman, Feynman conducted his own investigation. He arranged a series of private briefings over a weekend at NASA's Washington headquarters. He concentrated his attention on engine problems and in particular on the long history of difficulties with the O-ring seals under low temperature conditions. Feynman's colleague on the commission, General Donald J. Kutyna, wanted to bring the problem of potential loss of O-ring resiliency out into the open, but he wanted to do it without jeopardizing his sources of information within NASA. He accomplished this by helping to focus Feynman's attention on the issue. Feynman, following up on Kutyna's lead, requested O-ring test data from NASA, but he was sent irrelevant documents. Refusing to be put off, Feynman conducted his own experiments in his hotel room the night before the scheduled televised Commission hearing.

At the hearing the next day, Feynman, using ice water and a rubber O-ring sample, demonstrated with stunning simplicity to a national television audience of millions the physics of the shuttle disaster. He proved that cold temperatures could, and tragically in this case probably did, impair the resiliency of the shuttle's O-rings, causing a leak in booster fuel that ignited and resulted in the explosion. With this dramatic performance, he convincingly solved the mystery of the *Challenger* explosion, rattled the Washington bureaucracy down to their well-polished black shoes, and shattered the official silence on one of the most disturbing scandals of the 1980s.

Commission member General Kutyna (now retired) told how he

and Feynman first teamed up. An initial get-together had been held at the State Department offices of William Rogers, where the chairman had stressed the importance of not leaking information to the press. "That evening, as we walked out down the steps of the State Department—[former] Secretary Rogers, of course, had a large black limousine come and pick him up; Neil Armstrong had a big limo pick him up; even Sally Ride had a limousine pick her up—Feynman looked at me, with my two stars on my shoulder, and said, "Where's your limo?" I told him, 'Two stars don't get a limo in Washington. I ride the subway.' He put his arm around me, and he said, 'Kutyna, any general that rides the subway can't be all bad!' And that started a warm relationship between the two of us."

Kutyna decided to tutor Feynman in the ways of Washington bureaucratic procedures. The public hearings were almost scripted in advance; they were bland, unsensational, and there were to be no surprises. The executive sessions were much more productive, but they were under the tight control of the chairman. Feynman insisted on talking to the technical people directly, and a reluctant Rogers gave him permission to do so. It was during these briefings that Feynman learned of the history of trouble the shuttle launching had encountered.

At Kutyna's suggestion, Feynman looked into the effect of cold on rubber seals. They found that the temperature at the time of the *Challenger* launch had been 29°F and that the coldest previous launch had been at 53°F. Feynman knew, of course, that rubber gets stiff and loses resiliency under cold conditions. On February 11, the day of the ice-water experiment, Chairman Rogers was overheard telling Neil Armstrong in the men's room that "Feynman is becoming a real pain in the ass."

In the end, Feynman refused to sign off on the Commission's bland final report unless it included an appendix documenting the results of his O-ring research. Chairman Rogers had little choice but to allow Feynman his appendix—although he did his best to see that it was not widely distributed. The Commission's full report was published in five volumes, which were not broadly disseminated. The much more widely available summary version that was sent to the press did not contain Feynman's Appendix F. Despite this attempt to censor Feynman's findings, his dramatic television demonstration had made a stunning impression, and the fact that the O-rings had probably caused the disaster had become common knowledge.

Last Days

Feynman developed abdominal cancer in the 1970s, and, after years struggling against it, he died in 1988 at the age of sixty-nine. A story is told that when he was dying, he asked his physician what his chances were and was told, "It's impossible to talk about the probability of a single event." Feynman replied, "From one professor to another, it is possible if it's a future event."

The degree of esteem and affection in which Feynman was held by both the students and faculty at Caltech had been strikingly attested to several years before. During surgery in the fall of 1981, Feynman's aorta split, and he needed massive blood transfusions. Some seventy pints of blood were required, and much of it was donated by Caltech faculty and students. This affection was expressed powerfully again upon word of his death when the students hung a huge vertical sign on the side of the Millikan Library building. In large letters, it said:

> We
> Love
> You
> DICK.

Science is considerably richer for Richard Feynman's contributions. He was irreverent, earthy, insatiably curious, and in love with life. He once summed up his efforts to understand nature by saying, "Nature is a great chess game being played by Gods, which we are privileged to watch. The rules of the game are what we call fundamental physics, and understanding these rules is our goal."

But what might be a more fitting epitaph is a line found written on the blackboard in his office after his death: "What I cannot create, I do not understand."

Although Feynman would have denied it, his was one of the most extraordinary minds of our time.

Chapter Eight

MURRAY GELL-MANN

Now this, O monks, is noble truth that leads to the cessation of pain; this is the Noble Eightfold Way: namely, right views, right intention, right speech, right action, right living, right effort, right mindfulness, right concentration.

Aphorism attributed to Buddha,
about the appropriate path to Nirvana

What does the Buddhists' search for enlightenment and bliss have to do with the hard science of physics? It is the physicists' challenging pursuit not only to understand the cosmos—the behavior of the largest

213

objects in the universe such as the planets, stars, and galaxies—but also to search for the smallest objects, the fundamental unit from which all matter is made. This search led scientists to the concept of the atom, first proposed by the Greek scientists Leucippus and Democritus in 450 B.C.

The atom was long accepted as the one indivisible entity of matter until it was discovered, around the turn of the twentieth century, that the atom itself had an internal structure consisting of electrons and a nucleus. In examining the electrons and the nucleus, scientists discovered that electrons are themselves elementary—they cannot be broken down into still smaller constituent parts. However, scientists suspected that the nucleus was another matter (pun intended). The nucleus, they eventually found, is comprised of two components: neutrons and protons.

Was that it then? Were electrons, neutrons, and protons the fundamental units of matter? The hunt for the basic building blocks of nature is the story line for this chapter, and the major protagonist will be the brilliant theoretical physicist Murray Gell-Mann, now with the Santa Fe Institute in New Mexico. In addition to theoretical physicists like Gell-Mann, Richard Feynman, and George Zweig, the tale includes a large supporting cast of experimental physicists. This is the story of the field of particle physics, the study of the smallest known structures of matter and energy.

Just as exploration of the cosmos requires tools and equipment, specifically telescopes and satellite-borne sensors, so does exploration of particle physics require the use of specialized equipment, especially the devices known as accelerators. Sometimes called the largest and most expensive pieces of laboratory equipment in the world, accelerators (or atom smashers, as they were once popularly called) have evolved into gigantic, powerful machines that fire protons, electrons, and other subatomic particles at nearly the speed of light through vacuum tunnels that are miles long. There, the subatomic particles ultimately smash into one another, shattering into component particles. The resultant short-lived new particles are, of course, too small to be seen, but by using sensitive instrumentation, physicists can record their tracks. The patterns, lengths, and shapes of these tracks provide clues about the nature and properties of the newly discovered particles, some of which live only a few billionths of a second. In effect, accelerators recreate the high-energy collisions that occurred during the first moments after the Big Bang, when the building blocks of matter were first created.

On our tour of the strange world of particle physics we will encounter "strangeness," the eightfold way, quarks, and finally the standard model, physicists' best current explanation of the world. Murray Gell-Mann is the guide.

Prodigy

A prodigy is a child having extraordinary talents or ability. As a child, Murray Gell-Mann fit the definition of *prodigy* and then some. Born in New York in 1929, when he was only three he was taught to read (from a Sunshine cracker box) by his twelve-year-old brother, Ben, and he has never slowed from that fast start. Gell-Mann credits his older brother with much of his early education. The family lived in New York City, mainly in Manhattan, and the two young explorers roamed the city's parks and museums. Ben introduced Murray to bird watching, natural history, botanizing, and insect collecting—all of which became subjects of lifelong interest. When not on nature walks, Ben and Murray visited art museums, especially those that contained archaeological material, and the two boys even learned to read some inscriptions in Egyptian hieroglyphics. They also studied Latin, French, and Spanish, primarily for the challenge. Gell-Mann's lifelong fascination with languages can be traced in part to those early excursions.

Both Ben and Murray were prodigious readers, and Murray remembers being particularly impressed by the science fiction stories of H. G. Wells. Music was also not neglected, and the two brothers even tried to teach themselves to play the piano. They attended concerts when they could, but because the family was not affluent, radio was the prime source by which they learned about classical music.

Young Murray's precociousness was quickly recognized, and when he was eight years old he was transferred from his local public school to Columbia Grammar School, a school for gifted children that included high-school-level grades. He graduated in 1944 at the age of fifteen. In high school, Gell-Mann especially enjoyed playing soccer, but surprisingly found physics, at this level, "terribly boring." Gell-Mann's father pushed his son toward the physical sciences and mathematics anyway. An immigrant from Austria, Arthur Gell-Mann was a serious linguist who had taught himself to speak English without a trace of accent. He later formed a school of languages to teach other immigrants to speak English without a foreign accent. Speaking English (or any of the other five languages he knew) with extraordinary precision and accuracy has been a characteristic of Murray Gell-Mann noted by many journalists who have interviewed him over the years.

In addition to languages, Gell-Mann's father was interested in the sciences and taught himself mathematics, physics, and astronomy. Arthur Gell-Mann encouraged his son's interests in mathematics and prompted him toward engineering as a career. Murray resisted. As he related in his partly autobiographical book *The Quark and The Jaguar: Adventures in the Simple and the Complex*, he declared that he would rather starve than become an engineer. In his senior year in high school, Gell-Mann filled out an application form for admission to Yale. In it, he had to name the subject in which he would major. On his own, he would have chosen archaeology or linguistics, but his father, seeing little financial reward in either field, objected. They eventually compromised on physics, in part because Murray figured he could always change his major later. Physics was, ironically, the only subject in which Gell-Mann had done poorly in high school, but that was because he had been bored by it.

As an undergraduate at Yale, Gell-Mann found advanced physics far more interesting, and before he got around to changing his major, he was hooked on the theoretical aspects of relativity and quantum mechanics. In his own words, Gell-Mann "just happened to become a physicist."

Massachusetts Institute of Technology

After receiving his bachelor degree in 1948, he enrolled as a graduate student at the Massachusetts Institute of Technology (MIT). Like the subject of physics, MIT had not been his first choice. Gell-Mann had applied to several Ivy League graduate schools, but Yale would only accept him in mathematics, Harvard would take him if he paid full tuition, and Princeton would not take him at all. As Gell-Mann told the story, he then halfheartedly applied to MIT. He heard back almost immediately from the distinguished physicist Victor Weisskopf, of whom, oddly enough, he had never heard. Gell-Mann accepted an offer from Weisskopf to be his assistant, although with something less than full enthusiasm. MIT, after all, was known as a school for technical nerds, and Gell-Mann did not consider himself in this light. The joke he told later was that the alternatives did not convert; that is, he would try MIT first and suicide second, whereas the other way around would not work. In 1948, close to his nineteenth birthday, he joined Weisskopf at MIT.

The field of quantum electrodynamics was coming to the fore of physics at this time, and Professor Weisskopf told Gell-Mann to study the published papers of Richard Feynman, Jules Schwinger, and Freeman Dyson. Gell-Mann was not impressed with any of them, but then as now Gell-Mann was not easy to impress. He did recognize the originality and importance of the papers, but neither the math nor, in Feynman's case, the method of expressing ideas suited his demanding standards. Keep in mind that Gell-Mann was only a doctoral candidate at the time and was not yet officially in the game.

Strangeness

After receiving his doctoral degree in 1952, Gell-Mann left MIT and spent a year as a postdoc at the Institute for Advanced Studies at Princeton. He then joined Enrico Fermi at the University of Chicago. The fact that Gell-Mann was accepted by Fermi's research group is an indication of the promise he showed as a student. His status was greatly enhanced in 1953 when he proposed that certain subatomic particles possessed a quality that he called *strangeness*, a concept that attracted worldwide attention. Strangeness was a key step in bringing some theoretical order into the chaotic scene that was particle physics at that time.

Strangeness is defined as the property of elementary particles that governs the speed at which they decay. How does such an odd word used to describe a concept of physics fit in with the nomenclature of particle physics? Both *strange* and *degrees of strangeness* seem far too colloquial and fuzzy to be terms used in physics, which is supposed to be a hard science, not amenable to vague or nonspecific terminology. But the first particle physicists were exploring entirely new worlds, and they were forced to invent a new language—or borrow words from everyday language and use them in an original way—in order to talk to each other about their work. New particles behaving in an unpredictable manner could have just as easily been called *unruly* particles, but *strangeness* instead became the accepted terminology.

The idea of strangeness came to Gell-Mann because particle physicists had discovered that some of the particles created in their colliders were not behaving as expected. They seemed to take a much longer time to decay than had been predicted. They had been created by forces called *strong interactions*, and it was thought they should break down by these same forces, and in the same amount of time. Instead, they stayed around a lot longer. These amounts of time are fractions of billionths of seconds, but in the subatomic world this is a significant difference. Physicists thought the behavior of these particles was strange, so Gell-Mann decided to make it official and call them by that nomenclature.

Gell-Mann explained the unexpected decay rates of these new particles by showing that their energy states differed according to how each particle spun, like a tiny planet, on its axis. The energies he described and measured for the first time led to an explanation of the longer life expectancy of the strange particles.

Using his strangeness formulations (which were also proposed independently by the Japanese physicist Kazuhiko Nishijima), Gell-Mann successfully gave detailed predictions of numerous decay events of strange particles, as well as prophesying the existence of as yet undiscovered particles.

The Eightfold Way

By 1955, Gell-Mann had risen to the position of Associate Professor at the University of Chicago. He was only twenty-six, but he felt the time had come to move on. He visited Caltech for talks with its top physicist, Richard Feynman. The two native New Yorkers got along well, and Gell-Mann soon accepted an offer to join the faculty. He became a full professor in 1956 at the age of twenty-seven. This marked the beginning of a long and productive association with Caltech, during which time he proposed the oddly designated *eightfold way* and later the whimsically named, but vitally important, *quark hypothesis*.

Applied to particle physics, the eightfold way was Gell-Mann's answer to the particle population explosion of the 1950s. The first attempt to bring order out of the proliferation of new particles being discovered was to try to classify them according to their weight. The heavier ones, such as the proton and the neutron, were called *hadrons*, and the light ones, such as the electron, were called *leptons*. The hadrons were divided into the *baryons* and *mesons*, the mesons being of medium weight. This classification system helped at first, but problems arose. When the baryon population continued to expand, some new method of organization had to be developed.

Gell-Mann determined that he could group the known particles into families of eight particles with like characteristics. Each of the particles within the family had the same spin and baryon number, and they all had approximately the same mass. This method of classifying particles was called the *eightfold way* primarily because Gell-Mann chose to call it by that name, but also because it predicts that many hadrons can be grouped in sets of eight. The name is also a whimsical homage to the Buddhist path to Nirvana, and it is the first, but not the last, example of the fanciful nomenclature favored by Gell-Mann.

Unfortunately, the term encouraged the notion, popular in the 1960s, that particle physics and Eastern mysticism were related—that if you sat on the floor crosslegged and hummed you would gain insight into the complexities of nature. Gell-Mann called this idea "rubbish" and said his allusion to Buddhism was just a little joke that some people took too seriously.

At any rate, the eightfold way was the first successful attempt to show the fundamental connection between particles in different families, and it was developed independently by Murray Gell-Mann and Yuval Ne'eman, a physicist at Imperial College, London. The eightfold way bears the same logical relation to elementary particles that the well-known periodic table does to chemical elements.

The comparison between the eightfold way and the periodic table helped to make Ne'eman's and Gell-Mann's contribution more understandable and, therefore, is worth a brief review. During the late 1890s, the known number of chemical elements was proliferating because of so many discoveries, very much as the known number of particles was to proliferate in the 1950s. New elements seemed to be discovered every few months and the total had approached the hundred mark when the Russian chemist Dmitri Mendeleev (1834–1907) devised a table that arranged elements into horizontal rows (called *periods*) according to the elements' atomic number (number of protons in the nucleus) and into vertical columns according to related groups. Thus, the periodic table of the elements displays all the elements in such a way as to show the similarities in certain families or groups of elements. In addition to being a convenient way to display the elements, the periodic table also revealed gaps in the list of elements that correctly predicted the existence of elements that were discovered at a later date.

In the late 1950s, it was discovered that when protons and other subatomic particles were fired at each other in accelerators, new particles seemed to be created, not fragments of protons but brothers and sisters of protons, each as complex as the proton itself. These early experiments were producing such a profusion of new particles that physicists had to carry a notebook around to keep track. The search for fundamental particles was in a state of confusion. Science writer Jeremy Bernstein, writing in *American Scholar*, provided a glimpse of the frustration in the scientific community when he reported that he overheard J. Robert Oppenheimer suggest awarding a Nobel Prize to the first physicist who did *not* discover a new particle in a given year.

Gell-Mann, the scientific man-for-all-seasons, sought to explain the relationship between all known particles. He and Dr. Yuval Ne'eman, working independently, were able to group particles into families called *multiplets*. Each multiplet consisted of particles sharing common behavioral characteristics. In an effort to explain this approach without the mathematics, science writers at the time sometimes used the analogy of the numerous animals in a zoo. What Gell-Mann did was similar to turning a particle jungle into a particle zoo; that is, he looked at all the animals (particles) and decided which seemed related to one another. Ultimately, he found that there were five major categories of "animals," and he placed them in five huge cages—super multiplets. That completed, Gell-Mann noticed that some of the cages were short an animal or two, compared with the other cages. This in turn led to the ability to predict the existence of certain particles that had not yet been discovered.

This schematization was quite similar, if far more complex mathematically, to Mendeleev's achievement with the periodic table of the elements. Just as in Mendeleev's case with new elements, new particles were discovered because physicists theorized, based on Gell-Mann's hypothesis, that they had to exist. Taming the particle zoo was a major achievement in physics and, along with his previous contributions clarifying strangeness, moved Gell-Mann to the top rank of the world's physicists.

The Feynman–Gell-Mann Contrast

Caltech now had two luminaries: Murray Gell-Mann and Richard Feynman. A comparison of Caltech's two star physicists is revealing about both personalities. Whereas Richard Feynman was resolutely informal, most often teaching in his shirtsleeves, using colloquial English, and avoiding literary references of any kind, Gell-Mann was almost always seen in jacket and tie, expressed himself in precise sentences and accents, and often used esoteric cultural references, so much so that he risked losing his less-well-educated audiences.

At Caltech, Gell-Mann lunched at the Atheneum faculty club, where a special well-appointed table was reserved for him. Feynman most often preferred the so-called "Greasies" college cafeteria, where he could lunch while swapping stories with the grad students and postdocs.

A good feel for the contrast in their styles is revealed by the following comments on the field of psychoanalysis, for which neither showed much respect. Feynman put his opinion succinctly and amusingly. "Anyone who goes to a psychoanalyst," he said, "should have his head examined." Gell-Mann as usual expressed his views more elegantly and more exactly but no less skeptically. "I believe," he said, "that there is probably a considerable amount of truth in the body of lore developed by psychoanalysis, but that it does not constitute a science at the present time precisely because it is not falsifiable."

The two were colleagues, friends, and sometimes friendly rivals. In the 1960s, Feynman and Gell-Mann collaborated to create an important theory of the so-called *weak interaction*, which explains why nuclear particles sometimes decay by emitting electrons (or positrons) and neutrinos. One story nicely conveys the tone of their friendly sparring: During an argument over one aspect of the weak interaction theory, Feynman threatened to start spelling Gell-Mann's name without the hyphen; Gell-Mann promptly countered with the threat of inserting one in Feynman (Feyn-man).

Quarks

Fruitful as his collaboration with Feynman was, Gell-Mann's work was taking him into new areas, very much on his own path. Attempting to refine the eightfold way system of classification led him and his collaborators to the conclusion that some of the fundamental particles of the atom could be better understood if they were made up of even smaller components, an idea that lead to the concept of *quarks*.

Quarks are now accepted as the basic and fundamental building block of all matter—more fundamental than the proton and the neutron, once thought to be *the* elementary particles. (Electrons are still considered fundamental.) The original quark hypothesis was independently proposed in 1963 by Murray Gell-Mann and George Zweig. They postulated that all of the properties of the many particles could be better understood if these particles were built up from other, even more elementary, particles. Gell-Mann named these new hypothetical entities *quarks*, while Zweig called them *aces*. Because Gell-Mann's arguments about the existence of the particles were generally more persuasive, his nomenclature caught on.

The story of how Gell-Mann came up with the odd name *quark* is an interesting diversion. He recalls that he decided that a sound like "kwork" (pronounced to rhyme with "cork") might do as the tag for the new particle. Then, while rereading James Joyce's novel *Finnegan's Wake*, Gell-Mann came across the phrase "three quarks for muster mark" and decided to adopt Joyce's spelling of the word that each of them, separately, had coined. As used by Joyce, the term does not rhyme with "cork," but, on the other hand, the number three fit perfectly with the way quarks occur in nature. Gell-Mann decided to use the term in spite of the pronunciation disputes.

At the time he named his hypothesized fundamental particle in a two-page paper introducing his theory, Gell-Mann had little confidence in the theory. For example, he did not try to publish this paper in *Physics Review*, the usual medium for the exchange of ideas in the field, because he did not think it would be accepted. Rather, he published his ideas in *Physics Letters*, a journal published by CERN, the European Organization for Nuclear Research. Gell-Mann knew that the publishers of *Physics Letters* were looking for papers and might not be too critical. He might have given his hypothetical triplets the somewhat whimsical name at least in part because he thought only a few scientists would be paying attention.

In a still further diversion, I would like to offer a possible derivation of the term to explain what Joyce himself may have meant by the word. The line in Joyce's book is uttered by seagulls, as he puts it "shrillgleescreaming" above Howth Castle, and it is quite possible that Joyce meant that the quarks bestowed on Muster Mark below were bird droppings. Like much of Joyce, and practically all of *Finnegan's Wake*, this derivation is open to interpretation, but it seems to me to be within the realm of possibility that Murray Gell-Mann had made this interpretation too and was having a little fun by using the word. Gell-Mann's own story is that he had been enjoying paging through the book for years trying to understand bits and pieces of it, in particular the new words that Joyce invented. "It took Joyce seventeen years to write it," Gell-Mann has said, "so why shouldn't it take us at least seventeen years to read it?"

Gell-Mann also commented that he could easily have followed tradition and concocted "proper, pompous names for things, based on Greek. I know how to do that. But usually they were based on ideas that turned out to be wrong: *Proton*, for example, meaning first; *Atom*, meaning uncuttable. All these things turned out to be wrong! So I figured it would be better to come up with something playful."

Playful or no, Gell-Mann's terminology is nowadays accepted in all physics textbooks.

The original quark hypothesis called for three types, or flavors, of quarks: the *up*, the *down*, and the *strange* (*u*, *d*, and *s*). All ordinary matter can be constructed from just the *u* and *d* quarks. The *s* quark was added to explain certain particles created by high-energy events that have the strangeness property of existing for longer periods of time than predicted. One of the noteworthy features of quarks is that they carry an electric charge that is a fraction of the charge carried by the electron (usually designated by *e*), which was previously considered the fundamental unit of charge. The *u* quark carries a charge of $+2/3$, and the *d* quark a charge of $-1/3$.

Quark theory postulated that the protons and neutrons of the nucleus of the atoms are made up of quarks. The proton is made of two *u* quarks and one *d* quark; its total charge is then $2/3 + 2/3 - 1/3$, or 1.

Similarly, the uncharged neutron is composed of one *u* quark and two *d* quarks.

Structure Within the Atom

The basic structure of the atom was reconceived with the introduction of quarks, and further refinements to the structure were soon required as the experimentalists discovered still more new particles. In 1974, Burton Richter and Samuel Ting simultaneously discovered the J/psi particle. The properties exhibited by this particle required the postula-

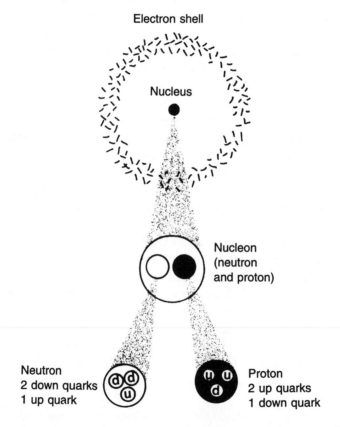

Electron shell

Nucleus

Nucleon
(neutron
and proton)

Neutron
2 down quarks
1 up quark

Proton
2 up quarks
1 down quark

Subatomic structure   Atoms consist of an electron or electrons orbiting a nucleus. The nucleus is composed of protons and neutrons, which are in turn composed of quarks.

tion of a fourth quark, which was given the whimsical name *charmed*, or *c*, quark. Later the *bottom*, or *b*, quark was added. Finally the *top*, or *t*, quark was theorized in order to create a complete hypothetical picture. The term *charmed quark* was the subject of numerous comments at the time.

A whimsical reader of the *New York Times* once wrote a letter asking the late Walter Sullivan, their science reporter and editor, what a charmed quark was and if they made good pets? This was Mr. Sullivan's reply:

"With regards to your recent inquiry as to what charms the quarks, it is the imagination of theoretical physicists that charms them.

"You inquired as to the cost. The best bargain is the mating of a charmed quark with a charmed antiquark. The cost ranges from 3 to 5 billion electron volts.

"Where can you buy such an object? The people at Stanford or Brookhaven might sell you one; but, because they survive less than a millionth of a second, special measures would be necessary to get it home before it vanishes."

Properties of Quarks

Quarks	Mass (GeV*)	Charge
Up	0.378	$+2/3$
Down	0.336	$-1/3$
Strange	0.540	$-1/3$
Charmed	1.500	$+2/3$
Bottom	4.720	$-1/3$
Top	174.000	$+2/3$

*GeV = Gigaelectron volts—or billion (10^9) electron volts.
It might seem strange that mass is measured in volts unless you remember that Einstein showed that mass and energy are equivalent and can be equated one to the other or converted one to the other by the formula $E = mc^2$.

In developing the theory that led to an orderly explanation of the relationships among the particles, Gell-Mann established some rules of quark behavior. Quarks, which are heavy, can stick together in one of two possible ways: either in quark triads or in quark/antiquark pairs. The triads produce heavier particles called *baryons*, which include the neutron and proton, the heaviest particles in the atomic nucleus. The quark/antiquark pairs make up the particles now called mesons.

Quantum Chromodynamics (QCD)

With time, the quark theory became more complex, and this complexity required still more in the way of terminology. The theorists, principally Gell-Mann, were up to the challenge. First, they postulated that each flavor, or type, of quark was actually three quarks. This property they called *color*. Each of the six postulated quarks can have any one of three colors, usually called red, blue, and green. *Color*, as the physicists used the word, has nothing to do with the usual meaning of the term. Quarks would not appear to be red or blue if they were visible. Color is a property of quarks, such as electric charge, that enables them to join together to form particles such as the proton. The theory behind the color force is called *quantum chromodynamics* (QCD). Gell-Mann named this theory by using the Greek root *chromo* meaning color.

Nobel Prize in Physics

Recognition of his accomplishments in elementary particle research and worldwide fame came to Murray Gell-Mann in 1969 when King Gustaf VI of Sweden presented him with the Nobel Prize for Physics in the traditional elegant ceremony in Stockholm. Gell-Mann was forty years old.

He had been appointed Robert Andrews Millikan Professor at Caltech in 1967 and was now at the peak of his career.

He was married at that time to the former J. Margaret Dow, and they had two children, Lisa and Nicholas. He told reporters at the time of his award that he enjoyed skiing, mountain climbing, and studying wildlife. Asked what he intended to do with his Nobel prize money, a question often asked by reporters (possibly in order to avoid getting into the science), he said that he would like to buy a small stretch of wild land somewhere so he could get away from big-city life.

In the glare of press attention that followed the Nobel prize, Gell-Mann revealed an arrogant and prickly aspect to his personality that has plagued his public persona ever since. In response to one request for a comment about winning the Nobel, he said (echoing Newton's comment that if he had seen farther than others it was because he stood on the shoulders of giants) that if he, Gell-Mann, could see farther than others it was because he was surrounded by dwarfs. This astonishing remark did not come as a surprise to his associates. Long before this incident, Gell-Mann had been diagnosed by many scientists as having a severe charm deficiency.

Science writers, journalists, and interviewers have not generally been flattering to Gell-Mann. In part, he brings this on himself. In general, he does not treat science writers with particular respect, and they, in turn, have often been moved to retaliate. In an interview with John Horgan published in the *Scientific American* (March 1992), Gell-Mann is quoted as saying that science writers and journalists, in general, are "ignoramuses" and "a terrible breed."

A short, compactly built man with a white crewcut and black glasses, Gell-Mann speaks his mind forthrightly—some might even say bluntly. His manner of speaking, erudite and cultivated as it is, still retains a slight New York hard edge, and his natural mode of communication is didactic rather than conversational.

Gell-Mann is a man of wide-ranging intellectual pursuits and often displays an expert knowledge on everything from botany to ornithology, from archaeology to natural history, from quarks to jaguars. It has been said that he ranks as one of the world's great physicists not because he has a particular aptitude for physics, but because he deigned to include physics among his many specialties. Almost above all is his love of language. He is notorious for correcting strangers in the pronunciation of their own names or the names of cities in their countries.

The *New York Times Magazine* profile on Gell-Mann by David Berreby was headlined "The Man Who Knows Everything." Perhaps a better title would have been "The Man Who Wants To Know Everything." He is a polymath who wants to become a totimath. He gives the impression that he has never forgotten anything he has ever read and that he will happily tell you all about it. In his defense, it should be noted that his mania for the smallest detail combined with his passion to know everything are two of the character traits that make him a great scientist.

Above all, he is an intellectual in the full sense of that sometimes misused term. His own explanation of his exceptional range of interests is that he is an "Odyssean" man. Whereas most people, he tells us, are either "Apollonian" (detached and analytical) or "Dionysian" (involved

227

and intuitive), he combines both traits. This rare combination, he says, is called *Odyssean*, after Odysseus, the protagonist of Homer's *Odyssey*, who sailed far and wide and gathered great wisdom from his range of experiences.

Gell-Mann has certainly proved that he has great wisdom, and it is remarkable how thoroughly his theory has been corroborated by experiments over time. But whether or not his theory would be upheld by experiments was for some time a question of dispute. Even Gell-Mann himself did not think quarks would ever be observed.

Mysterious Objects

At the time that Gell-Mann won the Nobel prize, quarks were still only hypothetical, and they were not detectable by experimental means: Their existence was established but only in the formal world of mathematics. Compelling as that mathematics was, a major obstacle to the acceptance of the theory of quarks was the suggestion by Gell-Mann and Zweig that quarks could not be seen, even if better experimental equipment were available. Did this suggestion not smack of theology rather than physics? Indeed, theology usually begins with an assertion that the subject matter is not visible, whereas physics has always been largely an experimental science. Gell-Mann now argues that his suggestion in an early paper that quarks were "mathematical" rather than "real" entities was misunderstood and that he did not mean to say that quarks were not real. At the time, he thought that quarks would always be trapped inside hadrons and, for this reason, that it would always be impossible to isolate and detect them individually. But, physics being the science that it is, in order for the compelling quark theory to win widespread acceptance, it would ultimately have to pass the test of observation and experiment.

Search for the Elusive Quark

Experimental physicists, in particular those associated with accelerators such as the ones at the Fermi National Accelerator Laboratory near Chicago and the Stanford Linear Accelerator Center (SLAC) in California and the large collider at CERN, near Geneva, Switzerland, eagerly took up the challenge of finding the particles Gell-Mann had theorized. They started looking for actual experimental proof of what Gell-Mann and other theoretical physicists told them they should find.

In a 1969 experiment at SLAC, scientists fired 20-billion-volt electrons into protons contained in a tube of liquid hydrogen and measured the energy that the electrons lost as they deflected off the protons. They calculated that if the electrons lost energy, it meant they had collided with moving parts of the proton, possibly the quarks that Gell-Mann predicted to be there. Results of these experiments indicated that the electrons did indeed lose significant amounts of energy, and the experimenters concluded that there was indeed something inside the proton. Other experiments showed that the parts inside a proton have a property called *spin* in precisely the amount theoreticians had predicted.

The actual number of components inside the proton, however, remained to be established. At CERN, scientists worked out a scheme to use yet another particle, the neutrino, to look for quarks. The *neutrino* is another bizarre particle—it is thought to have little, or possibly no, mass and no electrical charge. Neutrinos were first postulated in 1930 by Wolfgang Pauli, who said at the time, "I have committed the ultimate sin. I have predicted the existence of a particle that can never be observed." Enrico Fermi named the mysterious particle *neutrino*, which means "little neutral one" in Italian.

Experimental scientists eventually took up the challenge of finding neutrinos, and by 1959 they finally accomplished this difficult task. One experiment involved mounting optical detectors on the walls of large tanks of ultrapure water buried deep underground, and then recording the flashes of light produced when there is the rare occasion of a neutrino encountering an atom of water. Usually neutrinos pass through millions of miles of matter without interacting with any atoms, but there are so many neutrinos that the occasional encounter does happen. In an important CERN experiment involving much patience over a long period of time, scientists made millions of photographs of neutrinos colliding with protons and shattering them into other particles. By measuring the tracks of the particles, the experimenters were able to calculate the net number of parts inside the proton. Within an acceptable range of experimental error, that number was three, exactly as predicted by the quark hypothesis. Additional measurements seemed to verify that each part came in a fractional charge, again just as Gell-Mann had predicted.

The decade of the 1970s, called "the golden age of particle physics," saw the quark firmly established as a fundamental unit of hadronic matter. This is the way science like things to happen. One by one, experimental physicists seemed to confirm the expectations of the theoretical physicists. It could now be said with increasing confidence that quarks did indeed exist and that they appeared to be a fundamental unit of matter.

Physicist Leon Lederman, in his delightful book *The God Particle*, had a lot of fun discussing the relationship between the theorists and experimenters in particle physics. He pointed out that physics in general progresses because of the interplay between its two branches. Having said that, however, Lederman, who is an experimenter, went on to poke fun at theorists. They are the ones who write all the popular books on science, he said, because they are the ones with all the spare time. Lederman compared the roles of a theorist and an experimenter in discovery to the roles of a farmer and a pig in hunting for truffles. The farmer leads the pig to an area where there might be truffles. The pig searches assiduously for the truffles. Finally, the pig locates a truffle, and just when he is about to eat it, the farmer snatches it away.

Discussing this essential relationship between the theoretical and the experimental in physics, Gell-Mann once talked about what is needed to be a theoretical physicist. "The tools are simple," he said. "All you need are a pencil, paper, eraser, and a good idea." The problem, he went on to explain, is that most ideas are not good ones, and the equations and scribbles that result from looking into them too often appropriately end up in wastebaskets.

Accelerator/Colliders

The tools that the experimentalists use are not so simple. The most elaborate and the most effective of the experimental tools used in particle physics are, as has been discussed, accelerators, also called colliders. In modern accelerators/colliders, particles are first accelerated to velocities close to the speed of light (186,000 miles per second) and then made to collide head-on with other particles traveling in the opposite direction. The resulting explosion produces exotic particles that can then be analyzed. Colliders are machines that enable physicists to "see" inside the atom. The collider method of accomplishing this has been compared to smashing together two Swiss watches to find out what is inside. As the scientists try to find smaller and smaller particles, they need larger and larger colliders. Their goal, working with the theoreti-

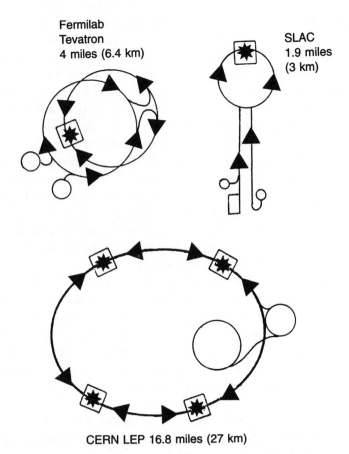

Fermilab
Tevatron
4 miles (6.4 km)

SLAC
1.9 miles
(3 km)

CERN LEP 16.8 miles (27 km)

Colliders Colliders are machines that enable physicists to see inside the atom. Shown are CERN's large electron–positron collider, Fermilab's Tevatron, and the Stanford Linear Accelerator. Subatomic particles are speeded up to velocities near the speed of light and made to collide with other particles traveling in the opposite direction.

cians, is to answer the big questions of subatomic physics: What is the universe made of? What are the forces that bind the parts of the universe together?

The three largest colliders in the world are Fermilab's Tevatron, a circular tunnel device that is 4 miles (6.4 km) in circumference; Stanford's Linear Accelerator, a machine that shoots electrons and positrons down a 1.9-mile-long (3 km)straightaway and then loops them through two semicircular sections into a collision course; and CERN's large electron–positron collider, called LEP, a circular device that is 16.8 miles (27 km) in circumference. Dwarfing all of these would have been the 54-mile (87-km)-circumference U.S. Superconductor Supercollider, which was to have been built at a site in Texas before Congress decided not to spend $8 billion on something that most of the American public, and the members of Congress, did not understand.

The use of these gigantic tools has produced precisely the results that were hoped for. The experimentalists have confirmed just what the theoretical physicists postulated. In the 1970s, experiments at SLAC were the first to show that the proton and the neutron in the atomic nucleus are themselves composed of smaller, more fundamental objects— quarks. This work was later recognized by the awarding of the shared Nobel Prize in Physics to Jerome Friedman and Henry Kendall of MIT and Richard Taylor of Stanford's SLAC.

Researchers at SLAC concluded that they could do a better job of examining the inside of the atom if instead of having their accelerated beam strike a stationary particle, it could be sent around a high-energy storage ring and then made to collide with a beam traveling in the opposite direction. To this end, their storage ring (SPEAR) was constructed. Using the SPEAR resulted in the discovery of an elementary subnuclear particle called the *psi* that was a combination of a quark and an antiquark of an entirely new kind. Before then, only three types of quarks were known, but the discovery of this fourth type of quark (called *charm*) served as further convincing evidence that the basic idea of the quark structure of matter was valid.

This pioneering work at SLAC was recognized with the award of the 1976 Nobel Prize in Physics to Burton Richter, leader of the research team, and shared with Samuel C. C. Ting of the MIT for his concurrent discovery of this new particle at the Brookhaven National Laboratory.

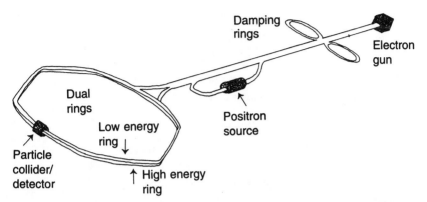

Stanford's Linear Accelerator   The Linear Accelerator (LINAC) uses the electron gun to release electrons from a heated metal source into the two-mile-long track where the particles are accelerated and injected into the dual rings.

Another revolutionary discovery made while using the SPEAR was a particle called the *tau*, which turned out to be the third in the sequence of electrically charged particles called *leptons*. Martin Perl of SLAC was recognized as the discoverer of the tau lepton.

The Fermi National Accelerator Laboratory (Fermilab) in Batavia, Illinois, was also heavily involved in the cooperative research effort. In 1977, researchers there announced the discovery of the bottom quark, the fifth and by far the heaviest of the quarks discovered until that time. In 1988, that work was recognized with the awarding of the Nobel Prize in Physics to Fermilab director Leon Lederman. Step by step, out of the showers and jets of particles created in the high-speed crashes in their accelerators/colliders, physicists, both the theorists and the experimenters, were fashioning what is now known and accepted as the standard model of particle physics.

The Standard Model

What is the universe made of, and what are the forces that bind its parts together? The answer is known as the *standard model*, which attempts to describe the nature of matter and energy as simply as possible. This model postulates that nearly all known matter, from the book you are reading to the distant galaxies, is composed of just four particles: two types of quarks, which make up the protons and neutrons inside the

---

Standard Model
of Particle Physics

FERMIONS
matter constituents

Ordinary Matter

Leptons		Quarks	
●	●	●	●
Electron	Electron Neutrino	Up	Down
0.511	?	5	8

Exotic Matter

●	●	●	●
Muon	Muon Neutrino	Charm	Strange
105.7	?	1,270	175
●	●	●	●
Tau	Tau Neutrino	Top	Bottom
1,784	?	174,000	4,250

The estimated mass of each particle is shown in the energy equivalent, expressed in millions of electron volts. The highly diverse masses have yet to be explained.

BOSONS
force carriers

Photons	**Gluons**	**Intermediate Vector Bosons**	**Gravitons**

ANTIMATTER

Matter made of particles with identical mass and spin to particles of ordinary matter, but with opposite charge—for every particle type there is a corresponding antiparticle type.

Standard model of fundamental particles and interactions It is now believed that all matter is composed of the twelve fundamental particles (fermions) plus the particles (bosons) that transmit the four forces of nature. Each particle has an antimatter equivalent.

nuclei of atoms; electrons, which surround the nuclei; and neutrinos, which are fast-moving, electrically neutral, virtually massless objects that can pass through millions of miles of solid lead with only a very slim chance of being involved in a collision. These particles of matter are acted upon by four forces: (1) the strong nuclear force, which binds quarks together in atomic nuclei; (2) the weak nuclear force, which triggers some forms of radioactive decay; (3) electromagnetism, which builds atoms into molecules and molecules into macroscopic matter; and (4) gravity. A completely separate class of particles called *bosons* are the agents that transmit these forces back and forth between particles.

But is it quite that simple (if any of this can be called simple)? The basic family of particles just described is supplemented by two more exotic families, each of which has a parallel structure: two quarks, a type of electron, and a type of neutrino. These two exotic families do not exist in the modern universe. They are thought to have existed in the first microseconds of the Big Bang—the unimaginably hot and dense fireball that 15 billion years ago gave birth to the universe and all it contains. It is only through the use of accelerators that conditions similar to the Big Bang can be recreated and the exotic particles detected.

A few more terms are necessary to complete our picture of the Standard Model. Physicists have grouped particles into classes according to their functions. *Fermions* is the term used for the class of particles that constitute all *matter*. Fermions, in turn, consists of two subclasses: leptons and quarks. Leptons are the subclass of elementary particles that have no measurable size and are not influenced by the strong nuclear force; that is, they are not locked inside larger particles and can travel on their own. Electrons, muons, and neutrinos are leptons. Quarks are a type of fermion that are trapped inside larger particles and are never seen by themselves.

Bosons, as I said, is the term used for the class of particles that transmit the *forces* of nature. There are four of these: photons, gluons, intermediate-vector bosons, and gravitons. Photons are the particles that make up light and carry the electromagnetic force. Gluons are the carriers of the strong force between quarks. Intermediate-vector bosons are the carriers of the weak force, which is responsible for some forms of radioactive decay. Gravitons are the yet-to-be-discovered carriers of the force of gravity.

We are almost there now, but I have to test your patience just a bit more by bringing up the concept of *antimatter*. Antimatter is still a bit of a puzzle to physicists, but it cannot be ignored. Antimatter is matter made of particles with mass and spin identical to those of ordinary matter, but with opposite charge. Each particle has an antimatter counterpart, which can be thought of as a sort of mirror image. Antimatter had been produced experimentally but is seldom found in nature. Why it is seldom found in nature is one of the unanswered questions of physics.

In the preceding description as well as in the accompanying chart depicting the Standard Model, I have divided all particles into two main classification: matter particles (fermions) and force particles (bosons). But this is not the only way to classify the many constituents of the standard model of fundamental particles and interactions. A different approach would be to arrange particles in accordance with their interactions with the electromagnetic force; for example, particles that are involved only in the weak interaction—that is, in slow radioactive decay—are called *leptons* (from the Greek for "small"). All other particles, with the exception of photons, are involved in one way or another with the strong interactions and are called *hadrons* (from the Greek for "strong"). In this approach, where particles are classified by interaction, the photon is generally put in a class by itself because it is the particle that mediates the electromagnetic interaction.

Two other approaches to classification involve the process of decay, or change from unstable to stable. The governing factor in the first approach is the end product, the makeup of the resulting stable particle. There might be only leptons and photons in the final collection, or there might be a proton as well. The presence or absence of a proton thus becomes the criterion for this method of classification. Particles in which a proton does appear in the end product of the decay process are called *baryons* (heavy ones). Particles in which a proton does *not* appear—the final collection of decay particles is made up entirely of leptons and photons—are called *mesons*. The governing factor in the other approach based on decay is the speed of decay: This leads to *strange* and *nonstrange* particles.

Elementary particles can also be grouped together in relation to their internal dynamics, that is, their rotational spin. There is no one official method of classification of the particles that make up the standard model. The various methods are just different ways of imposing order on a large group of seemingly unrelated objects. Using the various classification systems is similar to the way that the Census Bureau uses the results of a census. All the inhabitants counted can be grouped by sex, by age, by height, by income, by education, or by any other method that helps understand the overall population. The classification system is ultimately an aid to communication, and that is how it should be regarded.

Top Quark

The triumphant announcement in March of 1995 that physicists at the Fermilab had finally discovered evidence of the top quark brought an end to an eighteen-year effort to verify the actual existence of one of the last remaining pieces of the standard model. Physicists had long postulated the top quark's existence, but without experimental proof. Now, using the world's most powerful accelerator, the Tevatron, scientists managed to isolate the evasive, transitory bits of matter, confirming the comprehensive theory that holds that the entire universe is built from only a handful of fundamental particles and forces. As I pointed out earlier in this chapter, quarks vanished as independent entities at the beginning of time, when the original Big Bang that created the universe began to cool. Since then, they have existed only bound inside the nuclei of atoms.

Scientists had their best chance of finding the top quark once the Tevatron was completed at Fermilab. It smashes protons and antiprotons together at 1.8 trillion electron volts. At this energy level, experimental physicists thought that a top quark should be made once for every few billion collisions. This monumental project required the efforts of 440 investigators from thirty-six cooperating institutions, prompting jokes about the number of physicists needed to install a lightbulb.

The top quark flashed into reality for only a trillionth of a trillionth of a second in the bursts of colliding matter and antimatter. Over the years, the physicists had diligently probed trillions of beam collisions to detect in the burst of mysterious particles the "signatures" that computers then analyzed to confirm the existence of the until then hypothetical top quarks. These infinitely tiny particles proved to be incredibly massive—as heavy as an entire atom of lead and more than 180 times heavier than protons.

The successful discovery of the top quark brought a sigh of relief to the theoretical physicists worldwide. "There was tremendous theoretical expectation that the top quark is there," said Steven Weinberg of the University of Texas. "A lot of us would have been embarrassed if it were not."

Murray Gell-Mann had put it a little differently some time before. "If the experimentalists do not find the top quark in the energy range where it is now being sought, we theorists will have to 'fall on our fountain pens,' as my former colleague Marvin Goldberg used to put it."

Now that all six quarks postulated by Murray Gell-Mann and his colleagues have been found, describing their properties in detail will help understand why all matter has mass; why the universe contains far more matter than antimatter; and how the energy of the Big Bang turned all the particles and forces into stars, planets, galaxies, and ultimately into life itself.

Burton Richter, the Nobel Prize-winning director of the Stanford Linear Accelerator Center said, "The Fermilab people are fully justified in saying they have found the missing link in our theoretical model that tries to understand how the universe evolved from its birth." The conclusion to be drawn from Fermilab's important discovery is that the standard model is correct when it describes the fundamental particles and forces of the universe and that Murray Gell-Mann and his fellow theorists were on the right track.

It does not mean, however, that elementary-particle research has reached the end of the road. This latest accomplishment cannot be viewed as the completion of the standard model. Missing is something called the "Higgs boson," the hypothesized mechanism that would explain why particles have the masses that they do. It is thought to lie well beyond the reach of the Tevatron. One of the main purposes of the cancelled Superconductor Supercollider was to find evidence of the Higgs boson.

The Quark and the Jaguar: Adventures in the Simple and the Complex

The title of Murray Gell-Mann's book (published by W. H. Freeman, New York, in 1994) comes from a poem by Arthur Sze, a friend of Gell-Mann. Sze avers holistically that: "The world of the quark has everything to do with a jaguar circling in the night." Gell-Mann was struck by this line of poetry when his second wife, the poet Marcia Southwick, read it to him. He decided that it was the perfect title for the book on which he had been working for some time.

The Quark and the Jaguar is Gell-Mann's personal story of finding the connections between the study of particle physics and his fascination with natural selection, species diversity, and other fields. He clearly believes that in nature, the simple (a quark inside the nucleus of an atom) and the complex (a jaguar prowling its jungle territory) are closely linked.

It is Gell-Mann's central point that simple laws of nature can lead, through repeated application and interaction, to the appearance of complex phenomena whose properties could not have been predicted from those underlying laws. He uses examples of complexity and adaptation that range from biology and ecology through linguistics and sociology to scientific theories, which he sees as having a life and evolution of their own.

The book is in four parts, each of which reflects an area of Gell-Mann's interests. The first part describes the basis of Gell-Mann's fascination with complexity. The second section is on quantum mechanics and is really the intellectual heart of the book. Clearly Gell-Mann knows what he is talking about—in contrast to his less convincing theme (at least to me) of complexity as a new science. For some reason, Gell-Mann tells the readers that they may skip the quantum mechanic parts of the book. This, I suggest, would be a mistake for anyone interested in the subject matter. Although it is not always easy to follow, this section presents both a primer on quantum physics (although Gell-Mann claims that it is not), as well as insight into Gell-Mann's methods of thinking.

The third section, which looks at complex adaptive systems, is, in my view, not completely successful. Murray Gell-Mann, however, is worth a reader's attention on whatever topic he wishes to hold forth, relevant to the subject under discussion or not. For my part, I find Gell-Mann's sometimes rambling musings on subjects as diverse as Greek word derivations to continental drift to be the best parts of this fascinating book.

The final section of the book is a heartfelt plea for greater rationality in human affairs, in particular the need for biodiversity and environmental conservation. In a time when the nation seems to be busy dumbing down national problems to the level of talk-radio bombastics and bumper-sticker simplicities, his perspectives on global problems is refreshingly intelligent.

The writing of this book was reportedly not an easy task for Gell-Mann. He said that it was "the hardest thing he ever did." He went through two publishers and numerous would-be collaborators. In the end, he wrote the entire book himself, with only an editor's help. He nearly exhausted the patience of his eventual publisher, W. H. Freeman & Company, with his last-minute changes and corrections.

Has the former ogre mellowed a bit in his mature years? Judging by his performances on his book-promotion tour, he most certainly has. In several TV and radio interviews I have heard, Gell-Mann was gracious, patient, humorous, and self-deprecating—in short, a thoroughly charming spokesman for science. He handled questions from listeners with considerable tact, even those that might have elicited a sharp and cutting response from the "old" Murray Gell-Mann.

On one occasion in San Francisco, he was responding to a very high level of call-in questions when without any warning a breathless caller announced that he "had worked out the Grand Unified Field Theory" and went on to ask Gell-Mann if he had a pen and paper so he could share it with him. After the briefest of pauses, Gell-Mann said dryly, "I'll remember it."

Renaissance Man of Science

Today, Murray Gell-Mann is the cofounder and director of the Santa Fe Institute. He is also a Director of the John D. and Catherine T. MacArthur Foundation, where he serves as Chairman of its Committee on World Environment and Resources. For his contributions on behalf of the world environment, he has been named one of The Global 500 by the United Nations Environmental Program. He has also received awards from the Franklin Institute, The Atomic Energy Commission, and the National Academy of Sciences.

As for physics, the former wunderkind is now something of the elder statesman. Unlike Einstein, who fought hard against the new ideas and concepts of quantum physics, Gell-Mann is an enthusiastic supporter of new ideas, in particular, the superstrings theory of physics. In this theory, elementary particles are assumed to consist of tiny vibrating strings. (Four physicists at Princeton who are currently involved in this field are now known collectively as the "Princeton string quartet.") It is, however, a hypothesis yet to be demonstrated in the laboratory. Gell-Mann still believes that superstrings theory might eventually unify quantum physics with Einstein's relativity, shedding light on the origin of the universe in the bargain.

Asked on several occasions if quarks themselves would eventually be broken down into something even smaller, he has been cautious in his answer. "Quarks," he has said, "are as fundamental as electrons." This does not mean that at some time in the future both electrons and quarks will not be subdivided. As a scientist, he cannot rule out the possibility.

Gell-Mann spends his days now in New Mexico, working on topics ranging from quantum mechanics to the human immune system, the evolution of human languages, and the global economy as a complex evolving system. The former child prodigy from Manhattan has truly become the Renaissance Man of Science.

Epilogue
The Why of Physics

Our journey has taken us from the infinite (Newton's cosmos) to the infinitesimal (Gell-Mann's quarks), and the quest goes on. Today, physics has moved into a world governed entirely by mathematical and highly speculative theorizing, little of which can be empirically verified as yet. String theory, a ten-dimensional universe, black holes, white holes, wormholes, parallel universes, time travel, and the origin and fate of the universe—these are the subjects of concern to the young physicists.

So far, the *who*, *when*, and *what* of physics have been discussed. It seems appropriate to end with a few words on the *why* of physics: the philosophy of physics. Scientists and science writers, when speaking before public groups, are often asked questions that border on the metaphysical rather than the scientific. There are several reasons for this. First, there are aspects of quantum physics that are mysterious and little understood. Second, there is an important natural desire to make some sense out of all this science—to relate the equations and the mathematics to an overall view of the world. The German term for this is *Weltanschauung* (worldview), or comprehensive concept of the universe and of humanity's relation to it.

As we have seen, the science of physics has come a long way since the days of Thales and the other Greek philosophers who began to ask questions about the universe and the natural world. Today, science, and in particular, physics, can explain much about the natural world around us. At one time, nature seemed an inexplicable mystery. Today, although there are still some aspects of the natural world that science does not fully understand, the principles that govern the way they work are known.

One problem is that as science has discovered more and more fundamental physical principles, they seem to have less and less to do with us. Almost all of the particles that appear in the standard model of particles and interactions decay so rapidly that they are absent in ordinary matter and play no role at all in human life. Muons and tauons, for example, hardly matter at all in our daily existence. Because of this seeming irrelevance, pure physics is losing its audience.

Those who look to science for help in finding answers to the big philosophical questions, such as the purpose of the universe or the meaning of life, still look in vain. Physicists can explain almost anything in the objective world, yet we understand our own lives less and less. In response to this dilemma, there have been many attempts to mix physics and metaphysics. Two recent examples are the anthropic cosmological principle and the Gaia hypothesis, each of which implies that life on Earth is part of a larger purpose.

The anthropic cosmological principle, postulated by the English physicist Brandon Carter in 1974, is as exalted as it sounds. Briefly, it states that if the physical parameters of the universe were any different than they are, life would not be possible; therefore, the universe must have been organized by some supreme being to support life. This is a variation on the early reaction to Newton's clocklike universe. If the universe truly was as mechanically predictable as a huge watch, then there had to be a watchmaker.

One example of the anthropic principle is that the energy Earth receives from the Sun is precisely correct to nurture life. The term used in science for this energy is the *solar constant*, which is defined as 1.99

244

calories of energy per minute per square centimeter. If Earth received much more or less than 2 calories per minute per square centimeter, the water of the oceans would be vapor or ice, leaving the planet with no liquid water or reasonable substitute in which life could evolve. It is only because Earth is 93 million miles away from a Sun that produces 5,600 million, million, million, million calories per minute that life is possible.

For another example, it has been calculated that if Earth were just 5 million miles closer to the Sun, the intensity of the Sun's rays would have broken apart water molecules in the atmosphere and eventually turned the planet into a dry and dusty wasteland. If Earth were only 1 million miles farther from the Sun, the cold would have frozen the ocean solid.

Scientists explain that Venus, Earth, and Mars probably started off with fairly similar climates. However, Venus is too close to the Sun. The heat boiled off the water. Then solar radiation broke down the water molecules in the upper Venusian atmosphere, and the hydrogen escaped into space. With no rain to precipitate it, carbon dioxide accumulated in Venus's atmosphere causing a runaway greenhouse effect. The result is surface temperatures of 900 degrees Fahrenheit, hot enough to melt lead.

Mars is more of a mystery. Scientists tell us that 3.5 billion years ago Mars was warm and wet and liquid water flowed across its surface. It is even possible that there was life. There is no evidence of life now, and the question is what happened? Mars is much smaller than Earth, and without much gravity, it had a difficult time keeping its atmosphere from evaporating into space. Mars also lacked tectonic forces. On Earth, colliding tectonic plates are crucial to life. The carbon in atmospheric carbon dioxide dissolves in water and forms calcium carbonate, which piles up on the ocean floor and on the bottom of lakes. But some of the Earth's crust gets subducted under adjacent tectonic plates, is heated, and is spewed out from volcanoes, with the vaporized carbon rejoining the atmosphere. Without having this kind of tectonic interaction, Mars could not recycle its carbon, and gradually the carbon dioxide in the atmosphere diminished. The greenhouse effect disappeared, and Mars got colder. Finally, the surface water evaporated or froze. Most scientists define a *habitable planet* as one that can support liquid water. It is possible to imagine strange life forms that do not require water, but most researchers have concluded that water and the complex chemistry it supports make the chance for life much greater. Too hot or too cold for life are the norms in this universe, except, so far as is known, on this unique planet Earth.

Most cosmologists today agree that the universe began with a Big Bang and has been expanding ever since. Scientists believe that if the expansion rate of the universe were a little slower, the Big Bang could not have occurred. If the expansion rate were a little faster, there would not have been time for any kind of matter to coalesce, and there would not have been any stars. If something called the *fine structure constant* (the square of the charge of the electron divided by the speed of light multiplied by Planck's constant) were slightly different, atoms would not exist. Our very existence, yours and mine, seems to be the result of either an extraordinary, well-designed miracle or an accident.

But what preceded the Big Bang and why the universe has expanded in just the way it has seem to be questions for philosophers or theologians as well as for physicists. Does the very fact of our existence mean that some celestial clockmaker designed the machinery of the universe and set the parameters just right for life to evolve? Or was it just chance? In *The Anthropic Cosmological Principle* (1986), authors John D. Barrow and Frank J. Tipler argue that life is not just a chance occurrence but necessary, that a universe must have observers in order to exist. However, many scientists find this anthropic cosmological principle closer to metaphysics than to physics. The cosmologist Joseph Silk has likened the anthropic principle to the satisfaction felt by a colony of fleas in a dog's coat. They were secure in the knowledge that everything in their world had been ordained just right for their existence—until the dog's owner purchased a flea collar. One might also imagine a colony of ants floating downstream on an old log. Everything was perfect for their well-being, and it might seem that the log was a world designed for them—and then the log reached the waterfall.

The Gaia hypothesis, proposed in 1972 by James E. Lovelock, holds that the Earth and its living creatures have evolved together in a self-regulating system that maintains conditions that are optimum for life. Dr. Lovelock maintains that this self-regulation is just a natural property of the system, and he denies that he is imputing a purpose or design. But the Gaia (the name means "mother goddess of Earth") hypothesis quickly became mystical because it strongly implies that the reason the Earth has a benevolent greenhouse atmosphere is because there is an omniscient and omnipotent being in charge of the thermostat—there is no need to worry about any environmental problems because they will all self-correct under the watchful eye of the kindly Earth mother. Again, this is comforting but not supported by much in the way of science.

Both the anthropic principle and the Gaia theory are interesting ideas, often expressed in scientific language by scientists who long for a glimpse of some transcendent purpose in the universe. But neither concept is testable or verifiable. Science is a system of inquiry based upon the empirical. Theories must evolve from verifiable facts and explain what is, not what we would like it to be. In *The First Three Minutes*, a popular book about the Big Bang theory of the origin of the universe, physicist Steven Weinberg described the Earth as "a tiny part of an overwhelmingly hostile universe," itself doomed to end in utter cold and dark or a final fireball. "The more the universe seems comprehensible," he concluded, "the more it also seems pointless." That is a hard and difficult concept for many to accept, including some physicists. They try to force some meaning into the physical concept of the universe. There have been a number of books in the last few years—*The Dancing Wu Li Masters* by Gary Zukav and *The Tao of Physics* by Fritjof Capra, for two examples—that try to explain modern physics in terms of Eastern religion and mysticism. To me, they are reminiscent of King Ptolemy of Egypt, who, possibly taken back by the amount of homework required of him, asked Euclid if there was not an easier path to understanding geometry. You will remember that Euclid disabused the monarch of that notion by telling him that there was "no royal road to geometry"—likewise I'm afraid that there is no easy road to physics. Both of the recent books mentioned contain a lot of good physics, but both make huge jumps from proven concepts in science to metaphysical ideas based on faith, not on fact.

Disillusionment with science as the final answer to philosophical questions has led numbers of intellectual academics into an antiscience attitude. They pigeonhole science as a white, European, bourgeois, male view of the world. Therefore, many members of the humanities and social science faculties of our leading universities (and literary intellectuals generally) now consider the knowledge produced by science to be no more reliable than that produced by what they call "other ways of knowing." In their recent book *Higher Superstition: The Academic Left and Its Quarrels with Science* (Johns Hopkins University Press, 1994), Paul R. Gross and Norman Levitt challenge this basically antiscience position. As Gross, a biologist, and Levitt, a mathematician, put it: "Once it has been affirmed that one discursive community is as good as another, that the narrative of science holds no privileges over the narratives of superstition, the newly minted cultural critic can actually revel in his ignorance of deep scientific ideas."

The deep gulf between the literary intellectuals and the scientific culture, described by C. P. Snow in his now famous 1956 essay *Two Cultures*, has clearly widened over the ensuing years. The literary intellectuals who teach today's undergraduate students in the liberal arts that there are "other ways of knowing" do their budding lawyers, teachers, journalists, sociologists, businesspeople, and whatever a severe disservice. Science is devoted to the effort to see things as they are. Investigating nature's mysteries takes hard, sustained, disciplined thought— the results of which must be explainable in theory, submitted to critical peer review, and validated by reproducible experiment. When one does that, one is doing science.

Should scientists then abandon their attempts to find deeper meaning in their understanding of nature? I think not and I do not mean to suggest this. Efforts to link theology and science will continue because it is human nature too seek the *why* of life. Recently, Dr. Paul Davies, a mathematical physicist who has written and lectured on connections between science and theology, was awarded the $1 million Templeton prize for his contributions to religious thought and inquiry. Davies, a professor of natural philosophy at the University of Adelaide in Australia, is the author of more than twenty books, including *The Mind of God* (Simon & Schuster, 1992), which discusses ideas about the origin of the universe, order in nature, and the nature of human consciousness.

The Templeton prize was created in 1973 by the investor Sir John Templeton, an American-born British subject who is founder of several mutual funds. He required that the prize be given annually to an individual judged to have shown singular creativity in advancing public understanding of God or spirituality. He further stipulated that the cash value of the prize exceed the Nobel prizes, which he thought overlooked religion. Dr. Davies is the third physicist to receive this prize. In a telephone interview with the *New York Times* at the time of his award, Davies said, "Most people think that as science advances, religion retreats. But the more we discover about the world, the more we find there's a purpose or a design behind it all."

Physics can be expected to continue because it is, by its nature, open-ended and exploratory and because, at its heart, science is simply people asking questions—and there are still questions to be answered. Likewise, the philosophical issues touched on in this brief epilogue can also be expected to be with us as long as the human species continues to wonder.

Chronology of Physics

?	Arabs, Egyptians, and others develop the current numbering system, early geometry, and basic mathematics.
525 B.C.	Pythagoras derives synthesis of mysticism and mathematics, turning away from myths to numbers as the source of truth.
340	Aristotle argues that the Earth is a round sphere rather than a flat plate.
295	Euclid publishes *Elements*, codifying classical geometry.
260	Aristarchus of Samos postulates that the Earth orbits the Sun in a gigantic universe.
240	Archimedes develops classical mechanics and elementary physics.
200	Eratosthenes derives technique for measuring the circumference of Earth.
100	Claudius Ptolemy constructs complex Earth-centered model

of the universe that is the basis of astronomy for over 1400 years.

1515 A.D. Leonardo Da Vinci makes significant observations in the fields of mechanics, hydraulics, and aerodynamics.

1543 Nicolaus Copernicus publishes *On the Revolutions*, postulating a Sun-centered universe.

1572 Tycho Brahe observes a nova (or new star), evidence that the universe is changing.

1610 Galileo Galilei first observes the night sky through a telescope and announces discoveries that support Copernician concept of the universe.

1619 Johannes Kepler demonstrates that the orbits of planets are elliptical and develops laws of planetary motion.

1687 Isaac Newton publishes *Principia* and demonstrates that gravitational force obeying an inverse-square law accounts both for falling bodies on Earth and for the motion of the Moon in its orbit.

1799 Pierre-Simon De Laplace establishes mathematical basis for Newton's hypothesis of gravitation; develops probability theory and helps establish metric system.

1831 Michael Faraday discovers electromagnetic induction.

1824 Karl Friedrich Gauss postulates non-Euclidean geometry.

1824 Christian Doppler discovers that emissions (light or sound) from a moving source will appear to a stationary observer to be higher in frequency if the object is approaching, lower if the object is receding—the "Doppler Shift."

1848 William Kelvin determines absolute zero.

1849 Jean-Leon Foucault develops methods for measuring speed of light in air, and finds that its speed in water and other media diminishes in proportion to the index of refraction.

1860 Robert Bunsen and Gustav Kirchhoff develop the basis of spectral analysis, enabling laboratory materials to be compared with those of the Sun and stars; in effect, enabling scientists to identify the material composition of astronomical bodies.

1864   James Clerk Maxwell publishes *Treatise on Electricity and Magnetism* that makes possible a much greater understanding of the phenomena in this field.

1879   Albert Michelson uses Foucault principles to determine speed of light.

1887   Albert Michelson and Edward Morley perform precise experiments demonstrating that space cannot be filled with the ether that had been thought to be the medium for transmitting light.

1894   Heinrich Hertz demonstrates that electromagnetic waves travel at the speed of light and can be reflected, refracted, and polarized like light.

1895   William K. Roentgen discovers X rays, for which he receives the first Nobel Prize in Physics.

1898   Marie and Pierre Curie identify the radioactive elements radium and polonium.

1900   Max Planck postulates the quantum theory of radiation; develops basis for quantum physics.

1904   Ernest Rutherford proposes that the amount of helium produced by radioactive decay of minerals in rocks could be used to measure the age of Earth.

1905   Albert Einstein publishes papers on special relativity, photoelectric effect, and Brownian motion; special theory of relativity postulates that measurement of space and time are distorted at high velocity and that mass and energy are equivalent.

1906   J. J. Thomson establishes the existence of electrons.

1911   Ernest Rutherford demonstrates that most of the mass of atoms is contained in their tiny nuclei.

1913   Niels Bohr formulates theory of atomic structure.

1916   Albert Einstein publishes the general theory of relativity in which gravitation is portrayed as an effect of curved space; general relativity is a fundamental theory of the nature of space, time, and gravitation.

1924   Prince Louis de Broglie suggests that all matter, even objects ordinarily thought of as particles (such as electrons) should also display wavelike behavior.

1925   Wolfgang Pauli postulates the exclusion principle, essential to understanding spectral lines of stars and nebulae.

1926   Erwin Schrödinger develops equation that describes how the de Broglie waves move from place to place; considered the central equation of quantum physics.

1927   Georges Lemaitre proposes Big Bang theory of the origin of the universe as a solution to Einstein's field equations.

1927   Werner Heisenberg formulates principle of uncertainty, a fundamental limitation to the accuracy of experimental measurements.

1927   Jan Oort determines that the Milky Way galaxy is rotating; later uses radio telescope to map the spiral arms of the Milky Way.

1928   P. A. M. Dirac postulates the existence of antimatter—particles that have electric charges equal but opposite to those of their ordinary matter counterparts (e.g., positron or antielectron).

1929   Edwin Hubble determines, by means of spectral analysis, that the universe is expanding as Einstein had predicted.

1931   Wolfgang Pauli predicts the existence of neutrinos.

1932   James Chadwick discovers the neutron; receives 1935 Nobel Prize in Physics.

1938   Lise Meitner and Otto Hahn discover nuclear fission; Hahn receives Nobel prize for this discovery (Meitner had to flee Nazi Germany before their work was completed but is generally credited for their joint efforts).

1939   Leo Szilard conceives concept of chain reactions in atomic physics; coauthors letter to President F. D. Roosevelt (signed by Einstein) pointing out potentialities of uranium fission and the atomic bomb.

1942   Enrico Fermi supervises development of world's first nuclear reactor as part of the Manhattan Project.

1945   J. Robert Oppenheimer directs production of first atomic bombs as part of the Manhattan Project.

1946   George Gamow predicts that the Big Bang should have produced cosmic background radiation.

1960   Alan Sandage and Thomas Mathews discover quasars, the most distant galaxies from Earth.

1961   Murray Gell-Mann and Yuval Ne'eman independently derive plan for classifying subatomic particles that Gell-Mann calls "eightfold way."

1963   E. N. Lorenz publishes first paper on chaos theory.

1964   Murray Gell-Mann and George Zweig independently propose that protons, neutrons, and other hadrons are composed of still smaller particles, which Gell-Mann labels "quarks."

1965   Richard Feynman shares Nobel Prize in Physics with Tomonago and Schwinger for their theory of quantum electrodynamics, considered an important step in the search for an understanding of nature.

1965   Robert Wilson and Arno Penzias detect radiation in deep space, confirming theory of Big Bang.

1968   Experiments conducted at the Stanford Linear Accelerator Center support quark theory.

1981   Alan Guth postulates that the early universe went through an "inflationary" period of exponential expansion.

1995   Scientists at the Fermi National Accelerator Laboratory find evidence for the "top quark," the last undetected member of a family of particles that are believed to constitute the basic building blocks of all matter.

Glossary

absolute space Newton's concept of three-dimensional space in which the lengths of objects are independent of the motion of the reference frame in which they are measured; refuted by Einstein.

absolute time Newton's concept of time as being universal with the agreed upon notion of simultaneity of events as well as universally agreed upon time interval between two events; refuted by Einstein.

accelerator (Short for *particle accelerator*; sometimes called *atom smasher*.) A device, such as a cyclotron or linear accelerator, that speeds charged particles or nuclei to high velocities and high energies useful for subatomic-particle research.

alpha decay A nuclear emission process in which an unstable heavy nucleus emits an alpha particle and transforms itself into a different and lighter nucleus; one of the three processes (the others being beta decay and gamma decay) that make up nuclear radioactivity.

alpha particle (alpha rays) One of the three types of radiation (the others being beta rays and gamma rays) discovered in early studies of radioactivity around 1900.

antimatter   Matter made up of particles with mass and spin identical to those of ordinary matter, but with the opposite charge.

black-body radiation   The continuous spectrum of radiation emitted by a body that, when cold, is a perfect absorber at all wavelengths. (The reconciliation of the observed spectrum with a theorectical formula by Max Planck in 1900 was the beginning of quantum theory.)

bosons   Elementary particles, including photons, gluons, intermediate-vector bosons, and gravitons, that are the carriers of the four forces of nature.

chain reaction   A self-sustaining phenomenon in which the fission of nuclei of one generation of nuclei produces particles that cause the fission of at least an equal number of nuclei of the succeeding generation.

charm   The fourth flavor of quark. (Predicted by theory, charmed quarks were first discovered in 1974. Quarks exist in pairs called flavors, and one pair consists of an *s*, or strange, quark and a *c*, or charm, quark.)

classical mechanics (Newtonian mechanics)   Concept of theoretical dynamics based on the idea that particles travel in precisely definable trajectories according to Newton's laws of motion.

closed universe   Cosmological theory that envisions the expanding universe as "closed" or destined to stop expanding at some future time, which is to be followed by a collapse of all the galaxies in a sort of reverse Big Bang and then a rebound into a new expansion phase.

confinement   The trapping of quarks inside hadrons.

cosmic rays   Charged particles, mostly protons, from outer space.

critical mass   In physics, that amount of a given fissionable material necessary to sustain a chain reaction.

decay, radioactive   The progressive decrease in the number of radioactive atoms in a substance by spontaneous nuclear disintegration. (An atom decays when it changes from instability to stability; radioactive decay is a natural process going on all the time.)

Doppler effect   The apparent change in wavelength of radiation—whether sound or light—emitted by a moving body, noticeable when the source of sound or light is moving toward or away from an observer.

(If the source of the waves is moving toward the observer, the frequency of the wave increases and the wavelength is shorter, producing high-pitched sounds and bluish light (called blue shift). (If the source of the waves is moving away from the observer, the frequency of the wave decreases and the wavelength is longer, producing low-pitched sounds and reddish light (called red shift).)

duality The phenomenon by which, in the atomic domain, objects exhibit the properties of both particles and waves.

eightfold way In physics, a method of classifying particles into families of eight, based on group theory; developed independently by Murray Gell-Mann and Yuval Ne'eman in 1961.

electron The fundamental negatively charged particle that is a constituent of all atoms.

elementary particle A subatomic particle regarded as an irreducible constituent of matter (sometimes called *fundamental particle*).

energy In physics, the potential for work. (Energy and mass are interchangeable in accordance with Einstein's formula: $E = mc^2$.)

entropy A measure of the degree of disorder, or tendency toward the breakdown, of any system.

equivalence principle The principle, developed by Einstein in 1911, that life in a freely falling laboratory was equivalent to life with no gravity; conversely, that the effects of gravitation and of being in an accelerated frame are indistinguishable; the basis of Einstein's General Theory of Relativity.

expanding universe The concept, first postulated by the American astronomer Edwin Hubble in 1929, that distant galaxies are receding from Earth, and from each other, at a constant rate.

fermions Constituents of matter. (Leptons and quarks are fermions as are protons, neutrons, and electrons. On the other hand, particles that carry the forces of nature are called bosons.)

fission, nuclear The process in which the nucleus of an atom splits, either spontaneously or under external stimulus, into two fragments plus one or two surplus neutrons.

flavor In physics, the term used to designate types of quarks: up, down, charm, strange, top, and bottom.

force   The agency responsible for change in a system. (According to the standard model, there are four forces in the universe controlling the ways in which objects interact: electromagnetism, gravity, the strong nuclear force, and the weak nuclear force.)

frequency   The number of cycles per unit of time of a periodic phenomenon.

fusion, nuclear   Atomic interaction in which nucleons are fused together, creating new atomic nuclei and releasing energy.

Gaia hypothesis   The theory that suggests that Earth is a superorganism, the sum of all organisms, that can modify and maintain its own optimum environment. (This superorganism is Gaia, the mother goddess of Earth.)

general relativity   Einstein's laws of physics in which gravity is described by the curvature of space–time.

gluons   According to current quantum theory, fundamental units of energy. (The strong nuclear force, one of the four forces of nature, is carried by gluons.)

grand unified theories (GUTS)   Theories attempting to establish that the strong interactions, the weak interactions, and electromagnetic interactions are different aspects of one fundamental force. (The ultimate goal is to incorporate the gravitational interaction into these same all-encompassing theories.)

gravitons   The fundamental unit (or quanta) of nature thought to convey gravitational force.

Hubble constant   The number found by dividing a galaxy's recessional velocity by its distance from Earth. (This number is called the Hubble constant after Edwin P. Hubble, the discoverer of the expanding universe.)

inertia principle   Newton's first law of motion—every body (or mass) persists in a state of rest or of uniform motion in a straight line unless compelled by external force to change that state.

kinetic energy   The energy inherent in moving bodies; equal to one-half the product of its mass and the square of its speed. (Called *kinetic* from the Greek word meaning "to move.")

K-mesons   A subatomic particle with a mass about halfway between that of an electron and a proton. (Mesons are elementary particles that have zero spin.)

LEP Large electron-positron accelerator; located in Geneva, Switzerland, and operated by the European Organization for Nuclear Research (CERN); considered the largest scientific instrument ever built.

leptons The subclass of elementary particles that have no measurable size and are not affected by the strong nuclear force; consist of electrons, muons, taus, and their respective neutrinos.

mass Usually defined as a quantity of matter as determined by either its weight or by Newton's second law of motion, that is, the amount of force necessary to move it. (Einstein showed that mass is actually a very compact form of energy.)

matter The substance or material of which any physical object is composed.

molecule The smallest physical unit of a particular element or compound; made up of atoms.

muon A short-lived elementary subatomic particle with a negative electrical charge. (Muons are leptons.)

neutrino A particle that is believed to be massless, electrically neutral; experiences only weak interactions.

nucleons The constituents of an atomic nucleus, consisting of protons and neutrons.

nucleus, atomic The positively charged mass within an atom, composed of neutrons and protons; possesses most of the mass but occupies only a small fraction of the volume of an atom.

open universe Theory or cosmological model in which the universe continues to expand forever.

particle physics The branch of science that deals with the smallest known structures of matter and energy.

photons Discrete units of electromagnetic energy; the smallest indivisible unit of electromagnetic radiation.

physics The scientific study of the interaction of matter and energy. (Classical, or Newtonian, physics refers to the scientific studies made prior to the introduction of the quantum principle. Modern physics sees both matter and energy as being made up of discrete units, or quanta.)

Planck's constant   The formula for relating the energy content of a quantum (or unit of energy) to the frequency of the corresponding electromagnetic wave. (Max Planck expressed this relationship in an equation utilizing a very small number (6.624×10^{-27}), which gives the exact proportional relationship.)

positron   In physics, an elemental particle having the same mass as an electron but having a positive charge equal in magnitude to the electron's negative charge; the antiparticle of the electron.

probablistic   Pertaining to the probability of the occurrence of an event.

proton   A massive particle with positive electrical charge that is found in the nucleus of atoms; composed of two up quarks and one down quark.

quanta   Fundamental units of energy (singular, *quantum*).

quantum mechanics   The mechanics of atoms, molecules, and other physical systems that are subject to Heisenberg's uncertainty principle and Planck's quantum principle. (The term is interchangeable with *quantum physics*.)

quantum physics   Theory of physics based upon the quantum principle—energy is emitted not as a continuum but in discrete units.

quark   Elementary particle; comes in six types (flavors): up, down, charm, strange, top, and bottom.

radiation   All of the ways that energy can be emitted by an atom; includes X rays, alpha rays, gamma rays, and beta particles.

redshift   A displacement toward the longer wavelengths of the spectral lines of light coming from the stars of distant galaxies that is caused by these stars moving away from Earth. *See also* Doppler effect.

simultaneity, absolute   Newtonian concept that two events could occur at the same time, regardless of the position or relative motion of the observers; replaced by Einstein's concept of relative simultaneity.

simultaneity, relative   Einstein's concept that the time of occurrence of an event is relative to the position and motion of the observers.

singularity   A point in space–time at which the space–time curvature becomes infinite; the term used by physicists and mathematicians to designate the point in the universe where the equations of Einstein's general theory of relativity break down; the time of the Big Bang, when all matter in the universe was contained in one single point.

space–time According to Einstein's general theory of relativity, refers to the four-dimensional "fabric" that results when space and time are unified; the fusion of the three ordinary spatial dimensions of length, breadth, and height with time as the fourth dimension.

space–time curvature According to Einstein's general theory of relativity, the effect in space caused by the presence of matter. (Gravity is viewed as the consequence of the curvature of space that is induced by the presence of massive objects.)

spectrum The range of wavelengths or frequencies over which electromagnetic radiation can be propogated.

spin Property of an elementary particle; similar to spin of a spinning top.

standard model In physics, the theories or sets of equations that state that all matter in the universe is made up of fermions (matter constituents), bosons (force carriers), and antimatter or the mirror image of the fermions and bosons.

strange One of the six types (or flavors) of quarks. Others are up, down, charm, top, and bottom.

string theory A theory in which elementary particles are assumed to consist of tiny strings.

strong force One of the four known fundamental forces of nature; holds together the protons and neutrons inside an atom.

synchrotron An accelerator in which magnetic fields and accelerations are synchronized to keep the particle at a particular radius.

tau lepton The heaviest known lepton.

time dilation effect Loss of time of a moving clock as observed by a stationary observer; postulated by Einstein in his Special Theory of Relativity. (At the relatively slow speeds of normal travel today, this effect is negligible; but, at speeds approaching the speed of light, time slows down appreciably. At the speed of light, time would stand still.)

ultraviolet light Electromagnetic radiation of a wavelength slightly shorter than that of visible light.

uncertainty principle Principle stating that it is impossible to measure both the position and the momentum of a particle at the same time.

virtual particle   A particle that only lives a short time (restricted by the uncertainty principle). (The four forces of nature are transmitted via virtual particles.)

wave–particle duality   The theory that matter and radiation alike, within the reduced dimensions of the quantum world, behave at times like a wave and at other times, just as convincingly, like a particle; one of the most perplexing mysteries of quantum physics.

weak interaction   Nuclear interaction that is responsible for the process of beta decay. (Named in contrast to the *strong interaction*, which is billions of time stronger.)

X rays   A form of penetrating radiation; electromagnetic waves, similar to light but thousands of times shorter in wavelength.

Z particles, or Z°   Recently discovered subatomic particle that carries the weak nuclear force, which is responsible for radioactivity and is one of the four basic forces of nature; short-lived massive bosons (100 times more massive than protons and nearly as massive as an atom of silver) thought to have been abundant in the early universe.

Bibliography

Asimov, Isaac. *Asimov's Biographical Encylopedia of Science and Technology*. New York: Doubleday, 1987.

———. *Atom: A Journey across the Subatomic Cosmos*. New York: Dutton, 1991.

———. *New Guide to Science*. New York: Basic Books, 1972.

Barrow, John D., and Frank Tipler. *The Anthropic Cosmological Principle*. London: Oxford University Press, 1986.

Boorstin, Daniel. *The Discoverers*. New York: Random House, 1983.

Brennan, Richard P. *Dictionary of Scientific Literacy*. New York: John Wiley, 1992.

Bronowski, Jacob. *The Ascent of Man*. Boston: Little, Brown, 1973.

Calder, Nigel. *Einstein's Universe*. New York: Penguin Books, 1980.

Capra, Fritjof. *The Tao of Physics*. New York: Bantam Books, 1980.

Cassidy, David Charles. *Uncertainty: The Life and Science of Werner Heisenberg*. New York: Freeman, 1992.

Christianson, Gale E. *In the Presence of the Creator: Isaac Newton and His Times.* New York: Free Press, 1984.

Clark, Ronald W. *Einstein: The Life and Times.* New York: World, 1971.

Coleman, James A. *Relativity for the Layman.* New York: New American Library of World Literature, 1958.

Davies, Paul. *God and the New Physics.* New York: Simon & Schuster, 1984.

———. *The Last Three Minutes.* New York: Basic Books, 1994.

Dawidoff, Nicholas. *The Catcher Was a Spy: The Mysterious Life of Moe Berg.* New York: Pantheon Books, 1994.

Dyson, Freeman. *Disturbing the Universe.* New York: Harper & Row, 1979.

———. *Infinite in All Directions.* New York: Harper & Row, 1988.

Einstein, Albert. *Relativity, The Special and the General Theory.* New York: Crown, 1952.

———. *The Meaning of Relativity.* Princeton, NJ: Princeton University Press, 1923.

Eve, A.S. *Rutherford.* London: Cambridge University Press, 1939.

Feinberg, Gerald. *What Is the World Made Of?* New York: Anchor, 1978.

Ferris, Timothy. *Coming of Age in the Milky Way.* New York: William Morrow, 1988.

Feynman, Richard P. *QED: The Strange Theory of Light and Matter.* Princeton, NJ: Princeton University Press, 1985.

———. *The Feynman Lectures of Physics.* Edited by Robert B. Leighton and Matthew Sands. Reading, MA: Addison-Wesley, 1963.

———. *Six Easy Pieces.* Reading, MA: Addison-Wesley, 1995. (Originally prepared for publication by Robert B. Leighton and Matthew Sands.)

———. *Surely You're Joking, Mr. Feynman.* New York: Norton, 1985.

French, A.P., and P.J. Kennedy. *Niels Bohr: A Centenary Volume.* Cambridge, MA: Harvard University Press, 1985.

Gamow, George. *Biography of Physics.* New York: Harper, 1961.

———. *One Two Three—Infinity.* New York: Viking Press, 1947.

Gardner, Martin. *Relativity for the Millions.* New York: Macmillan, 1965.

Gell-Mann, Murray. *The Quark and the Jaguar: Adventures in the Simple and the Complex*. New York: Freeman, 1994.

Gleick, James. *Genius: The Life and Science of Richard Feynman*. New York: Pantheon Books, 1992.

Goudsmit, Samuel A. *Alsos*. New York: Henry Schuman, 1947.

Gribbin, John. *In Search of Schrödinger's Cat, Quantum Physics and Reality*. New York: Bantam Books, 1984.

Hawking, Stephen. *A Brief History of Time: From the Big Bang to Black Holes*. New York: Bantam Books, 1987.

Heilbron, J.L. *The Dilemmas of an Upright Man: Max Planck as Spokesman for German Science*. Berkeley, CA: University of California Press, 1986.

Hofstadter, Douglas R. *Gödel, Escher, Bach*. New York: Basic Books, 1979.

Holloway, David. *Stalin and the Bomb: The Soviet Union and Atomic Energy*. New Haven, CT: Yale University Press, 1994.

Kaku, Michio. *Hyperspace*. New York: Oxford University Press, 1994.

Krauss, Lawrence. *The Fear of Physics*. New York: Basic Books, 1993.

Lanouette, William (with Bela Silard). *Genius in the Shadow: A Biography of Leo Szilard: The Man Behind the Bomb*. New York: Scribner's, 1993.

Lederman, Leon (with Dick Teresi). *The God Particle*. New York: Dell, 1993.

March, Robert H. *Physics for Poets*. Chicago: Contemporary Books, 1978.

Mehra, Jagdish. *The Beat of a Different Drummer: The Life and Science of Richard Feynman*. New York: Oxford University Press, 1994.

Moore, Ruth. *Niels Bohr*. Cambridge, MA: MIT Press, 1985.

Motz, Lloyd, and Jefferson Hane Weaver. *The Story of Physics*. New York: Plenum Press, 1989.

Pagels, H. *The Cosmic Code*. New York: Simon & Schuster, 1982.

Pais, Abraham. *Niels Bohr's Times, in Physics, Philosophy, and Polity*. Oxford: Oxford University Press, 1991.

———. *Subtle Is the Lord: The Life and Science of Albert Einstein*. London: Oxford University Press, 1982.

Index

Rutherford, Ernest *(continued)*
  radioactive decay, 108, 120
  sonar, 128

S

Schrodinger, Erwin, 103, 160,
  161
  cat, 171–172
Schwarzchild, Karl, 74
Schwinger, Julian, 185, 199, 201
simultaneity, 60–63
Snow, C. P., 129, 183, 206, 248
Snyder, Hartland, 74
space, curved, 71–72
space shuttle (*Challenger*), 209–
  211
space–time, 67, 200–201
spectroscopy, 137–138
standard model, 233, 237
Stanford Linear Accelerator
  Center (SLAC), 67, 198,
  228, 231–233
strangeness, 217–218
string theory, 240–241
Stukeley, William, 14, 24
Sullivan, Walter, 225
Szilard, Leo, 82, 147–148

T

tau lepton, 244
telescope
  Galileo's, 8–9
  Newton's, 27
Thales, 1–2
thermodynamics, 88, 120
Thompson, Joseph John, 111,
  115–116, 123, 128, 133

thought experiment, 57, 58
time (*see* relativity)
time, dilation, 64
Ting, Samuel, 224
Tomonago, Shin'ichiro, 185,
  199, 201

U

ultraviolet catastrophe, 89–94
uncertainty, principle of 105,
  143, 162–166
uranium, 145, 148
  atom, 146
  critical mass calculations,
  180, 181
universe, expanding, 73

W

wave–particle duality, 104, 142,
  160–162
Weinberg, Stephen, xi, 238,
  247
Weisskopf, Victor, 175, 209,
  216–217
Weizmann, Chaim, 78, 121
Wheeler, John Archibald, 74,
  145–147, 193
Wigner, Eugene, 82, 148, 193–
  194

X

X rays, 112–113

Z

Zeeman effect, 156–157
Zweig, George, 214, 222, 228